ST. CLOUD

Picture Research by John J. Dominik

FACING PAGE
A variety of businesses had already been established
on the north side of St. Germain Street when this
photograph was taken in 1877. Notice the *St. Cloud
Journal* reporters and pressmen leaning out of the
second-floor windows, watching the photographer.
Courtesy, Stearns County Historical Society

American Historical Press
Sun Valley, California

ST. CLOUD

The Triplet City

An Illustrated History

John J. Dominik and John C. Massmann

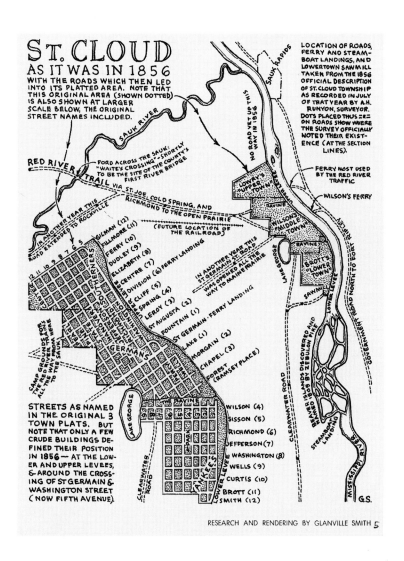

© 2002 American Historical Press
All Rights Reserved
Published 2002
Printed in the United States of America

Library of Congress Catalogue Card Number: 2002105489
ISBN: 1-892724-28-6

Bibliography: p. 198
Includes Index

Contents

PREFACE 7

Chapter 1
THREE INTO ONE: 8
The Birth of St. Cloud

Chapter 2
THE CIVIL WAR AND THE DAKOTA CONFLICT: 28
Fighting on Two Fronts

Chapter 3
BIG BUSINESS BEGINS: 44
Granite, Car Shops, and Automobiles

Chapter 4
PROHIBITION AND DEPRESSION: 70
Zeal, Repeal, and New Deal

Chapter 5
EDUCATION AND INFORMATION: 80
Schools and the Media

Chapter 6
EXPANSION AND MATURITY: 94
Growth in Size and Spirit

Chapter 7
CONTINUITY, CHANGE AND CHALLENGE : 128
1980–2002

Chapter 8
CHRONICLES OF LEADERSHIP 146

A TIMELINE OF ST. CLOUD'S HISTORY 192

SOURCES 198

ACKNOWLEDGMENTS 200

INDEX 201

Culture in a number of forms was always present in St. Cloud. Here the St. Cloud Union Band of 1888 poses under the trees near a bandstand that looks as if it might not have been able to hold the entire band. Courtesy, Stearns County Historical Society

Preface

The history of a community, especially one that is more than a century old, is difficult to write if one is limited to a book smaller than the average unabridged dictionary. It becomes apparent early in the research that the harder task will not be finding the information (a lively and well-stocked historical society is a boon!), but deciding what *not* to use. There is an urgent tendency to treasure every bit of hard-earned information and every once-lost name uncovered in research and to use it somehow.

Because knowledgeable readers may not find their favorite historical tidbit here, they are entitled to know the criteria used to select the information that was included.

Those episodes and people that contributed to the character of St. Cloud have been included whenever possible. As the chronological narrative moves along, the historical facts — and those legends that have survived so long they have the texture of facts — are reported if they highlighted a major turning point in the area's development, if they left a strong legacy to the uniqueness of St. Cloud, or if they represented some aspect that conveyed the ambiance of a particular time.

Admittedly that choice will be arbitrary, made differently by different people. The turning points and the facts that best describe them are the author's choices. Another sifter of history might easily — and justifiably — make other choices.

John J. Dominik

The difficulty in telling the story of a community's past in many ways is even harder when covering recent times. Rather than trying to cover everything the focus has been placed on how St. Cloud and the surrounding area has expanded and changed from the 1980s to the opening of the 21st century.

St. Cloud remained a vibrant community at the close of the 20th century. Its 19th century roots in agriculture, granite, commerce and transportation remained. Its population was still strongly rooted in north European and Christian roots. Optimism, growth and expansion remained strong.

Under the broad similarities, however, important changes were taking place. The spread of the automobile and interstate highway system and modern communications helped St. Cloud emerge as a regional medical center and a community with an increasingly diverse economy. Some areas, like the railroad, processing of agricultural products and the granite industry, declined in importance and influence while others like its growth as a regional commercial center continued.

More than the economic structure of the community was changing. No longer was growth fueled by north European immigration, especially German Catholic, as it had been in the 19th century, but the immigrants of the late 20th century often spoke new languages and had different colored skin, contributing their cultures to the area. The community has become less of what some critics call "White Cloud," while retaining many elements of its majority European roots. St. Cloud citizens have reacted optimistically to these new challenges.

John C. Massmann

1

Three Into One

The Birth of St. Cloud

The undulating prairie of central Minnesota is cut by the path of the Mississippi, the Father of Waters, as it meanders down from its source in northern Minnesota and, south of the twin cities of Minneapolis and St. Paul, reaches and forms the eastern border of the state.

Through this northern part of its course the river is normally a tranquil, even a placid stream, flowing relentlessly but gently through northern forests, central plains, and between the sheer cliffs of the southern bluffs. Only in its southern reaches, in the lower states, has the river, swollen suddenly in the north with spring snow melts or long rainstorms, spread serious devastation in its flood plain.

In modern times the Mississippi has been tamed effectively by the dams and locks of the lower, navigable portion, south from the Twin Cities. The river seems content to serve both business and pleasure on its broad, silty, lazy surface much

as it served in pioneer times when settlement began along the waterways of the wilderness, for this was frequently the fastest and usually the easiest means of travel, summer and winter. This mid-Minnesota portion of the river had also been the watery highway for the war canoes of the Dakotah and Ojibway Indians as they warred for dominance at this interface of their traditional territories.

Unknown to the Indians during their struggles and of course without their permission, other nations, across an ocean these central-plains Indians had no knowledge of, were claiming and counterclaiming the land that now includes Minnesota and specifically St. Cloud. Standing on a beach, Columbus, with as much knowledge of the interior as the Indians had of the ocean, claimed it for Spain in 1492. Sieur de la Salle, at the mouth of the Mississippi, claimed it for France in 1682. France, in 1762, gave the territory it claimed west of the Mississippi to Spain, and the following year ceded the land east of the river to England. (Had the *status* remained *quo*, East St. Cloud would today be ruled by Queen Elizabeth and St. Cloud by King Juan Carlos.)

By the Treaty of Paris in 1783 England gave up

John Lyman Wilson was given the title Father of St. Cloud, not only for his generous gifts of land to the city, but also because his plat of St. Cloud became the central portion of the business district. Courtesy, Stearns County Historical Society (SCHS)

all territorial claims east of the Mississippi, and by the secret Treaty of San Ildefonso, March 1801, Spain returned the future St. Cloud's site to the French; Napoleon sold it to the United States three years later to get the money to wage war against England.

Finally owned by the United States, the area that is now Minnesota became, first, part of the Territory of Missouri in 1805, the Territory of Michigan in 1820, the Territory of Wisconsin in 1836, and the Territory of Iowa in 1838. When Iowa became a state in 1846, Minnesota's first attempt to become a territory by itself failed; there were only 600 white men in the area. In 1849, when a census revealed that the population had grown to 4,780 inhabitants in addition to the 317 soldiers at Fort Snelling, territorial status was granted. Statehood wasn't achieved until 1858, but the condition has been permanent since then.

Although no white man could legally own property in this area until 1847, when the federal government paid the Sioux Indians for the land, explorers and fur traders had visited the area long before, the most famous of the explorers being Zebulon Montgomery Pike, sent by the government in 1805 to explore the headwaters of the Mississippi. On his way up the river, Lieutenant Pike made an entry in his journal for Thursday, October 10, in which he mentions the islands in the river below the present Tenth Street bridge in St. Cloud.

Came to large islands and strong water early in the morning. Passed the place at which Mr. Rienville and Mons. Perlier wintered in 1797; passed a cluster of islands, more than twenty in the course of four miles; these I called Beaver Islands from the immense signs of those animals, for they have dams on every island and roads from them every two or three rods . . . Encamped at the foot of the Grand Rapids.

The Grand Rapids of Pike's journal are the rapids between St. Cloud and Sartell. The next morning Pike and his party had to work their boats through them.

Both boats passed the worst of the rapids by eleven o'clock, but we were obliged to wade and lift them over the rocks, where there was not a foot of water, when at times the next step would be in water over our heads. In consequence of this, our boats were frequently in imminent danger of being bilged on the rocks. About five miles above the rapids, our large boat was discovered to leak so fast as to render it necessary to unload her, which we did. Stopped the leak and reloaded.

Later travelers on the Mississippi who left a record of the journey include Lewis Cass who, while territorial governor of Michigan, led an expedition to find the source of the Mississippi, the upper reaches of which were then under his jurisdiction. On his return from the lakes near the source, he came down the river, passing the site of St. Cloud on July 29, 1820. In his party were about a dozen white men, perhaps twice as many Indians, and the scholarly frontiersman, Henry R. Schoolcraft. When Cass became Secretary of War he sent another expedition to further explore the source of the Mississippi. Schoolcraft was also a member of this group, which passed St. Cloud's site during July of 1832. This expedition gave the name Itasca (from the Latin *veritas* and *caput*, meaning true head) to the lake that is the source of the Mississippi.

By this time, although the land east of the Mississippi was being settled rapidly by pioneers moving west, the great river was superstitiously believed to be the western limit of civilization. Only little by little did the Indian trader, the trapper, and the hunter move cautiously across the natural barrier of the river. By the late 1840s it was time for the agricultural pioneer, the farmer with his wife and family, to replace the lone woodsman who, along with the Indian, had been the only human roaming the plains west of the upper Mississippi.

John Lyman Wilson, a millwright from Columbia Falls, Maine, who is regarded as the Father of St. Cloud, came to Minnesota in 1851 to build saw mills. He had already constructed mills at Sauk Rapids and at Little Falls when, around 1853, he bought the claim of Ole Bergeson, a Norwegian

ABOVE
John L. Wilson married Mrs. Harriet Corbett (pictured here) in 1855 after his first wife died. Harriet Wilson lived until 1897. (SCHS)

ABOVE LEFT
Lewis Cass, governor of the Michigan Territory from 1813 to 1831, led an expedition to seek the source of the Mississippi. As he came down the river, he passed the future site of St. Cloud on July 29, 1820. Later, as Secretary of War under President Andrew Jackson, he sent another expedition to find the river's head. Courtesy, National Portrait Gallery

LEFT
Henry Rowe Schoolcraft's interest in the American Indian led him up the Mississippi and past the future site of St. Cloud at least twice. Engraving by Wellstood and Peters. From Cirker, *Dictionary of American Portraits,* Dover, 1967

squatter, for $100. The claim, about 320 acres, was bordered by the Mississippi River on the east, roughly by ravines on both the north and south, and included Lake George near its western border.

(St. Cloud is located near the center of the state, straddling the Mississippi. By 1980 approximately 75 percent of the city lay west of the river in Stearns County, for which St. Cloud is the county seat, while east of the river 14 percent of the city is in Sherburne County and 12 percent is in Benton County.)

The two great ravines at the north and south of Wilson's purchase determined the boundaries of the three settlements which eventually became St. Cloud. The settlement above the northern ravine became known as "Upper Town," while Wilson's settlement between the two ravines was known as "Middle Town"; the settlement below the southern ravine was known as "Lower Town."

All three towns were established at about the same time, from 1853 to 1855. Their settlers were in many ways typical of the settlers who migrated from the East to establish homesites along the west bank of the Mississippi: they were both farmers and frontier entrepreneurs, and they based their claims, and their hopes, on the lands to the west of the great river.

Wilson's Middle Town, which later became the central business district of St. Cloud, was platted in September 1855. He laid out a town on his newly purchased property and induced settlers to establish there by giving sites to a considerable number of them in return for pledges to erect buildings. He also contributed landsites for the erection of public buildings, including a courthouse for Stearns County, which was established in 1855.

Wilson's town was settled principally by industrious German Catholics, including tradesmen and shopkeepers who had come to the area from Evansville, Indiana seeking a location for a German colony. The St. Cloud site appealed to the Indiana group's leader, John W. Tenvoorde. He had read the reports of the pioneer missionary Father Francis X. Pierz, who had written about the favorable life in central Minnesota.

It is commonly believed that Wilson named his settlement St. Cloud after the Paris suburb of the same name. Wilson, who was of French Huguenot ancestry, was fond of reading about the life of Napoleon. One biography of the emperor related an incident which occurred when he was away from France fighting in Russia. Napoleon's wife Josephine was at that time residing at their summer palace in St. Cloud, and when Napoleon's messengers from France arrived one day to report on the state of affairs at home, the lonely emperor asked, at the end of their official report, "And how are things in St. Cloud?" It is said that Wilson remembered this incident at the time he filed his plat, and thus gave the Triplet City its French-bred name. (Ironically, though John L. Wilson is considered the Father of St. Cloud, for 100 years there was nothing in St. Cloud named after him. Both Wilson Avenue and Wilson Park in East St. Cloud are named after his brother Joseph, who was instrumental in founding Lower Town.)

A tradition in the Triplet City's long-established Mockenhaupt family would challenge John Wilson's right to the sobriquet "Father of St. Cloud." Ancestor August Mockenhaupt is said to have laid claim to the land from the present 8th Avenue on St. Germain Street west to 16th Avenue prior to Wilson's claim. But when he went back to Germany to bring back his future wife, he discovered upon his return that his claim was not recognized. But for the error of a recording clerk, August Mockenhaupt might today be considered the Father of St. Cloud—if the story is true.

Wilson's Middle Town grew slowly, and by 1858 it had only about a dozen families. Some of the town's early settlers were Germans from nearby Sauk City, who had been prevented by city ordinance from brewing and selling beer in their shanties. The beer-loving Germans decamped from Sauk City and soon populated the more lenient Wilson's town.

Upper Town, the area between the northern ravine (around 5th or 6th streets) to the present-day Sauk Rapids Bridge, grew faster in its early years than Wilson's Middle Town. The several hundred acres north of Wilson's settlement had been claimed, in 1853, by Gen. Sylvanus B. Lowry, a slave-holding Southerner from Tennessee. Lowry acquired his pseudo-military title from having been appointed adjutant general by Minnesota territorial governor Willis A. Gorman in return for a political favor. (Lowry was active in Democratic politics.)

Lowry had maintained a fur trading post north of Sauk Rapids at Watab and had also worked as an Indian interpreter, but he preferred to build and to live in his large, Southern-style house in Acadia—the name he chose for his potential city to the north of Wilson's Middle Town. Lowry's was the more cultural town in the beginning, attracting wealthy, educated Southerners who quickly developed closer social contacts with the people in Sauk Rapids than with the more parochial Germans in Wilson's Middle Town, or, later, the Yankees in Lower Town. Lowry's plantation-style home, however, did not hold up well under the harsh northern climate, and his town of Acadia, well populated at one time, fell eerily silent at the advent of the Civil War.

For several years Lowry's Upper Town had been, of the three communities, the principal business center. Steamboats plying the Mississippi frequently landed there, and stores and warehouses were erected on the river flats to accommodate them. But when hostilities between North and South erupted into war, the Southerners of Upper Town, some of whom owned slaves in the area, abandoned the settlement.

Lower Town came into being in 1854, when George Fuller Brott, a 30-year-old townsite developer from New York state, purchased squatter Martin Wooley's claim south of Wilson's settlement. Brott formed a townsite company and by September 1855 he too had the area platted and filed: The name he chose for the townsite was St. Cloud City. The striking similarity to Wilson's choice may be because John Wilson's brother Joseph was a member of Brott's townsite company. Also a member of Brott's St. Cloud Township Company was Charles T. Stearns, Brott's father-in-law and the man for whom the county is named.

St. Cloud City, or Lower Town, prospered at

George Fuller Brott was the developer of St. Cloud City or Lower Town. Brott described himself as "farmer, wagon and carriage maker, sheriff, postmaster, real estate dealer, editor, townsite promoter, owner of flour mills, steamboats, steamships, and sailing craft, wholesale and retail merchant, member constitutional convention, colonel of engineers, canal and railroad president, and inventor." He died in Washington, D.C., in 1902, probably of overwork. (SCHS)

ABOVE
The Stearns House, located on Eighth Street South between First Avenue and the Mississippi, was built in 1857. It was St. Cloud's leading hotel during the Civil War and a popular resort hotel with Southerners eager to escape the heat. (SCHS)

FACING PAGE
Henry Z. and Elizabeth Mitchell are pictured here about 1890. Henry's letters to his wife in Pennsylvania provide a picture of early life in pioneer St. Cloud. (SCHS)

first, mainly through the energetic promotional efforts of its developer. Advertising principally in the East, the promoters attracted settlers from New England and the mid-Atlantic states. The early residents were mostly Protestant, temperance-loving, anti-slavery Yankee merchants, and by 1857 the town could boast, in newspaper editor Jane Grey Swisshelm's words, "a grist mill, a planing mill, a sash and door factory, two churches, the Everett school and library, a large temperance hotel . . . over a hundred dwellings and stores, and a fine lyceum." The "temperance hotel" referred to was the Stearns House, a three-story luxury hotel managed by Charles T. Stearns, at which alcoholic beverages purportedly were not served. The hotel was frequented mostly by Southerners who came north to escape the heat (Sauk Rapids had become, by this time, a vacation spot for Southern sportsmen) and the establishment's temperance ideals may have been somewhat compromised by its guests' propensity for cool mint juleps on hot afternoons.

Lower Town's Everett School was a small, frame, single-room building erected with private donations. There had not been enough money collected in the school's first year of existence to finish lathing and plastering of the building, and surviving the Minnesota winter was part of the students' curriculum that first year. The teacher, Amelia Talcott, had come from Connecticut to visit her brother and, seeing the need for her services, offered to stay. Tuition at Everett School was $1.50 a year, and this, from 25 students, was the teacher's salary.

When Lower Town lawyer Christopher C. Andrews sent a copy of his dedicatory address to the famous orator Edward Everett of Boston (for whom the school had been named), Everett responded with a gift of about $200 worth of selected books. Although the shipment was held up on the east side of the river until school authorities could raise funds to pay transportation charges, the books eventually became the nucleus of the town's library—indeed, they *were* the library.

Insight into the everyday life of early St. Cloud may be found in the letters written by Lower Town storekeeper Henry Zehring Mitchell to his wife Elizabeth in Pennsylvania. The Mitchells had first come west to scout the area in the spring of 1856, then returned to Pennsylvania. But Mitchell came back to Minnesota alone in the fall to arrange for construction of a home and store in Brott's community. While waiting for lumber with which to start construction, the lonesome Mitchell kept his wife and family informed of local activities through his letters.

In his first letter to his wife in Wilkinsburg, a suburb of Pittsburgh, written on November 16, 1856, he tells her that he walked the 60 miles from St. Paul to Lower Town. "We arrived here on Friday evening pretty tired you may be sure. Never had such a walk in my life before, never want to again."

Mitchell thought Lower Town had improved

since his previous visit in the spring, although he was disturbed by the lack of lumber. "I find I have no more lumber here for my house than was secured from the ruins of the old sawmill after it was burned." Nonetheless, he wrote cheerily, "business seems quite brisk and things seem to move along quite lively." Social life that November centered around the Stearns House, Mitchell reported to his wife. He and a friend had been taken there one evening by early settler John Taylor, and Mitchell noted that Taylor had lost two pianos when the boat on which they were being shipped to St. Cloud sank in the Mississippi. But, he wrote, a "Mr. Sisson has brought on two pianos as far as St. Paul—so you see St. Cloud is going to be a musical place."

A week later—three weeks since Mitchell had seen his wife—he still had not received a letter from her and he was berating the mail service (it was nothing to write home about, or via) but it was all that was available. "The weather was holding," he wrote, and was "fully as pleasant as we are accustomed to have it at the same season in Pennsylvania." The date was November 23 and results of the recent presidential election had not yet reached St. Cloud, although Mitchell wrote "rumor says Buchanan is the man." But even the presidential election was a secondary concern to other news Mitchell had.

"There has been a large operator here from St. Paul, buying property; he has bought quite a

number of Lots in Upper Town. He bought one house and Lot in this town for 1,500 Dollars (a small frame)." In another letter written November 30 Mitchell complained that the river had not yet frozen solid, making the ferry crossing dangerous because of the running ice. Three days later he reported that it had finally closed and people were crossing and re-crossing at pleasure. He also noted the honesty of the pioneers on this western frontier:

Mr. Taylor had a load of goods lying on the opposite shore, exposed to the weather or anything else that might choose to destroy or appropriate them, for about a week. Folks must be little inclined to thieving as many of the packages were so small that any person might have carried off several of them at a time, such as boxes of Raisins, Sardines, etc. I wonder how long they would have been safe exposed similarly near Pittsburgh?

In describing a short trip he and friends had taken, Mitchell provides a picture of country life in the 1850s:

On Friday last about 3 o'clock the Doctor [Benjamin R. Palmer], Henry [Swisshelm, Mitchell's brother-in-law] and myself started over to Capt. [Joshua] Briggs'. We had a very pleasant ride going over ... Now all is mantled in one broad garment of pure white snow, and the thermometer at 12 to 20 degrees below zero. We have had so far, however, the finest winter I ever saw.

Well, we found Cap't Briggs and family all well. Mrs. Briggs as happy apparently as a bird. They seemed glad to see us and entertained much better than I thought they could, circumstances as they are. They are still in the old shanty, have not yet commenced their new house.

We had plenty of fresh and corned fish, fresh Beef roasted, and fresh Pork boiled, while there, accompanied with many other luxuries and dainties, not the least of which was cranberries. On Saturday (yesterday) the Cap't hooked his fine span of bays to our sled and after Breakfast, we

started over Lakes and Brooks; a merry ride had we, and did not return until about 3 o'clock, when Mrs. Briggs had served up for us a most excellent and bountiful dinner/supper and if You had seen us eat, You could have thought there was need for the abundance (at least) with which her table was supplied.

Well, after supper, which was near night, we left for St. Cloud. It was dark when we left ... and we soon after lost the road, the snow having drifted the tracks full. After driving over prairies, grubs, and hazel bushes about an hour and a half, we found ourselves back [at Briggs' house] when without stopping we took the road again and with better success as the moon had risen. We got here about 9 o'clock last night, having traveled about 8 miles without stopping.

Mitchell wrote his wife that the carpenter had finally started work on their house but was making little progress.

It is going to be a pretty expensive affair—I have to pay 20 Dollars for Lumber and 6 Dollars per thousand for shingles. Everything is high here this winter except the thermometer; that is always the lowest. ... Flour is selling at 13 Dollars pr barrel, Corn Meal $7 per cwt, Beans $8 pr Bushel, Beef 12 1/2 cts pr lb by the gross, Hogs $15 per cwt, chickens $1.50 a pair, Butter 40 to 50 cts when it can be had. No person pretends to use milk in their coffee or tea; coffee and sugar 20 cents per lb. Molasses $1.50 pr Gal. Clothing seems to be the most abundant article in the trade here, and sells lower than anything else in proportion. ...

I have sent You this price current that You may be able to answer interrogatories and when they ask You how I like this country, tell them I don't like any other.

When Mitchell returned East to visit his family, including his newborn son, he was kept abreast of St. Cloud news by a letter from his friend, Dr. Palmer. The doctor was one of only two physicians in the area at the time, which kept him busy, but not too busy to enjoy an active social life in a place where one might suppose there would be none. The doctor wrote to Mitchell:

> *Last week Henry [Swisshelm] and John Taylor and Brott and myself with ladies attended a party at Mr. Woods, Sauk Rapids, and I don't think that in Pittsburgh or any of your cities a more refined, accomplished, and well-dressed party could be collected (your humble servant, of course, excepted), or that any host could entertain more hospitably and handsomely than Mr. and Mrs. Wood.*
>
> *Two days afterwards we got up a very pleasant party from St. Cloud to Stevensons at Clear Lake, where we had a capital time.*

After Mitchell's return to St. Cloud, he and Henry Swisshelm (brother-in-law of Jane Grey Swisshelm) were joined by another Pennsylvania friend, Stephen Miller, in the large building Mitchell had finally finished. Mitchell used half of the building for his general store. According to William Bell Mitchell's history of Stearns County, his father stocked "a large and well assorted stock of calicoes, gingham, bleached and brown muslin, denims, hoop skirts, mantles, glassware, queensware, a large variety of ready-made clothing, and assorted confectionary."

The other side of the building was used as a grocery store by Stephen Miller and Henry Swisshelm, who also operated a real estate and land warrant office there. Within a few years, Stephen Miller would leave to fight in the Civil War and later would become governor of Minnesota.

Within a year or so, more businesses could be added to Jane Grey Swisshelm's list: Charles F. and William Powell had started a hardware store; Josiah Elam West, one of the most productive of the area pioneer builders, had a general store; the Northwestern Fur Company had an office (later occupied by the *St. Cloud Visiter* when that newspaper's office was destroyed); and the blacksmith shop of Thomas Jones was handy for repairs as well as for shoeing horses. Lower Town also boasted James M. McKelvy's law office, Silas Marlatt's drug store, E. C. Smith's boot and shoe store,

Grandmother's Garden

·FIRST·AVENUE·SOUTH·
·SAINT·CLOUD·MINNESOTA·
·TELEPHONE·627R·
·RUTH·MITCHELL·

Henry Mitchell's home was converted into Grandmother's Garden by his granddaughter, Ruth Mitchell. Here Ruth served "Luncheon and Tea-Box Lunches." (SCHS)

Francis Talcott's jewelry store, and the small log building which housed St. Cloud's first newspaper, the *Minnesota Advertiser*, predecessor of the *Visiter*.

But difficulties developed for Lower Town on two fronts. After George Brott had sold and deeded lots, it was discovered that he had claimed title to the property under the provisions of a mail contract, before the government had made a survey. (Martin Wooley's claim, purchased by Brott, represented only part of Lower Town.) After the survey was completed, the claim was found to be in an old section of land the government had previously granted to the St. Paul & Pacific Railway. Most businessmen in Lower Town were reluctant to make improvements on lots under a clouded title, and by 1860 a number of business houses had moved—physically, in many cases—to Wilson's Middle Town. The state legislature eventually cleared Brott's title but too late to save the commercial life of Lower Town.

The second problem could be attributed to the influx of Germans who settled in the St. Cloud area. Brott's townsite had attracted Yankee merchants from the East — mainly Maine, Pennsylvania, and New York. Most farmers in the vicinity of the three towns were Germans, lured to the

rich Sauk Valley farmland from Germany or states to the east by the writings of people like the Catholic missionary to the Ojibwe, Father Francis X. Pierz. They preferred to do business with the German-speaking storekeepers in Wilson's town.

The slow ebbing of commerce from Brott's development left the area free of the bustle of business but richer in larger residences; many businessmen had built their living quarters in conjunction with their stores, and the empty business space was converted into living quarters.

Lowry's Upper Town suffered a similar fate. A question over title to the land brought development almost to a standstill, and when businesses and warehouses moved across the ravine Upper Town became, like Lower Town, a nearly isolated residential community.

Transportation proved troublesome for all three communities in the early days of settlement. Early travelers reached the three settlements either by the territorial road that ran from Fort Snelling to Fort Ripley along the east side of the Mississippi River past St. Cloud, or they came by steamboat, which could reach Upper Town only at certain times of the year when the water was high. Even Lower Town was occasionally beyond the reach of the steamers due to low water.

General Lowry, in 1856, installed a ferry to carry passengers bound for Upper Town from the east side of the river to the west side. John Wilson soon followed suit. Brott also installed a ferry but took no chances; he bought a steam packet to bring travelers to Lower Town from St. Anthony. When high water allowed, the packet unloaded at Brott Street in Lower Town; when it didn't, passengers disembarked at Kilian's Landing two miles downriver on the east bank, came up the territorial road in wagons, and crossed to Lower Town on Brott's ferry approximately at 10th Street.

All three ferries were the swinging type, fastened by a long rope upstream and swung back and forth across the river by the swift current acting against the keel and rudder. Occasionally a ferry would slip its cable and spin out of control downstream with the current. Until the ferry was retrieved and in operation again, the freight and passengers who couldn't wait were taken across the river in skiffs. This was no small risk; logs floating freely downstream could easily upset the small boats.

Many of these logs were snaked out of the river at the sawmills and quickly turned into needed lumber, but because of the difficulty of getting longer lengths, buildings were necessarily small. John Wilson's frame house was only 15 by 20 feet with studdings of 11 feet. Even when the longer sawed lumber could be obtained, the houses built with it were often poorly constructed. The demand for skilled carpenters far exceeded the supply, and many men who had not held a hammer or used a saw seriously before were pressed into service to build houses. Attorney Christopher C. Andrews discovered this for himself.

When the work [on his house] was progressing, I was greatly surprised to see the carpenter nailing clap boards on the bare scantling [studding] without first having nailed boards on, and I remonstrated against it. They turned to the contract, which read that the walls should be sided. I knew that siding meant clap boarding but supposed it implied that clap boards should be put upon boards. They said they were doing it the

TOP
A solid river of logs moves slowly past the State Normal School buildings high on the left bank around 1897. (SCHS)

ABOVE
John L. Wilson's second home, built in 1856, was on the west side of Fifth Avenue and Second Street North. This picture, with Mr. Wilson at the right, was taken about 10 years before his death in 1910. (SCHS)

FACING PAGE
When the water was high enough, the Northern Line packet *Minneapolis* carried freight and passengers between Minneapolis and St. Cloud until 1874. Passengers continued to enjoy the scenic river route until the faster railroad and the unpredictable river made steamboats obsolete on the upper Mississippi. (SCHS)

way buildings were erected here. Although my house was to be lathed and plastered inside, I felt sure it would not be warm enough without being boarded, but the work was so far advanced and to avoid dispute, I let it go on.

The ceiling of my office was unusually high and although I had a good sized box stove, I suffered the ensuing winter considerably from the cold.

The next season, I had the walls of the building filled with sawdust, a drum put on my stove, and was much more comfortable.

Warmth was not the only problem with many of these early buildings. They were erected so quickly and inexpertly that they often lacked minimum strength. In May 1855, for example, the gabled attic of one such house was used as a chapel. The small space could not contain all who had come for the service, and many remained on the lower floor. During Mass the ceiling began to give way under the weight, and only the prompt action of those below, who improvised supports from nearby fence railings, prevented a serious accident.

In the summer of 1855, the plateau above the west bank of the Mississippi River was relieved only by the trees and two or three shanties. Two years later the population had blossomed to between 200 and 500, and by 1860, with a population of nearly 1,000, the Triplet City was called "a place of some importance," and "headquarters of the stageline to the West and the Northwest" by one Chicago newspaper.

The three communities soon saw the benefits of incorporating into one community, enabling them to share common services and gain political unity. The state legislature granted Acadia, St. Cloud City, and St. Cloud the right to incorporate into one political entity in March 1856. St. Cloud was chosen as the name for the new town, and on April 2, 1856 the new city's voters chose St. Cloud's first officers. Though they remained separated by their ethnic, political, and social differences for many years, the Triplet Cities soon melded into one community that grew from a "small but pretentious suburb of Sauk Rapids"

into a town "wearing more of an air of life and business than any other place in Minnesota."

The main contribution to this surge of growth was the well-dressed European and Englishman strolling down the streets of the more fashionable cities wearing his tall felt hat. The raw material for this stylish item—beaver pelts—was found wrapped around a small but prolific rodent populating Canada and the northern part of the United States. Until it was trapped almost to extinction, the beaver was the first link of a chain that went through the trapper, trader, shipper, and manufacturer to wind up on the head of a dandy. The trader bought furs from the trapper and shipped them out to the manufacturer by various methods: voyageurs (mostly Frenchmen) paddled large freight canoes over the waters of Canada and the Northwest while Métis (half-breed French Indians) drove ox cart trains over the land routes.

One of the early land routes wound down from Fort Garry (now Winnipeg) through northwestern Minnesota to Fort Snelling and St. Paul. This land route, known as the Red River Trail, branched into three routes across the state. The main branch of the East Plains trail met the Sauk River a mile or two west of St. Cloud. Drivers forded the Sauk River at the present site of the Waite's Crossing Bridge and crossed the Mississippi by ferry at St. Cloud before going down the territorial road to St. Paul. The drivers usually camped at the western edge of town before making the crossing.

The common carrier used to haul pelts down and merchandise back up the Red River Trail was the ox cart. Pulled at first by a single ox, later occasionally by a horse, this frontier freighter was a heavy, cumbersome, two-wheel vehicle made almost entirely of wood; rawhide thongs were the only other material used in its construction. The wheels were huge, five feet in diameter and three inches thick and were fitted onto the wooden axles and held in place with wooden pegs. No grease was used on the broad bearing area, and the carts shrieked with an unearthly, deafening howl when they were moving. As they approached a settlement—and they could be

heard coming for miles—all activity ceased, including church services, until the shrill, piercing din had either passed on or stopped. With great justification and some understatement, the Red River Trail traffic was called the Big Squeak.

Almost exclusively, the drivers of the carts were half-breeds from the northern community of Pembina. Known for their flashing eyes, vivid smiles, and native grace, they dressed in buckskin or coarse blue cloth decorated with brass buttons, and usually wore red Pembina sashes at their waists. They wore beaded moccasins and their shoulder-length black hair was either covered by a bandana, a skin cap, or a wide-brimmed hat worn at a jaunty angle.

Lieut. John Pope, topographical engineer of a military expedition from Fort Snelling to Pembina, observed the half-breeds who made up most of Pembina's population.

A string of Red River Trail carts—the Big Squeak— follows the crest of a hill on the way down to St. Paul from Winnipeg. These primitive but efficient wagons were the principal freight haulers for beaver and other peltry being shipped to eastern and European markets until they were replaced by faster stages and railroads. (SCHS)

21

Lieutenant (later General) John A. Pope's early exploration and maps led to the development of the Red River Valley, hence the Red River Trail. After an ambrotype by Mathew Brady. From Cirker, *Dictionary of American Portraits*, Dover, 1967

Some Métis rest on the prairie. Their carts were constructed without using metal of any kind. They did not have metal tires, nails, or iron reinforcement. Even their axles were wood. (SCHS)

They speak the French language, are nearly all Catholic with mild and gentle manners, great vivacity, generous and honest in their transactions and disposed to be a civil and orderly community.

They are hale and hearty, robust men, evidently accustomed to hardship and exposure, to which they submit cheerfully. They are brave and hardy, fine horsemen and skilled marksmen, and would make the finest soldiers in the world.

Noisy, colorful, infrequent visitors who stayed only long enough to rest their animals and buy supplies, the Red River Trail ox cart trains were the main attraction when they arrived at a settlement, much like the steamboats of the lower river towns in later years. Jane Grey Swisshelm, St. Cloud's pioneer woman editor, observed one train that came through town in June 1858:

One hundred and forty carts camped on the St. Cloud prairie [probably around 20th Avenue and 4th Street North] Saturday evening last and on the Sabbath afternoon proceeded on their journey, crossing at Fowler's ferry [in Lower Town].

They were enroute to St. Paul with pelfry. . . . The drivers were principally half-breeds and each displayed more or less bead work and bright colored sashes. There were several women in the train, each driving her own cart.

Another observer said that on pleasant evenings, "The young men on ponies gave free exhibitions of their horsemanship, on the prairie back of town, and did some wonderful tricks from the backs of their horses."

However necessary the Red River Trail carts and drivers were to the fur trade, they could not long maintain a monopoly on their route, nor on the valuable loads they carried. Their oxen and carts were slow, and the speed did not pick up appreciably when the oxen were replaced by horses. And they carried no passengers. The western country was opening to settlement and would-be passengers were seeking transportation.

Among the first to see the opportunity at hand were the Burbank brothers, James Crawford and

Henry Clay. They had a forwarding and commission business in St. Paul, begun in 1853, and they took over the Northwestern Express Company in St. Cloud, appointing Upper Town's Sylvanus Lowry as their local agent.

The freight business expanded rapidly, thanks largely to the beaver hat's continuing appeal, and Henry Burbank soon moved to St. Cloud to personally manage the local terminal. By 1859 the Burbanks had added a stage line.

To the freight wagons and the stage line, the Burbank brothers soon added a steamer that plied the river between St. Cloud and St. Paul with the freight and passengers the stages couldn't carry. All of this activity soon fostered an increase in the jobs available in St. Cloud. One new arrival, Samuel Holes, who had been born in England, arrived at St. Cloud after stops at several other settlements, and was hired as a "horse doctor" to care for the ox teams. He later managed the cart trains for the Burbank brothers.

Conrad Herberger, born in Baden (Germany), came to St. Cloud in 1856 when he was 22 years old. He described his job with the Burbanks:

In 1856 I started a blacksmith shop. In 1859 the first stage ran from St. Cloud to Georgetown [17 miles north of the present site of Fargo, on the Red River], a distance of 200 miles, and Burbank & Co. hired me to do their horse shoeing. My wife and self were stationed at Pomme de Terre to keep the night station on the stage line. I was to shoe the horses used on the line from Sauk Centre to Georgetown.

Pomme de Terre is twenty-two miles this way from Fergus Falls and twelve beyond Evansville. We got along there fairly well until the Indian outbreak, on August, 1862. At that time we were forced to return to St. Cloud. . . .

Travel on the Red River Trail increased rapidly. In the early 1850s the Big Squeak had made only one trip down and back each summer with two or three trains, each containing no more than five or six carts. The number of trips and carts, and the value of the cargo seemed to increase almost daily. One May day in 1863, the Burbanks brought down $5,000 in cash. In 1864 a train of 200 carts passed through St. Cloud. By 1865 the company

ABOVE
Henry Clay Burbank, of the Burbank Bros. freight lines, moved to St. Cloud to manage the local terminal of the flourishing business. Courtesy, Minnesota Historical Society

ABOVE RIGHT
James Crawford Burbank maintained the St. Paul office of the Burbank Bros. company. Their selection of St. Cloud as a terminus meant the first large-scale influx of a wide range of job seekers for the city. Courtesy, Minnesota Historical Society

FACING PAGE
Travelers on the Burbank stage line could catch a meal in Frank Kindler's dining room, far less primitive surroundings than they would find farther west in their travels. (SCHS)

was carrying $7,000,000 in cash and 1,000 tons of goods.

The stage line also prospered. By 1865 the trip was commonplace and the 700 miles between Pembina and St. Cloud could be covered in 7 1/2 days (the stage never traveled after nightfall). Every day between 40 and 50 passengers passed through St. Cloud on their way to points west, and they usually provisioned for their trip at this last stop in civilization.

When the U.S. treaty of 1863 minimized the threat of the Sioux in Minnesota, white settlers flooded into the Red River Valley in homesteaders' covered wagons. Their crops were later shipped out in freight wagons so heavily loaded that they required a six-mule team. The 1865-1866 gold rush in Montana brought still more traffic along the pioneer highway. But even this slightly more civilized traffic did not completely do away with the original commerce on the route. In 1867, within a 10-day period, 140 tons of furs came down from Pembina through St. Cloud for transshipment to Europe.

But change was coming. If it wasn't apparent by the disappearance of the buffalo from the prairie, it could be seen in the smudge of smoke moving on the horizon, snaking toward those cities and centers that had lasted through pioneer times and had settled into permanency. The railroad that would eventually drive the ox carts, the freight wagons, and the stages farther west to open new territory was traversing the land with tracks. New immigrants were making their way up from St. Paul. In September 1866 the first train of the St. Paul & Pacific Railway reached the depot on St. Cloud's east side.

The ox carts and the Burbank brothers had served their purpose; they had opened the area to settlement by establishing permanent lines of communication, travel, and commerce. Henry

Clay Burbank, the local presence of the Burbank brothers, (James Crawford Burbank lived in St. Paul) was described by William Bell Mitchell as a "delightful man, quick and accurate in judgment, with a large sympathy for all who were in need but firm when he made a decision." In May 1863, preparing for marriage to Mary C. Mitchell, the daughter of Henry Zehring Mitchell, Burbank had a house built for his bride. By now housing in St. Cloud no longer depended solely on lumber; Volz and Weber's brickyard was turning out a red brick and, according to an early resident, "new buildings no longer had those abominable old sheet iron chimneys so generally in use in early days." But red brick did not suit Mr. Burbank. He had yellow brick shipped from St. Paul for his home at Third Avenue and Second Street South. The house, known later as the McKelvy house, was razed in the 1950s to make way for the DeSoto

Bridge across the Mississippi, but its elegant woodwork was still a point of pride at the time the house was demolished.

But how far had St. Cloud come since its founding days? Was the Triplet City really gaining in sophistication? Minnesotan Oliver Hudson Kelly, founder of the Grange movement, gave his opinion of St. Cloud in 1865:

> *St. Cloud, though the most northern town of any importance in the state and where an Eastern man would hardly expect to find much beauty and fashion, yet it is here in all its gorgeous hues and attractions—pianos, Brussels carpets, ...greenbacks, crinolines, and all the other accompaniments which add happiness to the soul of handsome and accomplished women wherever they may be found.*

That the three towns had solidified into one city was fortuitous, for they faced, with the rest of the nation, the terrible specter of a civil war, and, more locally, the threat of an Indian rebellion that would unify the city in spite of the differences spawned by the national tragedy of slavery.

ABOVE
The Minnesota House barn not only rented wagons but also stabled the horses of overnight visitors. Its convenient location, at Sixth Avenue South between First and Second streets, placed it near the center of commercial activity. (SCHS)

LEFT
Oliver Hudson Kelley was a government clerk who, with six associates, founded the National Grange in Minnesota in 1867. Courtesy, National Grange. From Cirker, *Dictionary of American Portraits*, Dover, 1967

FACING PAGE, TOP
The forerunner of the Grand Central Hotel, the Central House, was only one of several hotels in the area catering to the customers of the stage line. (SCHS)

FACING PAGE, BOTTOM
The Grand Central was located on the corner of Fifth Avenue and St. Germain Street and was at least the third hotel erected on the site. In its heyday it was known as "the finest hostelry in central Minnesota," and the three floors of elegant rooms featured a large dining room on the main floor where Buffalo Bill once entertained his guests. It was razed in 1972. (SCHS)

2

The Civil War and the Dakota Conflict

Fighting on Two Fronts

With the firing on Fort Sumter in Charleston Harbor on April 21, 1861, years of tension between the North and the South exploded into civil war.

Minnesota governor Alexander Ramsey, who happened to be in Washington when Fort Sumter surrendered, immediately volunteered 1,000 Minnesota men for the Union Army. It was the first such offer made to President Lincoln.

While St. Cloud—and Minnesota—was far from the scene of any battle and never heard a shot fired in anger throughout the entire Civil War, the issue behind the war, slavery, was not alien to the city or to the state. Minnesota Territory's sparse white 1850 population included some southerners, especially among the army officers and the occasional business person, such as Sylvanus Lowry in St. Cloud. Southern plantation owners — and their slaves — spent summers at Lake Minnetonka in St. Anthony, at Sauk Rapids, and at St. Cloud. Only later did the farmers, lumbermen, and merchants, most of them opposed to slavery, come in from the northern tier of states and from Europe.

The dichotomy that existed in the states bordering the deep South existed also in this northernmost state: pro-slavery people lived next to abolitionists, who lived next to neutrals.

These forces, and their ensuing controversies, were quite evident in St. Cloud. Upper Town's Sylvanus Lowry had kept slaves, even though Minnesota was a free territory. Most of the Germans and Yankees of Middle and Lower Towns, however, were traditionally opposed to slavery.

St. Cloud's ardent abolitionist, editor/publisher Jane Grey Swisshelm, had herself come from Pennsylvania, and readily, if not always accurately, identified the supporters of the various sides of the slavery issue. Although she described Sylvanus Lowry as "one of those who are born to command," stating that, "He had a splendid physique and dignified bearing and possessed a superior intellect and mesmeric fascination," she was quick to point out that, "his life spent among negroes and Indians made him feel his superiority and assert it with the full force of honest conviction."

In the spring of 1861 Stephen Miller enlisted in the army as a private but was soon appointed lieutenant colonel of the First Minnesota Infantry. Photo by Whitney's Gallery; Courtesy, Minnesota Historical Society

ABOVE
Minnesota Governor Alexander Ramsey was the first to volunteer his state's men for President Lincoln's Union army. He was to be absorbed in a conflict in his own state when the Sioux Uprising would turn the southwestern part of the state into barricaded cities and abandoned farms. Courtesy, Minnesota Historical Society

FACING PAGE, TOP
General Sylvanus B. Lowry was the founder of Acadia or Upper Town, an Indian trader, adjutant general of Minnesota, an unsuccessful Democratic candidate for lieutenant governor in 1859, and manager of a forwarding and commission business. He died in St. Cloud in 1865. (SCHS)

FACING PAGE, BOTTOM
While Joseph Edelbrock's home may have nearly collapsed under the weight of those attending Mass in his attic, his place of business, on the southwest corner of Fifth Avenue and St. Germain, was more substantial in 1870. (SCHS)

Mrs. Swisshelm's own antislavery convictions grew out of a short but memorable stay in Louisville where she had seen slavery firsthand, and she was deeply convinced that it was evil. This conviction often colored her reporting of events. The Rev. Thomas Calhoun was killed when his horse bolted over the bridge spanning the ravine between Middle and Lower Towns, and Mrs. Swisshelm duly reminded her readers that the horse had been purchased with money from the sale of a slave woman and her baby. The implication of divine retribution was clear.

This was not the only time her convictions colored her interpretation of events. Some time later, as Sylvanus Lowry was driving across the same bridge at Washington and Fifth avenues, one of his horses fell, and in its struggles to regain its footing it nearly threw the carriage and riders into the ravine. Mrs. Swisshelm's antislavery views provoked this comment:

> *The carriage which Mr. Lowry uses was bought at the time that the horse which was killed in the Calhoun accident was, and both were the price of blood. They were bought in exchange for that Minnesota baby and its mother who were sold into southern bondage. God has a controversy with the Lowrys and will pursue them until they restore that woman and her child to freedom. No one else ever met with an accident on that bridge.*

Many in St. Cloud were like early settler Joseph Edelbrock, who was identified by Mrs. Swisshelm as a "whole-hearted, slavery hating, German Democrat." But there were other Democrats, like attorney Christopher C. Andrews, who believed that the North was bound to uphold the terms of the Missouri Compromise for the sake of the Union and peace.

So, despite Governor Alexander Ramsey's immediate and generous offer of soldiers, many St. Cloud men were loathe to rush into service. The 47 men of the Little Giants, the home guard unit, were reluctant to leave the state. In March 1861 the county board had allowed this group $25 for the purchase of ammunition, which they were to have "ready for use when called for." The Little

Giants presumed that this gave the county—not the governor—first call on their services.

Mrs. Swisshelm's immediate reaction to their reluctance was to call the guards "German Democrats, some few of whom were said to be badly frightened." Later, her opinion mellowed. "The reason for the apathy of our people is . . . that we are on the extreme frontier; the soldiers have been removed and many, apprehending trouble with the Indians, think that all our men should stay home. The Indians serve as a respectable substitute for various reasons not given."

Mrs. Swisshelm, considered by many the mother of Minnesota's Republican Party, was, ironically, not favorably inclined toward President Lincoln. She had wanted the nomination to go to William H. Seward and was disappointed when Lincoln received it. Her newspaper, the *Visiter*, did not "whoop" for Lincoln until the last week before voting. After his election, she remained aloof and seemed to distrust him. She had wanted a strong abolitionist, and Lincoln's patient attitude looked like weakness to her. One issue of her newspaper in September 1861

appeared in mourning because of the President's countermanding of General John Charles Fremont's order freeing the slaves in Missouri.

One of the first from St. Cloud to enlist in the Union Army was Stephen Miller. Miller was a business associate of Mrs. Swisshelm's brother-in-law, and an active abolitionist. He had been offered a commission in the regular army but preferred to enlist as a private and work himself up through the ranks. In a short time he rose to the rank of lieutenant colonel, generating such pride among his friends back in St. Cloud that they took up a collection and bought him a sword. (Miller would later be elected governor of Minnesota, the only Minnesota governor to have come from St. Cloud, and his sword was eventually returned to the city and the Stearns County Historical Society.)

Early apathy concerning the war grew into general lethargy. Christopher C. Andrews announced his intention to form a St. Cloud Volunteer Company in which he proposed to enlist as a private. (The enlistment of both Miller and Andrews as privates may have been a little more self-serving than it appears. Both were well-educated men and presumed they might be called upon to command their units, as they were.) Thirty names were enrolled the night of the announcement, but from then on enlistments waned. Andrews had had six months in residence at Fort Leavenworth but thought he needed more training in the manual of arms; he spent a week at Fort Ripley drilling under a "bright Irish corporal." But in the sparsely populated area around St. Cloud even a properly drilled recruiter found army life, especially with a war on, hard to sell.

When they realized that the federal government was not going to drain all the fighting manpower from the state and send it south to fight, the St. Cloud Guards, (the local volunteer militia) offered their services, but limited it to protecting the forts in Minnesota. (Brave they might be, but foolhardy they certainly were not.)

Slowly, the city began to reflect a more military atmosphere. In July 1861 two companies of Minnesota's Second Regiment, en route to Fort Abercrombie (30 miles south of Fargo) camped overnight near town. When she learned of the encampment, Mrs. Swisshelm organized a group who rode around St. Cloud soliciting food. That evening the soldiers were escorted to a picnic ground where tables were piled high with food donated by St. Cloud citizens.

But the citizens were yet reluctant to fully support their own men in uniform. During the entire Civil War period the state governments did little for their soldiers, leaving most of the responsibility to local communities, while the federal government left the responsibility to the states or the communities. Even the hospital supplies were supposed to be furnished by the local community. Many counties voted appropriations to outfit and supply their volunteers, but the political dissension in St. Cloud was still so deep that a resolution to support local men with a contribution could not be passed by the city council.

The lack of support was sometimes attributed to the political polarization of deeply entrenched beliefs. The division in St. Cloud was surprisingly equal. This was apparent in the 1860 election, in which the citizenry cast a total of 494 votes for Douglas and Breckenridge and 439 for Lincoln. (The Democratic Party had split in that election; Stephen Douglas had represented the Northern Democrats and John Breckenridge the Southern.)

As late as September 1861, Mrs. Swisshelm was complaining that only Republicans had answered their country's call to arms. "Not one of the Democrats who cast votes for Douglas or Breckenridge last election has gone to do any fighting." She overlooked Democrat Christopher C. Andrews' efforts to mount a company. He had not yet gone, but in October his company of 20—he appears to have lost 10 of the original volunteers—left for Fort Snelling by stage.

James McKelvy, one of the company's organizers with Andrews, decided at the last minute not to go because the company was to be consolidated with others and thus, he felt, would lose its distinctive "St. Cloud" flavor. The company *was* merged with a larger squad from Le Sueur County and became the nucleus of Company I of the Third Minnesota; Andrews eventually commanded it, first as captain, then as

lieutenant colonel, colonel, brigadier general, and major general.

Later in the month, the St. Cloud Guards, a German company under Captain Lueg, left for Fort Abercrombie, and five months later the following ad appeared in the *St. Cloud Democrat*: "WANTED—15 sober, able-bodied men to fill up Captain Charles Lueg's Company of the 4th Regiment to the maximum of 101 men." It isn't known whether he got those volunteers or not.

The next year, in April, Lueg's company and another returned to St. Cloud and were given a supper at John Wilson's Meeting Hall. Following the supper two kegs of Kraemer's Best Lager Beer were brought in and disposed of. For the Home Guards, war had not yet become hell.

Pictured here is the Second Minnesota Regiment at the battle of Missionary Ridge. In July of 1861 two companies of the Second Minnesota, while encamped near St. Cloud, were treated to a picnic dinner by Jane Grey Swisshelm and other St. Cloud residents who contributed food. Oil by Douglas Volk in the Minnesota Capitol. Courtesy, Minnesota Historical Society

A lone man looks out over the southern end of Lower Town below Tenth Street around the time of the Civil War. (SCHS)

In August 1862 the President issued a call for another 300,000 men, the second such request. Another company, the Annihilators, was formed in St. Cloud. At one meeting, after speeches had been made and the St. Cloud Brass Band had played stirring marches, 11 persons, mostly Germans, signed on the enlistment roll. Perhaps Kraemer's Best Lager Beer was the best recruiter. A volunteer group from Watab and Winnebago Prairie landed at the upper levee and were escorted to the office of the Annihilators by the Brass Band to be sworn in. But at the last minute, three of the 25 volunteers backed out.

St. Cloud had the unsettling distinction of furnishing one of the Union Army's youngest soldiers. Lawrence Garlington, a nephew of Captain James McKelvy, enlisted in November 1862 as a drummer boy in Company I of the Seventh Minnesota Volunteers, his uncle's company. At the time of his enlistment he was only a few weeks past his 13th birthday. He was discharged July 4, 1865 because of a disability.

While the men were organizing into the Annihilators, the Little Giants, and other military groups, the women were forming Soldiers' Aid societies. They sewed clothing and made "half

'kerchiefs," which were used as towels and bandages. One group solicited donations of money and in one day raised enough to purchase a good deal of muslin, shipping to Captain Andrews' company—"41 shirts, 26 slippers, 15 pairs of drawers, 4 pillow slips, 2 sheets, 44 handkerchiefs . . . and 350 yards of bandages."

To her credit, Mrs. Swisshelm's Northern patriotism was not limited to editorializing in her newspaper. During the war she moved back East and worked in hospitals treating the Union wounded. Some said she moved back because she didn't like long-distance sniping at the administration; she preferred to do it at close range and in timely fashion. She continued writing, mainly for Eastern newspapers, and occasionally sent a story back to her nephew, William Bell Mitchell, who had taken over the *St. Cloud Democrat.* She was in Washington at the close of the war and one of the stories she sent back, following Lincoln's assassination, strongly hinted that the President had been the victim of a poison attempt before he was shot. Her previous lack of enthusiasm for the President did not prevent her from later becoming a close friend of Mrs. Lincoln's in Chicago.

Despite the early reluctance to march off to war, 647 Stearns County men (from an 1860 population of 4,505) eventually enlisted in the Union Army. Many of them may have enlisted because of the threat of the Dakota (Sioux) Uprising, also called the Dakota War, but their service continued after the threat from the Dakota was eliminated, and they were sent to fight in Civil War battles.

Minnesota's men were involved in some of the Civil War's worst and bloodiest battles. The First Minnesota Volunteer Infantry fought at Bull Run (Manassas) on July 21, 1861, the first large-scale land engagement of the war and a Union disaster. Antietam, where Minnesota men also fought, was considered one of the bloodiest days of the war, and at Gettysburg the First Minnesota was sacrificed in a futile charge to buy time for the Union forces. Although local men undoubtedly fought in these battles, no specific records can be found.

In the late summer of 1862, while the rest of the nation's attention was held by the blue and the gray, Minnesotans in the southwestern corner of the state were anxiously watching the red and the white. They were shocked and frightened by the slaying of five white settlers at Acton, a small town a few miles south of present-day Grove City, on August 17, 1862. The murders were wanton, the immediate result of a dare issued by one member in a hunting party of four Sioux Indians. But the real causes, like those of the Civil War, burned deep into the past.

White settlers in growing numbers had encroached on the Indians' territory, taking lands that the Indians had once roamed and hunted freely. Now the prairies sprouted houses and fences. White trappers came and began to take wantonly what the Indians had taken only in need.

The federal government eventually and grudgingly recognized the Indians' claim to the land and made many treaties to buy the land, each succeeding treaty offering less than the preceding one. By the treaties of 1805, 1837, 1847, 1851, and 1858 the Dakota, without fully realizing it, had surrendered almost all of their Minnesota Land. Ultimately these proud hunters were forced onto two strips of land along the Minnesota River, roughly from present-day Franklin northwest to Granite Falls, and told to farm that land. But even portions of this land were eventually taken from the Dakota by the white settlers.

For the most part, the Indians lived peaceably with the white settlers. But they did not suffer every indignity quietly. In 1858 an Indian delegation from Minnesota led by Chief Taoyatedutah

(Little Crow) went to Washington to seek, among other things, more prompt payment of Indian annuities due under earlier treaties. Whether by design or not, the delegation was detained in Washington throughout the summer; and work on their farms had to wait until their return. In desperation they signed yet another treaty and hurried back to Minnesota.

The new treaty was given as much respect by the government as the previous ones. Resisting government pressure, the Indians had insisted on receiving their payment in gold, but when it was delivered, the white traders were allowed to take out what they claimed the Indians owed them. Unscrupulous and unfeeling Indian agents were commonplace. One of them, told that the Indians were starving because their crops had failed, replied, "Let them eat grass!" His retort filtered back to the Indians, and when his body was found after an Indian attack on the agency his throat had been stuffed with grass.

Most Indians knew the white settlers would react violently to the murders near Acton. They realized that acting quickly, before the settlers could organize, was their only chance for success. Little Crow, though he had been replaced as spokesman for his tribe, was asked to lead the warriors in driving the white settlers from the Minnesota River Valley, where the Dakota activity

THIS PAGE
Among the Dakota who traveled to Washington in 1858 to seek enforcement of treaty provisions were: Big Eagle, Traveling Hail, Red Legs, Medicine Light, The Thief, Taconlipeiyo, Has-a-War-Club, Red Owl, Mankato, and Wabasha. Photos by Fredericks, Washington, D.C. Courtesy, Minnesota Historical Society.

FACING PAGE
Twenty-five thousand Minnesota men fought in the Civil War. The Third Minnesota is depicted here entering Little Rock, Arkansas. Oil by Stanley M. Arthurs in the Minnesota Capitol. Courtesy, Minnesota Historical Society.

Editor's note: Dakota (Dakotah) is the anglicized version of the name used by the Sioux when referring to themselves. It is generally preferred in place of Sioux, a term derived from the Ojibwe (Ojibway) for their Dakota enemies. The Ojibwe prefer the use of this name rather than Chippewa.

was centered during the month of the conflict. The immediate target of their violence was the Lower Sioux Agency on the Minnesota River, but the tremors were felt throughout the southern half of the state.

First news of the attack reached St. Cloud the evening of August 20. By coincidence, Clark W. Thompson, superintendent of Indian Affairs from St. Paul; William P. Dole, United States Commissioner of Indian Affairs; Minnesota Senator Morton Z. Wilkinson; and John G. Nicolay, one of President Lincoln's private secretaries, were in St. Cloud on their way to negotiate a treaty with the Red Lake and Pembina Ojibwe Indians. While these officials hurried back to St. Paul, Governor Ramsey issued an order to the militia of northern Minnesota to "rendezvous at St. Cloud and serve as mounted guard for protection of settlements in the area."

The threat from the Dakota in the south was not the only one now worrying St. Cloud and the more northern communities. The reason for the pending Ojibwe treaty was an incident concerning Hole-in-the-Day, an Ojibwe chief. He had stolen three head of cattle from the agency at Crow Wing, north of Fort Ripley, a few days earlier, and escaped his pursuers. There were fears the Ojibwe would literally bury the hatchet and join their longtime enemies, the Dakota, in a war against the whites while many of the men were off fighting in the Civil War.

Hole-in-the-Day was only a surmised threat, and the Ojibwe never did join with the Dakota, but Little Crow and the Dakota were actually attacking settlements and massacring whites. The number of Dakota now actively participating in the uprising grew and the area under attack expanded. Some of the Dakota, called "cut-hairs" by the more militant, had originally refused to take part in the raids. Some of the cut-hairs were friendly with whites, and others felt it was too late to stem the tide of whites taking over their lands. But they changed their minds when they saw how many scalps the warriors were bringing back and how ill-prepared the settlers were to defend themselves. Few of the white settlers knew how to use guns effectively.

Two scouting parties were sent out from St. Cloud almost immediately after receiving news of

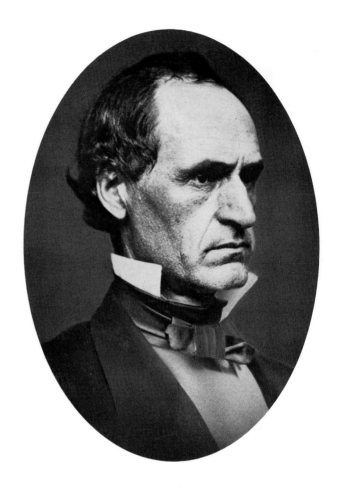

the attack. Ambrose Freeman, Chris Grandelmyer, and Sam Holes went to Paynesville, 25 miles southwest of St. Cloud, while Leander Gorton and J.H. Proctor went to Forest City, 25 miles south. The Paynesville party, returning on August 22, reported that 14 people had been killed at Norway Lake, 17 miles west of Paynesville, and much property had been destroyed by a marauding band of Dakota.

A volunteer company of 25 men from St. Cloud was quickly organized, armed, and supplied with horses. They started for Paynesville the next morning to help in getting the outlying farmers and their families to the larger settlements. Ambrose Freeman was chosen captain of the volunteer group.

When the company reached the Paynesville area they found it abandoned and all but two houses burned. The men went on to Norway Lake

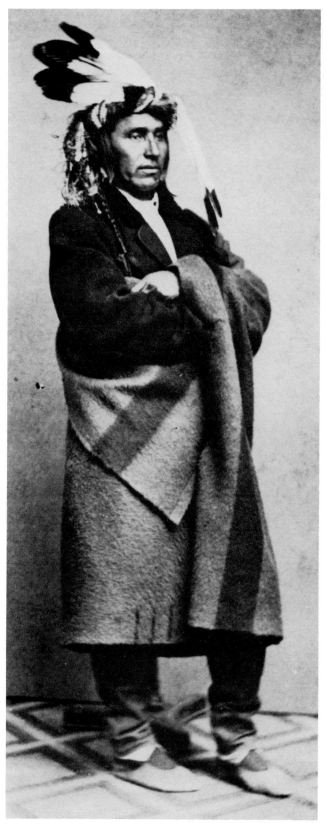

ABOVE
Taoyatedutah (Little Crow), the Dakota chief who led the militant Indians in their uprising in the fall of 1862, is depicted in this 1860 watercolor by Thomas W. Wood. Courtesy, Minnesota Historical Society

LEFT
Pogonaykeshick (Hole-in-the-Day) was an Ojibwe chief whose activities at the Crow Wing Indian Agency north of St. Cloud caused some concern at the same time Little Crow was leading the Dakota against southern Minnesota towns. Photo by Whitney's Gallery. Courtesy, Minnesota Historical Society

FACING PAGE
Minnesota Senator Morton Wilkinson was a member of the group whose purpose was to attempt a treaty with Hole-in-the-Day. Courtesy, The National Archives

but saw no Indians. The proximity of the attack at Paynesville, however, was enough to galvanize the residents of St. Cloud into providing for their own protection.

St. Cloud's residences and businesses were still spread out, difficult to defend against a concerted attack. Defenses were prepared, first in the area between what is now Sixth and Seventh avenues, which was enclosed and barricaded; the "command post" of this area was in the large, three-story brick building on the south side of St. Germain Street known as Broker's block, the ground floor of which was occupied by the Burbank brothers' store.

A more ambitious refuge, Fort Holes, was named for its designer, Sam Holes, and was built on the high ground facing present 10th Street South, between Second and Third avenues. The fort was a circular structure, 45 feet in diameter, and had a bulletproof tower with holes for sharpshooters. The fort held provisions for 500 people and was considered among the strongest defenses on the frontier. Neither Fort Holes (which was torn down in 1864) nor Broker's block were tested by an attack, although the fortifications did serve to provide shelter for refugees from outlying areas.

Returning from Paynesville, or what was left of

it, on August 24, Ambrose Freeman organized another company of mounted men, the Northern Rangers. The men left St. Cloud on September 3 bound for Forest City via Richmond. Indians had attacked Forest City and driven off all the horses. Freeman picked up the trail and followed it for about 10 miles to where a house had been burned and a number of hogs killed. But the trail had been lost in the destruction, and the men returned to Richmond.

While at Richmond on September 10, two of the men, sent out to secure horses, were fired on by two Indians hiding in the grass. Retreating, the men saw four Dakota on horseback attempting to cut them off, but they were able to raise the alarm and join the rest of the troop in pursuit of the mounted Indians. During the chase, another Indian was seen and shot. When it was discovered

FACING PAGE
The Broker block, a three-story brick building erected in 1861 by Joseph and Henry Broker, served as the northern defense of St. Cloud against possible Indian attack. The building, located on the present site of Fandel's, was destroyed by fire in 1872. (SCHS)

BELOW
The north side of St. Germain Street from Fifth Avenue looking west is pictured here about 1866. (SCHS)

that the dead Indian was a half-breed Ojibwe, and a scout from Company G of the Ninth Minnesota, the remaining Ojibwe scouts were so incensed that the soldier who had fired the fatal shot had to be sent back to Fort Snelling under arrest to forestall further hostility.

One company of men was now assigned to remain at St. Cloud for the protection of the citizenry, but on September 22, a message from Richmond caused Gen. Henry Zehring Mitchell to send 40 of the men to the aid of settlers who were being attacked. Soon 50 of the mounted Home Guards followed the original unit. They chased but did not catch up to the Dakota.

Some of the men in this contingent went on to relieve the men at Fort Abercrombie on the Dakota border, but even this fort did not provide total protection. While watering their horses at the river near the fort, the men were fired on by a party of Dakota, and John Weissing, a teamster from St. Cloud, was wounded. He died that night. John

Raymond, another St. Cloud soldier, was carrying water up from the river when a Dakota bullet pierced the bucket he was carrying, but Raymond escaped unharmed.

Southwestern Minnesota was taking the brunt of the uprising, with many towns suffering from the hit-and-run tactics of the Indians. Other towns suffered almost as much damage from preparing for attacks that never came. But by the end of September a unified command under Colonel Henry Sibley, a former fur trader and the first governor of Minnesota, succeeded in defeating the Dakota at Wood Lake. Many of the Indians left Minnesota for the Dakotas and were at Wounded Knee in 1890 where an armed Indian revolt was crushed in a bloody massacre.

Little Crow fled to the Dakotas with about

150 followers and spent the winter there. He returned to Minnesota quietly in June 1863 and was shot and killed while picking berries near Hutchinson.

Little Crow's band of militant Indians had failed in their original mission to regain control of their own land and destiny, but they had succeeded in unifying the divergent citizens of St. Cloud. (Or was it just that the Southerners and Southern sympathizers had moved out?)

A few years later, when Gen. Robert E. Lee surrendered the Confederate forces at Appomattox, those St. Cloud men who had served in the Union Army returned, eager to join others in building a community and in establishing businesses.

St. Cloud had passed out of its pioneer, frontier stage and was preparing to enter its industrial age.

ABOVE
In December of 1862, under orders of President Lincoln, 38 Dakota prisoners were hanged at Mankato for their part in the uprising. Courtesy, Minnesota Historical Society

FACING PAGE
Colonel Henry H. Sibley (1811–1891), the first governor of Minnesota, was asked by Governor Ramsey to direct the troops against the rampaging Dakota. From Cirker, *Dictionary of American Portraits*, Dover, 1967

3

Big Business Begins

Granite, Car Shops, and Automobiles

Certainly no city in the United States ever formed without businesses at the core. The three towns which became St. Cloud initially depended on fur—its trading and transshipment—as their main commercial activity. But as more pioneers came to the growing nuclei of the three towns, a broader range of business necessarily developed.

The greater number—and the greater variety—of commercial activities gravitated at first to Lower Town, George Brott's St. Cloud City, where the Yankee merchants from the East sought the company of like-minded men, especially in view of the alternative associates: Southerners, whose slave-holding they abhorred (although not all, perhaps, with the zeal of Mrs. Swisshelm); and Germans, whose language they didn't understand and whose beer-brewing and drinking many of them could not condone.

Once of the more successful early companies in St. Cloud was Julius Adams' Cigar Factory. In the background is the United States Post Office, which was demolished to make way for the Civic Center (SCHS)

The frontier to which these merchants came was a gamble: still patrolled by troops from small army posts; still under territorial law, which was often late in appearing where needed and usually fell short of what was expected; still underpopulated but with a high proportion of renegades, swindlers, ne'er-do-wells, and rough-hewn backwoodsmen.

These Yankee merchants had come from areas where civilization—white man's civilization, that is—had been developing for almost 200 years. Their Eastern cities, even the smallest and crudest, boasted established law and custom, orderly if occasionally corrupt government, and existing commercial lines of distribution and sale. Moving west was not precisely a leap into the unknown, but it was a daring move.

These early entrepreneurs were, in the main, small businessmen; they furnished the goods and services necessary for city living in a frontier area where inhabitants could not shoot or grow all of their own food nor weave and sew all of their own clothing. Though they provided needed ser-

ABOVE
Raymond & Dunnewold's Sash and Door Factory had all the work it could handle in the city's early days. The partnership between J.H. Raymond and Gerard H. Dunnewold was formed in 1895. Raymond died in 1906, the year this picture was taken, and Dunnewold entered a new partnership with Henry Sartell. (SCHS)

RIGHT
Gales & Strobel, wagonmakers, was a local business at 1022 St. Germain Street. In this 1895 view, business still appears prosperous, but the automobile would soon spell disaster for local wagonmakers. (SCHS)

vices, apart from the few clerks or helpers they hired, these early merchants did not furnish employment for large numbers of people.

The first large-scale employer was the Burbank brothers' freight line, established in the early 1850s. Hostlers, drivers, wainwrights, harness-makers, blacksmiths, clerks, innkeepers—these and a host of other tradesmen connected with moving heavy loads over great distances—found employment with the Burbanks either at or through the firm's St. Cloud headquarters. But with the advance of the railroad lines, this variety of employment dried up, to be replaced eventually by a localized form of employment based on the railroad.

Nonetheless, the Burbank brothers helped propel the city into a business boom. Concomitant with the Burbanks' freight line, other smaller but still valuable enterprises were begun. The sash and door factories that had supplied the early builders of St. Cloud now had the means to reach the opening markets further west. The brewers, despite Yankee disdain, found enough Germans— or converted enough non-Germans—to finance construction of several breweries in St. Cloud. (Not incidentally, in the early 1980s one of the few small independent breweries still operating in the United States brewed beer in nearby Cold Spring.) Flour mills, taking advantage of the nearby water power of the Mississippi and the grain produced in the fertile Sauk Valley, flourished into modern times. The last mill in the city operated into the 1960s, and one feed mill still operated less than half a mile north of the city limits at the mouth of the Sauk River; another still ground away in nearby St. Joseph until 1980.

Early St. Cloud businessmen, though they may have railed about the Mississippi River as a barrier to trade from the East, eventually realized that it gave them a certain advantage over merchants in the older, larger, more established Sauk Rapids on the east bank. The western plains were now being farmed by a growing number of settlers, and their business was important to St. Cloud merchants. The lack of a bridge across the Mississippi meant that their shopping was confined largely to the St. Cloud stores on the west side of the river.

But in 1886, a disaster struck which altered the destinies of both Sauk Rapids and St. Cloud. On April 14 a tornado spiraled out of the Minnesota sky. The funnel was first observed in an area southwest of St. Cloud. It moved north, circling the city, nibbling at the edges, and then crossed the Mississippi and struck Sauk Rapids. Every public or commercial building but one in that town was either sucked up or smashed flat.

A path of destruction 300 yards wide left 109 buildings, with a valuation of $176,000, destroyed; total property damage for St. Cloud and Sauk Rapids amounted to $300,000. St. Cloud suffered 20 dead and 75 injured; Sauk Rapids 38 dead and 64 injured.

The preeminence of Sauk Rapids as the major trading center of the area was destroyed that spring afternoon. Its commercial area was devastated, and by the time the city recovered and rebuilt, St. Cloud had taken the lead and would not relinquish it. Now the St. Cloud merchants clamored for a bridge across the Mississippi.

The industry with which St. Cloud was most identified for the longest period, and which was responsible for the city's sobriquet, "The Busy

Gritty Granite City," was initiated in 1863 by Breen and Young, a granite company, at a spot now within the walls of the Minnesota Correctional Facility, more commonly known as the St. Cloud Reformatory. Actually the first granite quarry in Minnesota was opened earlier in the same year, 1863, about 12 miles north of Sauk Rapids, but it closed down almost immediately when the operators, two Scotsmen, discovered that granite could be shipped to Chicago from

FACING PAGE AND ABOVE
The Mississippi & Rum River Boom Company was logging on the Mississippi in St. Cloud long after 1900. The stern-wheeler not only towed the necessary eating and sleeping barges, but it also furnished the power necessary for other purposes. Crews even managed to get logs over the shallower dams where openings in the weir allowed passage. (SCHS)

LEFT
The 1886 cyclone that destroyed the business section of Sauk Rapids also touched the residential area. The only wall left standing in this house had the window blown out, but the door was left closed. (SCHS)

Aberdeen in their native Scotland cheaper than they could cut and ship it from their quarry.

Breen and Young's choice of location was dictated as much by its proximity to established shipping lines as by the quality of the stone. Minnesota granite, the earliest use of which was limited to construction purposes—foundations, curbing, steps—was preferred for its strength rather than for its beauty. Only later, when advanced polishing techniques became less expensive and revealed

the natural beauty of the native granite, was this natural resource of Minnesota extensively used for building facades and other decorative purposes.

Early development of the granite industry depended on the skills of the immigrants who began moving into St. Cloud with the opening of more quarries. Scots and Scandinavians, especially Swedes, were skilled at working granite, which was native to their homeland. And it was because of the skills of these men, in management as well as with the stone itself, that the industry prospered.

Minnesota granite was exhibited at the 1876 Centennial Exposition in Philadelphia and won awards for its beauty, but it was nevertheless still relegated mostly to such structural use as foundation piers or railroad bridges, one of them in St. Cloud itself. One utilitarian use was sufficiently remunerative to keep the quarries around St. Cloud operating in the black until the other virtues of its granite were appreciated; this was the widespread use of granite paving blocks. St. Paul and Minneapolis, growing into larger cities, used the paving blocks to form the bed for their street railways. St. Paul was supplied with over a million and a half blocks, and 1,200 carloads of blocks were used on the extension for the Minneapolis car line. St. Cloud paving blocks were shipped as far away as St. Louis.

Structural use of St. Cloud granite was also

limited by the lack of municipal (hence substantial) buildings in what was essentially still a pioneer area. Federal and state buildings, heavy users of granite and other stone, were still confined to older, more established areas farther east, and only gradually, as St. Paul and Minneapolis (and much later St. Cloud) gained sufficient stature and permanency to require such edifices, did local (that is, state-wide) architectural use of area granite become a factor in granite production.

ABOVE
This comparatively shallow granite quarry shows that early granite companies found their material almost at the surface. From *Pictorial Proof of Progress,* Pan Motor Company, 1918

ABOVE LEFT
"Railroad and wagon bridges across the Mississippi at St. Cloud" was the description on this scenic postcard view, probably taken from the steeple of Holy Angels Church in 1870. A number of logs floating freely in the river were no longer a threat to ferry passengers; they could take the bridge. (SCHS)

FACING PAGE
A locomotive tries the new railroad bridge across the Mississippi. The barrels on the bridge may have been kept filled with water to douse any fires on the wooden trestles caused by sparks from the engine. (SCHS)

The Minnesota State Reformatory for Men at St. Cloud was built on the site of the state's first successful granite quarry and had the longest uninterrupted granite wall in the world. Many St. Cloud residents do not know that the wall was not completed until 1939. Photo by Mike Knaak. (SCHS)

Archbishop John Ireland of St. Paul was regarded with warmth by granite men; his choice of native granite, rather than Indiana limestone or Vermont granite, for the Cathedral in St. Paul led to its use for churches throughout the state.

Almost from the beginning, cemetery headstones and markers were the second mainstay of the industry. And it was this phase of the industry that enabled many granite companies to remain in the business when the more lucrative architectural work slacked off during times of depression. In fact, this business was so steady that many St. Cloud granite companies concentrated all their efforts on producing monuments, to their ultimate regret. In the 1940s, 1950s, and 1960s, when newer cemeteries opted for small, flat markers or none at all, those companies specializing in monuments exclusively found that their "certain" market had dwindled. They were unable

to produce enough smaller markers at a profit substantial enough to remain in business; they had few contacts in the architectural field; and they could not pick up the skill and knowledge quickly enough. One by one, the St. Cloud-based granite companies were acquired by the Cold Spring Granite Company, now the world's largest producer of granite in all its uses, with quarries throughout the United States and Canada. The Cold Spring company had maintained its architectural business, expanded it, and evolved manufacturing techniques and equipment that enabled it to produce monuments efficiently, keeping them a lucrative but secondary segment of the business.

While it was growing and prospering in St. Cloud, the granite industry was the source of livelihood for several St. Cloud families who had founded granite companies: the Holes, Campbell, Simmers, Gruber, Luckemeyer, and Trebtoske

families, among others, owned or operated quarries or finishing plants that employed a large number of St. Cloud's inhabitants. As subsidiaries of Cold Spring Granite and in some independent shops, many of the plants still maintain fairly large work forces.

The most remarkable reminder of the early days of the granite industry in St. Cloud now surrounds Breen and Young's first quarry. The quarry site was chosen in 1887 for the Minnesota State Reformatory for Men. In 1889 construction was begun on a wall to enclose the 55-acre prison grounds. The wall is 4-1/2 feet thick at the base, 3 feet thick at the top, and 22 feet high. The major portion of the wall was finished in three or four years, but the final section was not completed until 1939. The wall is 1,700 yards long, (200 feet short of one mile) and it was laid up of granite that was quarried on the site, cut, and placed by inmate labor. It is presumed to be the longest uninterrupted granite wall in the world. (The Great Wall of China is interrupted by gates.)

While the granite industry's growth in the area did not displace other industry, the railroad that reached St. Cloud in September 1866 clouded the future of the Burbank freight wagons, barges, and stage coaches. But although it pleased the passengers who no longer had to ride in dusty, bouncing stagecoaches, the railroad soon irked the city fathers. The St. Paul & Pacific railroad line paralleled the territorial road, which ran along the east side of the Mississippi. Passengers and freight still required ferrying across the river to the more rapidly developing west side. Because the railroad's government charter stipulated that it had to provide "rail service to St. Cloud," the city sued the rail line to force it to bridge the river, but the courts decided the depot on the east side was "in the vicinity" and was close enough. In 1882 another line was completed to St. Cloud from Minneapolis up the west side of the river, and this line, plus a connection between St. Cloud and the port city of Duluth, somewhat compensated the city for its loss of the suit. The bridge was built later anyway, and with St. Cloud granite.

While rail connections were important for the markets they opened both to and for St. Cloud,

FACING PAGE
An unidentified family group poses with its horse and buggy in front of the family residence. Photos similar to this one, taken in 1900, substituted for the usual formal family portrait. (SCHS)

RIGHT
James Jerome Hill, the Empire Builder, selected St. Cloud as the location for the Great Northern Railway's shops in 1890. The facility quickly became the largest single employer in the St. Cloud area. Courtesy, Minnesota Historical Society

BELOW
This train, one of four special ones, passed through St. Cloud on September 4, 1883. Distinguished American and foreign passengers were being taken to the celebration marking the completion of the Northern Pacific at Gold Creek, Montana. This was the opening of the northwest by the "first of the northern transcontinentals," a great event in U.S. railroad history. (SCHS)

their contribution in the form of employment, while welcome, was limited at first. The marshalling yards of the Great Northern on the northwest border of the city did require engineers, firemen, brakemen, switchmen, and other personnel, but the real boost in employment came when railroad entrepreneur James J. Hill, Minnesota's Empire Builder, decided to locate a facility in St. Cloud to build boxcars for his line.

Jim Hill and three partners had started in business in 1878 with the purchase of the first division of the St. Paul & Pacific line. Three years later they acquired the Minneapolis & St. Cloud railroad. The St. Paul & Pacific was consolidated later as the St. Paul, Minneapolis & Manitoba. In 1889 the name of the Minneapolis & St. Cloud was changed to the Great Northern, which then absorbed the St. Paul, Minneapolis & Manitoba.

When St. Cloud became the focus of Hill's plans for a car shop in the late 1880s, he acquired a 160-acre site abutting the Sauk River west of St. Cloud. The first five buildings erected in 1890 were the repair shop, paint shop, blacksmith shop, wood mill, and store room. Most of these buildings still stand. The car shops immediately became the

major employer in the area, soon hiring as many as 500 men. The area around the shops soon had enough residents to incorporate as Waite Park, and ordinances were passed regulating the speed of horses and mules, providing for the disposition of dead animals and "unwholesome substances," and penalizing drunkenness and nudity.

In the beginning, the facility's function was the construction of wooden boxcars, urgently needed for the rapidly expanding Great Northern. As the line's needs changed, so did the products of the car shops, and over the years the shops have turned out steel baggage cars, snow dozers, weed spray cars, and a multitude of specialized equipment. With the March 1970 merger of the Chicago, Burlington & Quincy, the Great Northern, the Northern Pacific, and the Spokane, Portland & Seattle into the Burlington Northern, the line has become the longest railroad in the United States, operating over 26,000 miles of track. The car shops in St. Cloud are now involved principally in performing heavy repairs on various types of freight equipment and in serving as the major material distribution point for the entire Burlington Northern system.

During World War II, when freight handling was at a peak, the car shops employed as many as 1,200 men, but since changing to a repair facility the labor force has stabilized to around 500.

The early history of St. Cloud is dotted with the names of many businesses that were begun to fill a particular need—sash and door factories, lumber mills, flour mills, brickyards, cigar and broom manufacturing, to name only a few. Many of the businesses either changed or faded into obscurity as that particular need changed or disappeared. Few of those early companies intended to make a dent in a national market; in fact, those that did aspire to national distribution could be counted on one hand. Some did attempt to grow in St. Cloud's early days, but they were born one at a time and they died young.

One of the earliest ones, with a rare product for its day, was the St. Cloud Fibre Ware Company. The flats below the hill in Lower Town had easy access to water power, and among the firms concentrated in an area served by early St. Cloud builder Josiah E. West's Water & Power Company was the Phoenix Iron Works, built in 1886. The iron works had been erected specifically to make milling machinery to produce flour by a new process. The owner of the iron works also constructed a flour mill nearby to utilize the process. Neither the iron works nor the mill succeeded; the new process may have been faulty, and/or, as is faintly indicated by the news stories of the day, the owner was. In 1888 the iron works was taken over by George Tileston, who owned a nearby flour mill. He put 25 coopers to work in the old

Phoenix plant making flour barrels for his mill.

In August 1889 the newspapers reported that a "gentleman from the East" (from Ohio, specifically) was looking over the property as a possible manufactory for "vulcanized fibreware." The process involved using molds to form a mixture of wood pulp and resin into tubs, pails, buckets, sinks, kegs, barrels, and even furniture. So eager was the city to aid the newly formed St. Cloud Fibre Ware Company that when, in 1890, the taxpayers voted a bond issue of $80,000 for city improvements and earmarked $50,000 for a bridge across the Mississippi at 10th Street South, $20,000 of the remainder was directed to be spent on improvements to make the Phoenix Iron Works building suitable for the new occupant. Claims were made by the investors that 100 men

ABOVE
Julius Adams' Cigar Factory furnished employment to enough people around the turn of the century to produce one million cigars during the year of 1903. (SCHS)

FACING PAGE
The car shops of the Great Northern represented significant employment for St. Cloud when James Hill opened them in the 1890s. Many of the buildings presently in use by Burlington Northern are the original buildings.

would be needed when the machinery for the process arrived; 600 would be employed when production began in earnest.

The Eastern gentleman was George W. Laraway of Akron. He had invented his process in 1840 and now had patents on the machinery needed to produce fibreware items. The process, he said, used "sawdust, popple wood, straw—any fibrous substance," in fact, and Mr. Laraway, soon on the scene in person, expressed regret that there was no lumber or pulp mill nearby as a source for his raw material. Josiah West, never one to miss an opportunity to erect a building, immediately constructed a pulp mill next to the Fibre Ware plant, which was still awaiting shipment of its machinery, being made in Akron. By the end of August 1890, the pulp mill was ready, turning out two tons of pulp a day. At Fibre Ware, one pail machine was in place and turning out a pail a minute, but the product was not as impervious to moisture as hoped. The company said that adjustments were being made in the mixture of gums and resins used in the process.

In March 1891 a larger disaster visited the old Phoenix building: the Fibre Ware plant burned down. Summer was spent rebuilding the plant and repairing the machinery, and in the fall the company was ready to try again. A news story describing the reopening listed the investors, and among the Akron stockholders were local investors Josiah E. West and William Bell Mitchell, as well as James J. Hill.

In January 1892 the Fibre Ware Company admitted it was still stymied; its pails still softened in wet use. The local investors became restless. Pulp from the pulp mill, built especially to supply the raw material for the Fibre Ware Company, was piling up. So several of the original investors formed the St. Cloud Paper Mill Company. West and Mitchell were joined by attorney F.E. Searle and investor Nehemiah P. Clark. It is likely there were others, but they remained in silent partnership. The paper company built a new 21x170 foot building and installed paper-making machinery in April 1892.

Testing was still going on at Fibre Ware and hope was high. In case that point was missed, Mitchell's newspaper printed a story about a

buyer from Wisconsin, N.H. Brokaw of the Menasha Woodenware Company, who visited the plant, saw the product and contracted for the entire output on the spot. But by the end of 1892 the product was still unsatisfactory, and Fibre Ware reported that chemists were now working on a new cream finish that would not affect taste or peel off when frozen. However, the company's contract with the city, which included a bonus of $10,000 after 90 days of successful operation, was in jeopardy. The time limit was running out.

The St. Cloud Paper Mill was now running in high gear, producing three tons of No. 1 manila paper a day. Late in February 1893 they were slowed down a bit by a fire that damaged the plant. It had been set by an arsonist, the young manager of the mill who had recently been fired.

Calamity was never far away, it seemed. No sooner was the paper mill humming along again when, in August, it was hit by a second fire. Both the pulp mill and the paper mill were completely destroyed. Only $17,474 of the reported $40,000 damage was covered by insurance. The proximity of the disaster seemed to finish off the St. Cloud

Fibre Ware Company, too. Or perhaps management was looking for an excuse to abandon the project. At any rate, this time it did not rise, phoenix-like, from the ashes.

Whether or not the experience with the Fibre Ware Company, or the Phoenix Iron Works, or other unpublicized financial fiascos were the cause, St. Cloud seemed to shy away from large industry that aspired to national status for many years. Thus, when another opportunity later presented itself the city gave it such support that when it died, in the national spotlight, the trauma of its passing lasted for a generation.

The public announcement in the city's newpapers on March 2, 1917 that the Pan Motor Company would locate in St. Cloud created such excitement that when the United States declared war on Germany a little over a month later, the news shared the front pages in local papers with the details of the new company's organization.

The Pan Motor Company was the brainchild of Samuel Conner Pandolfo, an ex-insurance agent from the Southwest. Looking for a new challenge, Pandolfo renewed an old interest in automobiles. Pandolfo was a portly, dynamic, wide-visioned man who had supreme confidence in his ability to accomplish anything he undertook. He lacked only two attributes needed for the success he craved: a modicum of caution, and the ability to accept advice from others, especially those who made less money than he did. He had energy to burn, ideas to spare, and unlimited audacity. His promotional activity for the new venture soon spread over the land—at least from the Mississippi River west—a blizzard of brochures and letters that concentrated more on selling stock in the company than it did on selling the company's cars. (Admittedly, the company had no cars to sell and would not have any for several months. It

Pictured here are the Tileston flour mill and elevator on the west side of the river below the Tenth Street dam. St. Cloud Fibre Ware was located in the same area. (SCHS)

ABOVE
With flags waving and bands playing, the first group of soldiers leaves to fight in World War I. (SCHS)

FACING PAGE
Samuel Conner Pandolfo was founder, president, and general manager of the Pan Motor Company. From *Pictorial Proof of Progress*, Pan Motor Company, 1918

would have none of its own manufacture for several years.)

Pandolfo's first contribution of many to the company concerned its organizational plan. During his presidency, only common stock would be issued by the Pan Motor Company. It carried a par value of $5 but would be sold for $10. Pandolfo wanted the Pan Motor Company stock to be "unimpaired." He understood this to mean that the par value of the stock would be used only for capital assets, not for organizational or advertising expenses. Thus, of each $10 taken in payment for a share, $5 went into the surplus fund and $5 into the capital fund. The surplus fund could be used at Pandolfo's discretion—for salaries (including his own), commissions to stock salesmen, legal fees, advertising, postage, and all other expenses until the capital fund contained $30,000. The capital fund would be used only for the purchase of land and the purchase of and erection of equipment for the plant.

Pandolfo explained this plan as he traveled through the Southwest in the summer of 1916, selling stock (to be issued later), and heading for Chicago where he would incorporate, gather a technical staff, and look for "habitation" for the Pan Motor Company.

From Chicago Pandolfo had sent letters to a number of communities, asking about the possibility of locating an automobile plant in the vicinity. Perhaps as early as January 1917, he had a reply from the Commercial Club (forerunner of the Chamber of Commerce) of St. Cloud. They could not give him land or other inducements, but

to persuade the company to locate in St. Cloud, many members would lend their names and prestige to the company, in addition to buying stock.

Before locating in St. Cloud, the company's board of directors consisted of Pandolfo, George Heidman, and Norman Street (two Chicago attorneys who had handled some legal work for the new company), and John Barritt, whom Pandolfo had hired away from the Cheyenne (Wyoming) Business College that Barritt had founded to be the secretary of the Pan Motor Company.

The St. Cloud men—a good part of the business community of the city—who joined the Pan Motor Company's board of directors were: Charles D. Schwab, president of the Farmers State Bank, the Farmers Loan and Investment Company of St. Cloud, and the First State Bank of Clear Lake; Charles F. Ladner, president of Ladner Hardware Company of St. Cloud, of the Retail Hardware Merchants Fire Insurance Company, of the Hall Hardware Company of Minneapolis, vice-president of the St. Cloud Iron Works and the Miner Theatre Company, and a director of the Security State Bank of St. Cloud (Ladner was not an original member of the board but joined early in 1918); Hugh Evans, president of the St. Cloud (wholesale) Grocery Company and a former mayor of St. Cloud; Fred Schilplin, publisher of the *St. Cloud Daily Times* and an owner of Security Blank Book and Printing Company (he would later, while on the Pan board, become postmaster of St. Cloud); George E. Hanscom, president of the Merchants National Bank of St. Cloud and of the First State Bank of Stewartville, and vice-president of the Mayer, Watertown, Maple Plain, and Long Lake state banks and the Farmers and Merchants State Bank of Sedan; Charles Bunnell, a trustee of the Nehemiah P. Clark estate, involving vast lumber, ore, and stock holdings; Peter B. Thielman, a director of Farmers Loan and Investment Company; and Hal C. Ervin, Jr., a director, secretary-treasurer, and manager of the St. Cloud branch of the H. C. Ervin (flour mills) Company, director and vice-president of the Beltrami Elevator and Milling Company, Bemidji, and director of the Merchants National Bank of St. Cloud.

The business connections are noted here for the same reason Pandolfo, who called his directors the "million dollar board," to their embarrassment, noted them: they were among the powers of the business community of St. Cloud.

Construction of a plant for the Pan Motor Company, north of the railroad tracks on 33rd Avenue, was pushed hard by Pandolfo, and perhaps because of its potential for war work, he had no difficulty getting the materials. But until it was completed, the business offices of the company were spread among various buildings on Fifth Avenue in downtown St. Cloud. Main offices were on the second and third floors of the First National Bank building on the corner of Fifth Avenue and St. Germain Street; advertising offices were in the Farmers State Bank building (now a restaurant) on Fifth; and mail preparation facilities were in the Board of Education building, which no longer exists, on Fifth Avenue between Third and Fourth streets.

While still in Chicago, Pandolfo had arranged that 10 demonstration cars being built in Indianapolis be brought to St. Cloud on the Fourth of July. He planned a welcoming celebration in the form of a giant barbecue. More than 15,000 pounds of beef were ordered, 8,000 loaves of bread were baked, and every pickle in St. Cloud

was searched out, sliced, and served up.

The cars on display at the barbecue were not really Pan cars. They had been hurriedly assembled from available parts by a consulting engineering firm in Indianapolis, and though a total of 10 had been ordered and were delivered, Pandolfo, who praised the cars publicly while he belittled them privately, told his technical staff to drop work on the ultimate Pan car and assemble an interim model the company could sell until production could start on the "real" Pan.

And there were other problems facing Pandolfo. St. Cloud had grown slowly but steadily over the years. Even the influx of employees for

ABOVE
On a temporary platform, Pandolfo addresses the crowd at the Fourth of July barbecue while other speakers, including Bishop Joseph F. Busch, await their turn. To the left a movie cameraman grinds away.

FACING PAGE
This aerial view of Franklin Manufacturing looking west indicates how much has been added to the original Pan Motor Company building, which was called Factory Building Number 2. Number 1 was the Engineering Building, no longer in existence, but located next to the tracks in the present parking lot across the street, where the long building is presently.
Courtesy, Franklin Manufacturing

the Burbank freight line had come in a constant stream rather than all at once, and many of them did not stay to live in St. Cloud. This slow, steady growth meant there were few homes for sale or rent in St. Cloud, and almost none at all in the west end near the Pan plant.

But now engineers, mechanics, specialists, laborers of all kinds, and salesmen from everywhere were pouring into town; and they could find few places to stay, even overnight. Pandolfo quickly erected the Motor Hotel a few blocks from the Pan plant for the transients. But for the more permanent staff he started his own small city, Pan-Town-on-the-Mississippi. The 58 homes that were built there were much closer to the lowly Sauk River, but Pandolfo knew that few outside of Stearns County had heard of that small stream, whereas the mighty Mississippi was known worldwide.

The company had faced some initial difficulties in obtaining permission from the state to sell its stock, but they were cleared up and, even in the

ABOVE
Pictured here about 1918 are some of the homes in Pan Town. Due entirely to Pandolfo's hard sell to the city, Pan Town had "white way" street lighting long before any other residential area in St. Cloud.

RIGHT
Developers were hoping that other areas of the city in addition to Pan Town would prosper with the location of the Pan Motor Company in St. Cloud. This brochure promoted North Side Park, a development in which P.R. Thielman, a Pan Motor Company director, had an interest.

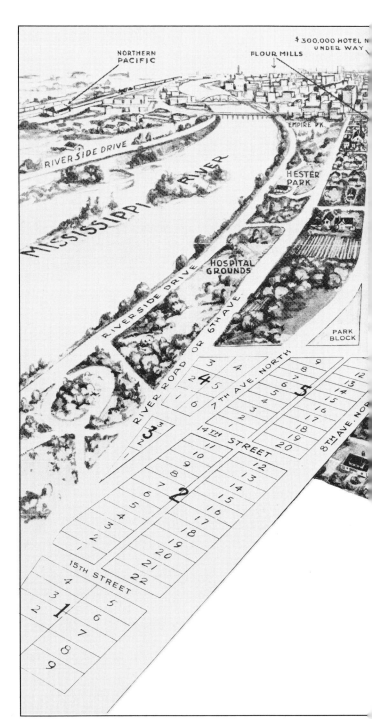

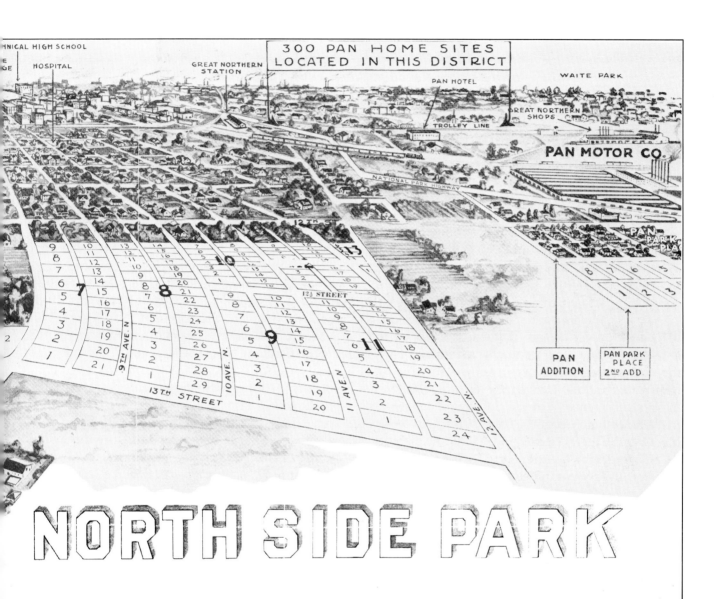

300 PAN HOME SITES LOCATED IN THIS DISTRICT

NORTH SIDE PARK

WE invite you to become part owner in North Side park and by so doing, share in the profits. We are giving you the benefit of wholesale prices on lots you buy and doing everything possible to promote the interests of all who take advantage of this offer. We need your help in developing this district, and we know you will appreciate as well as greatly profit by our efforts.

face of patriotic competition in the form of liberty bonds, money was soon flowing into St. Cloud at a rate that would have amazed a man with smaller dreams than Pandolfo's. In April 1918, 43,718 shares, at $10 each, were sold. One day in May more than $30,000 was taken in.

Pandolfo put the wealth to work at once. He was finally convinced by his staff that a newly designed car did not leap from the drawing board into instant production. Another source of income was needed, so the drop forge complex was pushed to early completion. The facility not only allowed the Pan Motor Company to contribute directly to the war effort, it also earned money by supplying parts for other automobile companies.

Still, with the heavy start-up expenses, the company was unable to pay dividends on its stock, and the various state regulatory agencies, if not the stockholders themselves, were questioning the company. Pandolfo insisted the fuss was raised by bankers, particularly in the Southwest where he had made some enemies. They didn't like to see money leave their control, he said, and he planned an answer to the questioners.

It began as a pamphlet and grew into a large format (12-1/2 x 9-1/2 inch) 270-page book. Filled with facts, figures, and photos, it was called *Pictorial Proof of Progress*, and it detailed the steps necessary to make and assemble a car. People, machinery, raw material, even holes in the ground (one was an open pit ore mine on the Mesabi range, the other a gravel pit on the Pan plant grounds) were pictured. Following an initial print run of 5,000, special copies with a gold-stamped cover—the rest were blind-embossed—were sent to every governor of every state and to every senator and representative in Washington.

However, neither the book nor Pandolfo's energetic and often vituperative defense of the company held off the federal government. Just five days after the November 11 armistice in 1918, a federal grand jury in Fergus Falls, Minnesota brought an indictment accusing Pandolfo and company secretary John Barritt of using the mails to defraud.

Up to this point Pandolfo had been dealing with innuendo, and at a distance, from his critics. Now

the charges were spelled out and would be tried in Minnesota. Or would they? As the company and attorney Ripley B. Brower prepared the defense, the government asked for a postponement to gather more evidence. Pandolfo cried, "Foul!" and the judge agreed. Delay would only harm the company; investors would avoid buying stock in a company under indictment and without a chance to clear itself. The government withdrew the charges rather than risk an immediate trial.

Pandolfo said it was a victory, but the damage had been done. Where money had been the least of the company's problems before the indictment, the lack of it now threatened its very existence. And the "victory" turned out to be short-lived; the "war" against the company was resumed in February 1919 when the government brought in a new indictment, this time in Chicago and this time naming all of the company's directors as co-conspirators. Along with the others, Fred Schilplin, St. Cloud's postmaster, found himself accused of using the mails to defraud.

What perhaps irritated Pandolfo most about the timing of the indictment was that the trial would be beginning in Chicago just when the Model A Pan, the model the company had labored two years to produce, was due to roll off the assembly line in St. Cloud.

The car was not a radically new design but it did have a number of features that made it unique. The engine, designed by Victor Gauvreau, was rated by the auto magazines of the time as a very efficient design. It was claimed to be the first commercially produced car to have a counterbalanced crankshaft running in ball bearings. But the feature usually associated with the car was the folding seat arrangement. The back of the Pan car's front seat folded down level with the back seat to form a bed. This was an instant hit with traveling salesmen if not with the mothers of nubile daughters.

The Pan car also featured a deterrent to those car thieves of the period who could hot-wire an ignition; its gear shift lever could be unlocked in neutral, waggling ineffectually from the floorboards until the key was inserted and turned, locking the gear shift lever to the shifting fork.

ABOVE
The Pan "Tourist Sleeper" Model was the only version of the A-model produced, although the company had plans for a closed sedan and a roadster. Approximately 500 autos of this model were built. From *Pictorial Proof of Progress*, Pan Motor Company, 1918

LEFT
Testing the Pan car in Minnesota's typical severe winter weather are, left to right, Victor Gauvreau, chief designing engineer; Ray DeVlieg, methods engineer; Ray J. Fitness, assistant designing engineer; and LeRoy Brown, production manager.

It was a firm, friendly, powerful little car that could have had a long and fruitful existence and certainly would have been a powerful addition to St. Cloud's industrial base had it survived.

Pandolfo's irritation at not seeing it into production was soon replaced by another overriding one: the case against the company would be heard beginning October 24, 1919 by Judge Kenesaw Mountain Landis. The man who would later be remembered as baseball's first and most high-handed commissioner was first a high-handed federal judge. Landis had earned a reputation as a brisk, opinionated jurist, and he lived up to it during and following the trial. An example of his ruling, and a point on which Pandolfo based the appeal of his conviction, was his decision regarding the showing of motion pictures of the Pan plant in action. He had ruled, late one afternoon, that the movies could be shown to the jury. The next morning when the photographer who had taken them testified to their authenticity, he said that Ben Forsyth, Pan Motor Company advertising manager, had accompanied him. Landis then ruled the movies inadmissable, saying that it was an advertising manager's job not to tell the truth. What made Pandolfo's appeal viable was that the remark was made within earshot of the jury.

But it was on Pandolfo's unique and highly remunerative salary arrangement that the prosecution concentrated its attack. Government attorneys frequently asked defense witnesses who were stockholders if they didn't think it unfair for Pandolfo to take as much as $500,000 to $600,000 in commissions when they weren't getting dividends from their stock. A typical answer was given by a St. Cloud board member who said he didn't think Pandolfo was being overpaid if he built a company that would later pay stockholders large dividends. "He is getting paid now," the witness said. "I'll get paid later."

The trial lasted more than a month, and when the jury returned their verdict on December 6, they found all board members innocent except Pandolfo.

Judge Landis gave his opinion of the Pan Motor Company at the time he sentenced Pandolfo. Given a 10-year sentence and fined $4,000, Pandolfo listened as Landis said he wanted it understood that the court's action was not intended to influence present or future holders of Pan Motor stock. "A United States citizen," the judge said, "has a right to throw his money away if he feels like it."

Later in December Pandolfo resigned from the company presidency although he remained one of the largest stockholders. He was replaced as president by Charles Ladner. Ladner's solid reputation and business sense, board members felt, would

earn back for the company the confidence of the investors it had lost in the trial. The company issued preferred stock to try to gain funds, a move first opposed by Pandolfo as being unfair to the common stockholders but later supported when he realized that it might be the only way to save the company. Ladner, whose health was poor, was soon replaced by Charles Schwab, who tried to set up a dealer network and also tried to introduce a Pan car with a new six-cylinder engine. The technical staff, sensing little future in the foundering company, began to drift off. Dealers and buyers, seeing this, were reluctant to invest in a car without a foreseeable future. Yet during this gloomy period the company produced—and somehow got rid of—close to 500 cars, more than it had sold previously.

The drop forge plant contributed to the company's solvency for a time, turning out a variety of parts for other manufacturers including a patented rake-hoe combination tool for a St. Cloud inventor. Pandolfo, meantime, was devoting his time, talent, and energy to another enterprise while pressing the appeal of his conviction. Called the Pandolfo Manufacturing Company and located just across the railroad tracks from the Pan Motor Company, Pandolfo intended it to turn out metal products under the trade name "Handy Pandy." The company's early and only catalog, called "Our Family Album," pictured some of the items: a coffee maker ("from sunny Italy"), a washtub, a folding metal chair for use in automobiles, and fenders for the Ford tractor. But this venture failed too, by overextending its resources, and the Pandolfo Manufacturing Company was foreclosed by creditors.

Exactly when the doors of the Pan Motor Company closed for good is difficult to determine. In January 1922 the company was sued by the Erie Foundry Company of Pennsylvania for payment owed on drop forge equipment. By September the plant, now shut down, was being inspected by Ralph De Palma, a former racing driver, with a view to reopening it on behalf of some "wealthy Minnesota men," but nothing came of it.

Placed in receivership, the Pan Motor Company exerted a strange influence on the stockholders, who retained loyalty to the company. From all over the West, many of them banded together to attempt to rescue their investment. They wanted to buy the auto plant and place it in the hands of an experienced manager: Samuel Pandolfo.

Within a week of their offer, in March 1923, Pandolfo's appeal was denied by the United States Supreme Court. Pandolfo now asked for a stay of sentence, saying, "There are 75,000 stockholders in the Pan Motor Company—the very people I am supposed to have defrauded—that say I am not guilty."

This argument, too, was rejected and in early April Pandolfo surrendered to a federal marshal in Chicago and was sent to Leavenworth to begin serving his sentence. The legacy he left St. Cloud was twofold and long-lasting. While many residents stubbornly upheld Pandolfo's innocence, others felt he had betrayed the confidence placed in him, even if unintentionally. He had made the city a laughingstock.

The experience certainly chastened the business community. Their attitude was usually concealed, but it was once expressed openly in a motion made by the Commercial Club after they were approached by a developer seeking help for a new business. They would not look at a new venture, they said, but they would certainly back a going concern.

The buildings erected for the Pan Motor Company were a source of jobs for many over the years. Following the Pan Motor Company demise, the Diamond Motor Parts Company occupied the main plant for a time. A variety of businesses later shared its large area, including a printing press and a bottling plant. During World War II the plant was used to make aircraft parts, and at the conclusion of the war it was taken over by Franklin Manufacturing. Now, with additions easily quadrupling the original space and a work force around 600, it turns out brand-name freezers.

The last, continuing, and finally profitable legacy of the Pan Motor Company is buried in Pan Town. At the time the houses were being erected in the Pan Addition the city was required to install a sewer line, the largest single municipal expenditure to that time: $300,000. To pay for it, the city issued dedicated bonds, basing repayment on land assessments payable with the Pan Town residents' taxes. When the Pan Motor Company closed, the Pan Addition became a ghost town, silent and dark. Most of the property owners lost their land to the state for nonpayment of taxes, and the assessments, intended to retire the bonds, were not paid.

Bondholders, seeking a legal decision, sued the city for payment, but the court ruled that the city was not required to pay off the bonds from other sources of income. The state legislature then passed a special act that set up a trust fund. The land in the Pan Town assessment district which had been forfeited for nonpayment of taxes was transferred into the fund. Owners of forfeited land in Pan Town were given the option of regaining their land simply by paying the balance of the assessments. Land not redeemed was sold and the proceeds were used to pay off the bonds.

Following World War II, when the city expanded north into the Centennial Addition, the trust fund began to grow until, by the middle 1970s, the city had retired all bonds in the trust and had a considerable sum left. In its capacity as trustee, the city asked the court to rule whether or not the city was required to pay interest on the bonds up to the time they were retired. The court held that the interest period of the original bonds was the only one the city was bound to honor. That period ran from the time of the original sale of the bonds until 1929, when they were to have been retired from payments of the assessments. In setting up and administering the trust the city had performed a service for the bondholders who otherwise almost certainly would have lost their total investment.

The city has recently considered using the money left in the Pan Sewer Trust to renovate a building to be used for additional municipal offices. So the Pan legacy has not totally disappeared from the city. Pan Town is still called Pan Town; Franklin still uses the plant to make freezers and provide employment for many in the city; and there's a street, a short one, in Centennial Addition called Pandolfo Place.

4

Prohibition and Depression

Zeal, Repeal, and New Deal

Despite the passion of its advocates, it was doomed to failure from the beginning, if not in the rest of the country, certainly in the area around St. Cloud. One would have thought that Andrew Volstead, the congressman who proposed the Liquor Prohibition Amendment in December 1917, would have known that. He was from Minnesota. But, in a little over two years, ratified by 36 states, the law went into effect. It stated simply: "the manufacture, sale, or transportation of intoxicating liquors within, the importation thereof into, or the exportation thereof from the United States and all territory subject to the jurisdiction thereof, for beverage purposes is hereby prohibited."

The reaction of the local populace to that ban had been mildly mirrored by Pope Pius IX many years earlier when Abbot Boniface Wimmer, later abbot of St. John's Abbey, had told him the German Benedictines at St. John's Abbey in Pennsylvania had no brewery. "Germans not drinking

beer," the pontiff had said. "That is much. St. Paul wrote to St. Timothy he should take a little wine for his weak stomach, and so you must have something."

No one publicly claimed papal sanction for violating Prohibition but if the violation went beyond "a little wine for a weak stomach" it was because everyone did not have the same tastes, or the same degree of "weak stomach." St. Cloud Germans had demonstrated a preference for beer, but they were not above drinking something stronger if it was available. And it was readily available.

In fact, it became available in such quantity that the question had to be raised: If a majority had ratified Prohibition, where were all these distillers and drinkers coming from? One answer—and a strange one—appeared after the fact in a book titled *The Amazing Story of Repeal*, published in 1940 and written by Fletcher Dobyns, a former Cook County attorney and, by coincidence, one of the attorneys Samuel Pandolfo had hired in Chicago in 1919 to conduct his defense against charges of mail fraud. Dobyns claimed that Prohibition had been working, that the stories appearing in newspapers about people drinking

When discovered, most stills were smashed on the spot, but these were apparently kept as evidence for the trial of several "shiners." (SCHS)

71

were planted by liquor interests anxious to get the amendment repealed.

Dobyns' theory notwithstanding, a short ride with federal agents—or a knowledgeable drinker—in the country around St. Cloud would have convinced anyone that the woods were full of alcohol cookers. Not all, or even most, of the moonshine in the area was imported; it was locally produced in large quantity by many small operators and a few larger ones.

Farmers had a ready opportunity to become midnight distillers. With farm prices low, a second income was not only welcome, it was often necessary. For this reason local law officials usually looked the other way when they spotted a lawbreaker from the area; they had little incentive to jail a man trying to support his family by making what everyone seemed to want despite the law. There were other motives for locating a distillery on a farm: isolation was one. The smell of fermenting mash was strong and pervasive. More than one rural distillery used the odor of a nearby manure pile to mask the powerful pungency of fermenting mash, thereafter claiming an improvement in the taste of the product, although never alluding to the source of that piquant flavor.

An additional reason for the farm-based distillery was the natural ingenuity of the farmer, who had to rely on his own resourcefulness when machinery broke down. Stills, even before Prohibition, were not a manufactured product, and certainly parts could not be ordered from a mail-order catalog. Most farmers were handy at the skills required to assemble a still, and the proximity of the farmer's clientele made for prompt feedback on the quality of his product. In a short time, the locally produced beverages were easily as good as—and often better—than the "imported brands" from larger illegal stills.

It was not that the farmer was less law-abiding than the city dweller who sought him out to buy his homemade product; the farmer just had less opportunity for alternate sources of income in a weakening economy. But an easily identifiable market, a well-hidden location, and distilling expertise did not insure success. Ingredients had to be purchased in several locations unless the proprietor was well-known to the buyer; the risk of buying in the large quantities necessary to make the effort worthwhile was that suspicions might be raised and a call would bring the feds.

Getting corn for mash was no problem for the farmer, but the amount of sugar and yeast required was a good deal more than a farmer's wife might need for a threshing crew. Recipes varied according to individual tastes, and booze was made from just about every plant except crabgrass. But in the St. Cloud area the usual base was a mash featuring a hybrid corn (Minnesota 13) developed by the University of Minnesota. Eventually, whether it used that corn as a base or not, most Minnesota moonshine was called Minnesota 13, and the illegal hooch became more famous than the corn that gave it birth. Federal agents reported people as far away as San Francisco and New York walking into their favorite "soft drink parlor" and asking for Minnesota 13 by name.

The still used to produce the liquor in most small operations was a wash boiler, the copper tub used to heat water for washing clothes. It was easily obtainable and caused no comment when purchased. With the lid welded on and a "worm," a coiled copper pipe, fitted to the lid to condense the steam and lead it into containers, this crude but efficient apparatus was at the heart of an industry that, while illegal, was the mainstay of many farm families in the Depression.

One pass through the still produced a drink of 80 to 140 proof, hardly more than soda pop with a little "kick" to a seasoned drinker. A second pass through the still raised the proof to a more substantial 160 to 180. It was now strong enough for the discerning drinker, but it needed aging. Properly done, this meant a week to 18 days, depending on the temperature, in charred oak barrels. But "proper" aging was frequently longer than most customers and therefore many moonshiners cared to wait. The process was speeded up by adding chips of charred oak to the mixture and heating it. This not only added a smoky quality to the taste but gave the clear liquid the desired golden color. After standing for a day, the liquor was strained to remove the chips. It was now ready for shipment and consumption. Ingenuity knew no bounds, however. One resourceful chef added charred peaches to the alcohol, reducing "aging" to one hour.

These were the specialists, brewing a few gallons for their own consumption and that of a few—say, 50—friends. One buyer said he would leave his house in the morning and place $2.50 under the doormat on his back porch. When he returned home in the evening he would find a quart fruit jar filled with pure, golden corn "likker" in plain sight of passersby.

There were others, out to satisfy a larger clientele, who did not bother with the small stills. For some reason they seemed to be concentrated in the Holdingford area near St. Cloud. These larger operations dwarfed the small one- or two-man stills. In one raid on a farm in the Holdingford area in mid-September 1925, federal agents found what they called the biggest, most comprehensive manufacturing operation in Minnesota. They estimated its cost at $15,000. It was equipped with 250-pound steam pressure boilers, daylight windows, and all modern factory conveniences. The

agents found two 400 gallon stills in operation, and confiscated 7,000 gallons of mash and 250 gallons of finished moonshine.

If it was hooch that put the noise in the Roaring Twenties, it was the federal agents who tried to mute the horn of plenty. According to the law, those who disobeyed it fell into one of three categories: distillers, runners, and drinkers. (Several versatile individuals fell into all three at one time or another.) The distillers were the most vulnerable; they could hide but they couldn't run. The runners were mobile; they couldn't hide but they could run—and did, at night in powerful cars and trucks over back roads at high speed. The drinkers seldom ran or hid, but could consume the evidence in a pinch.

Runners found their jobs dangerous but exciting, and they were well paid. One runner, loading 100 gallons of alky in his car at a remote meeting spot, heard a strange noise midway through the operation. Without waiting to identify it, he jumped behind the wheel of his car, which he had judiciously left running for just such emergencies, and tore away. In a short time he noticed head-

Normally a still would not be used near a combustible material such as hay, but this picture was taken long after this still had ceased being used for its original purpose.

The Triplet City

lights in his rear view mirror. He increased his speed, but the car was topheavy since he had not had time to balance the load. The car tipped over on the next curve, the booze spilling out of most of the smashed cans. Climbing out and resigning himself to arrest, he was startled—and relieved—when the following car pulled up and his suppliers jumped out.

"Why did you take off when the owl hooted?" they asked. "Here's the rest of your load."

No route was foolproof, but one runner had high hopes for a safe journey. He loaded his creamery cans of moonshine on a raft, and waited until darkness to push off in the river and float silently downstream, undetected. His steering apparatus lacked precision, however, and he snagged on a deadhead in midstream, hung up in plain sight with the sun coming up. Only the rescue operation of friends, who discovered him before the federal agents did, permitted his career as Huck Finn to end happily.

An interesting statistic is revealed in an October 1925 survey of Minnesota jails. While the state penitentiary and reformatories had only a few inmates over their normal number, the county jails, where violators of the Prohibition laws were "boarded," showed a dramatic increase. The Stearns County jail held 38 inmates at the time of the survey, only six of whom were not Prohibition violators. It had held only four prisoners 10 years earlier.

It was perhaps inevitable that with most stills being operated on farms, some episodes involving livestock would surface. Some wild ducks, for instance, were the downfall of one couple in the southern part of the state. The birds got into a barrel of mash hidden behind the barn and had their fill. Within a few minutes they were squawking so hilariously that they could be heard for half a mile. Agents in the area, attracted by the noise, carted the owners away, leaving the birds to sleep it off.

A local farmer's fowls weren't so lucky. His geese got into some discarded mash that was still potent enough to knock them out. The farmer, who had been testing his own product, discovered the prostrate fowls and, deciding they had been

shot, proceeded to pluck their feathers and throw the limp carcasses on top of his woodpile. Some time later, when the geese had recovered, the farmer was roundly shaken to see "New York dressed" geese walking gingerly but nakedly in his barnyard.

The reputation of the county as a major center for the production of illegal booze was acknowledged privately by federal agents and even publicly by local newspapers. One editor, noting the arrest of a Kandiyohi County man for bringing a load of "wort" (the mixture used to make moonshine) to St. Cloud, commented that "it required a sample of nerve for New London to presume to ship spirits to St. Cloud." This "coal-to-Newcastle" attitude was echoed by the federal agents.

As the county seat, St. Cloud served as the clearing house for the confiscated booze the federal agents seized in the county. A cargo of 500 gallons of 188-proof alcohol was taken near Albany one October day from two men who were running it to North Dakota, where the hooch would sell for $10,000. The market value in St. Cloud was then about $7,500.

The agents brought the alcohol to St. Cloud and began emptying it into the Mississippi behind the police station. A small crowd gathered in the cold to watch the ceremony, and about 300 gallons had been poured out when one of the interested spectators, lighting a match, accidentally set fire to his glove. Yanking the glove from his hand, he threw it into the pool of alcohol trickling its way to the river. The alcohol ignited, set fire to the dry grass, and the rapidly expanding flames threatened a police car parked nearby; the flames, whipped by the wind, snaked toward the city garage and were licking the walls but were soon brought under control by the fire department. Agents took the remaining 200 gallons to a remote spot out of town to dispose of it.

While federal agents were fired upon only once in local memory, they were disliked for their activities and were often harassed. Resentment was occasionally expressed openly when agents overstepped what their quarry considered fair play. One December day in 1928 a local newspaper office was visited by a delegation of Holdingford citizens who had come to express their disdain for the tactics used by federal agents who raided a farm in the Holdingford area.

As described by the visitors, the incident began when a force of agents drove into the yard of the farm, four miles northeast of town. The farmer was away at the time and when the agents could not show his wife a search warrant, she refused them entrance. They pried open a side window, entered, and climbed directly to the attic where they found a still, a pressure tank, and a quantity of liquor and mash. The woman claimed the agents tipped over the containers, letting the liquid run onto the floor and seep through the ceiling and into the living room below. The still was demolished and the pressure tank was broken open, catching fire in the process.

The agents then left the house and drove away. When the farmer's wife smelled smoke later, she went outside and saw that the roof of the house was burning. Her husband, returning from town, saw the flames from a mile away and raced home. But despite the help of neighbors (now part of the delegation), only a few pieces of furniture could be saved, and the farmer lost $190 in cash. The actions of the agents, the delegation claimed, were illegal and unfair. The newspaper printed the story, but no further action was taken.

Large and regular raids by federal agents only temporarily halted the traffic in moonshine. After several years of contesting each other, agents and violators seemed to reach an unspoken agreement whereby only the flagrant transgressors and repeaters would be apprehended. One area man caught operating a still pleaded guilty and was fined $100 and sentenced to a year in prison by an unrelenting judge. He left a wife and six children with no resources in a one-room flat. The wife wrote to President Herbert Hoover, explaining that the only reason her husband became involved in bootlegging was to provide for her and the children; that if he was pardoned he would never again be involved with anything illegal; and, if he could not be pardoned, she asked to take his place in prison so he could earn a living and take care of the children.

Her plea was supported not only by the prosecutor, who reminded the President that "the purpose of the law is to punish the offender, not his innocent family," but by area federal agents who raised $63 among themselves to help the family. A Presidential pardon, with timing worthy of a Charles Dickens novel, arrived by telegram at the Stearns County jail on Christmas Eve.

Estimates—no sampling survey would ever be accurate—claimed that four out of five residents in the county were involved in some form of illegal activity regarding Prohibition: either as purveyors of ingredients and aware of the intended final use (which was not, strictly speaking, covered by the law), as cookers, runners, or sellers, or as final consumers. It left few people within the law, and if this open disregard for the law was not making hardened criminals out of respectable citizens, it was breeding a disrespect for law and order in general and a kind of sniggling contempt for the government that would continue to prosecute a law so widely ignored, even by many government officials.

The eventual repeal of Prohibition in 1933 put many people temporarily out of work, but even these breathed a sigh of relief. They had seen repeal coming and, in many cases, had been saving their money. More than one legitimate business in St. Cloud was started on the proceeds of a bootlegging career.

If Prohibition touched many people in and around St. Cloud, the Depression, signaled by the stock market crash in October 1929, struck St. Cloud softly. This is not to say that there was no hardship, no privation, or no unemployment in the city, but it was on a quieter scale than in much of the country.

Like so many smaller towns, St. Cloud had grown slowly, depending upon no one or two single economic hubs for its vitality. The two major employers in the area—the car shops of the Great Northern, and the granite sheds of several companies—were not deeply affected by the national economy and were able to continue in operation, although there certainly were cutbacks and layoffs.

Because the city had grown slowly, many people knew each other or knew each others' families. The tendency was to share food from gardens and outgrown clothes with neighbors or relatives so that few really went hungry or cold for long. With a population a little over 20,000, the problem was never acute in numbers, only for individuals.

The "helping out" attitude was evident in all phases of urban life, from neighbor helping neighbor, to Mayor James Murphy's suggestion for a "Make Work Program" for the city. Although the *St. Cloud Daily Times* had started running free "Help Wanted" classified ads in November 1930, a policy it continued throughout the Depression, there were still many who desperately needed work. Murphy's proposal was both daring and controversial, and would be echoed by President Roosevelt in some of his programs a few years later.

In October 1931 Murphy suggested a program of city projects to be funded by a $25,000 bond issue where labor would be the major cost. After further study, the figure was raised to $75,000, with one-third to be raised in a bond issue, one-third by "popular subscription," and one-third to come from a portion of the city budget set aside for a "poor fund."

The business community endorsed the plan, as did a committee appointed by the mayor to study it. But when a special election was held to vote on it, only 2,800 votes were cast and the issue was defeated by more than two to one. The voters may have been influenced by continuing news stories in the local paper claiming that, although the city had a problem, it was not as severe as in similar communities around the country. Such civic pride led many to believe that the city, in fact, was not suffering severely.

But a charity drive, started the same day as the election, asked each wage earner in St. Cloud to contribute four days' wages to help those in need. With St. Cloud's Wheelock Whitney as chairman,

the drive passed its $25,000 goal less than one month after it started. Food purchased with funds from the drive were distributed to the needy at the Carter Building at the corner of Fifth Avenue and Second Street North. The Barr Canning plant, south of the city, canned meat and gave it to the poor.

Early in 1932 the city inaugurated its "War on Depression." Headed by the American Legion and joined in by other local civic groups, the drive was patterned on a national program sponsored by the Legion. Its aim was to generate more business activity, particularly in the construction industry. The program was so successful—raising over $800,000 to provide jobs—that Mayor Murphy proudly stated that federal aid was not needed in St. Cloud: "We can take care of ourselves."

The refusal of federal help was not total, however. A number of St. Cloud's young men and women joined the Civilian Conservation Corps (CCC), created in 1933 to enable young people to earn $30 a month doing conservation chores. They signed up for a six-month stint, and were given $5 out of their pay for their own use, while the rest was sent home to help support their families.

The Works Progress Administration (WPA), created in 1935 by the federal government,

LEFT
Williams Gardens, at Ninth Avenue and Second Street South, was demolished when Division Street was extended north of Lake George. Most people never knew, or forgot, the name of this park. A miniature golf course had been built on the site in the early 1930s. (SCHS)

FACING PAGE
Perhaps to compensate for the fact that liquor was now legal, Minnesota's legislature, responding to urging from Governor Luther Youngdahl, declared gambling via slot machines illegal. Sheriff Art McIntee takes a sledgehammer to several confiscated machines in the late 1940s. (SCHS)

FACING PAGE, TOP
A section of the mural painted by David Granham as a WPA project in 1938 is reproduced here. It hung in the old post office, now the Federal Building. (SCHS)

FACING PAGE, BOTTOM
St. Cloud has always had beautiful parks. Munsinger Park, named for Joseph Munsinger, the superintendent of parks who designed it and many others in the city, was built on the site of a sawmill. In this late-1930s view the buildings of St. Cloud State Teachers College (now St. Cloud State University) can be seen across the river. (SCHS)

BELOW
Pictured here is Munsinger Park looking north about 1938. Rocks were trucked in from miles away to form the pond and border the walks. (SCHS)

employed adults in various civic projects. The first one in St. Cloud involved remodeling and building an addition to St. Cloud Technical High School to provide an automotive training center and storage room. Later projects included the construction of the granite wall around Selke Field on the southeast side of St. Cloud, and the construction of granite walls on the dead-end streets near the Mississippi River. The granite was donated by the St. Cloud granite companies.

By 1942, the state caseload of WPA (now known as the Emergency Relief Administration) workers had gone from a peak of 68,000 in the depths of the economic crisis to slightly over 5,000, and the program was scheduled to close.

Wartime demands were taking men faster than the Depression had put them out of work. But even before the full impetus of World War II had wiped out the reality of the Depression, St. Cloud had weathered the worst shocks of the grim economy and had rebounded, ready for the next municipal contingency.

5

Education and Information

Schools and the Media

From its earliest days, St. Cloud exhibited strong support for education by establishing a public school system which has served both the city and surrounding areas with innovative education. Although as early as 1856 the Stearns County board had levied a one percent tax, one quarter of which was destined for school support. St. Cloud's first school, the Everett School, was privately built in 1857 and was supported at first by the Lower Town Yankees.

By the time Everett became a public school, receiving the support of taxes, a problem had developed in the German community. St. Cloud had created two school districts early in its history: the first was mainly in Lower Town, while the second included most of Upper and Middle Towns. When the Upper Town Southerners left at the inception of the Civil War, a German Catholic majority remained in the St. Cloud area. The German Catholics wanted their children to be taught

in German, and they wanted their children to have religious instruction as well as classes in academic subjects. In 1863, these German Catholics asked that their parochial school be placed on a tax-supported basis, yet retain religious instruction. But Bishop Grace of St. Paul, under whose jurisdiction the St. Cloud Catholics fell, refused to allow a tax-supported school to operate on church-owned property.

Persistent pressure by local Catholics finally wore down the state legislature, and in 1875 they allowed the creation of an independent school, supported by taxes, wherein religious instruction was given. The Independent School existed until 1914, when the "religious garb" law was passed, prohibiting teachers from wearing distinctly religious habits while in school.

Early schooling consisted of one or two terms during which the student was given a grasp of "reading, writing, and numbers." The Reverend Elgy VanVoorhis Campbell, considered the father of the graded school system in St. Cloud, noted the lack of graded schooling when he arrived in St. Cloud in 1864 to become pastor of the First Presbyterian Church, and he began a campaign for what he termed a "proper" school. His erudi-

Old Main, constructed in 1874, was the first building erected for the State Normal School (SCHS)

81

tion and persuasiveness made the effort successful and graded schooling began in St. Cloud in April 1867 with a primary level and a "higher" level.

A little over a year later, the St. Cloud school system got its first building—the former Fowler furniture factory—and named it the St. Cloud Academy. The school was soon so crowded that all nonresident students were asked to leave. In 1869 St. Cloud's first board of education was elected and a site was purchased for a new school building. Union School, built at a cost of $17,000 on 4th Avenue South between 2nd and 3rd streets, had a furnace, real desks, including three teacher's desks, and blackboards.

With a "proper" school building and two teachers—four were needed by the end of the first term—education began to come of age in St. Cloud. A nine-month school year was put in effect, and the curriculum was broadened to include subjects such as spelling and geography. Cultural subjects—music, art, languages—still

had a room designated as a high school; its occupants were taught separately by the principal. But the high school concept had not yet found universal acceptance. Ironically, the new Normal School (later Teachers College, still later St. Cloud State University) accepted students without a high school diploma, prepared them to teach, and sent them out to earn their living before the average student in "high school" completed his studies. Because of public dissension on the high school question, the high school room was discontinued in 1885; and special teachers were hired to teach high school subjects instead.

But by 1888 the pendulum of public opinion had swung and the district applied formally for a high school grade, which it obtained along with a $400 state grant. The 1890s saw the creation of the single school district, and curriculum as well as physical plant expansion. Enrollment in the Franklin School was down; not many parents still insisted on their children being taught in German,

had to be studied with a private tutor, however.

During the years following the establishment of Union School, increased numbers of students required continuing expansion. Not counting the students in the Independent (Catholic) School—which was more frequently called the German School and which by 1889 had changed its name to the Franklin School—there were now over 700 students in four schools in St. Cloud.

During this same period St. Cloud's first high school was formed. The Union School had always

and religious education was being fostered in a good English-language parochial school system. In fact, the St. Cloud school system was so attractive that other districts in Benton and Sherburne counties petitioned to join it. Legislation eventually called for the closing of outlying districts and the addition of five schools to the St. Cloud system.

In the first 15 years of the 20th century growth accelerated even more, as the school district saw increased enrollment and budget expansion. For

the first time, boys in high school outnumbered the girls. Previously, boys usually left school early to find work. It was during this period too that public school transportation was first employed to correct unbalanced teacher/pupil ratios due to population density in certain areas. And, the board now required teachers to have completed advanced normal school work or to have graduated from college.

The expansion, especially in the high school area, led the school board to consider creating an independent district for the high school system, and after a long campaign for public acceptance, Independent School District 28 was created in 1914. The next decision was the selection of a site for a new high school. The choices were narrowed down to either upgrading the old Union School or erecting a new building on reclaimed swampland near Lake George. The second option won out, probably because of its more ample space for athletics, and construction began on Technical High School in 1916. The name was a compromise, for although the school gave special emphasis to practical subjects, its thrust was still academic. The new facility featured a gym, a pool,

ABOVE
The Union School, constructed in the 1870s, served long into the 1970s as the older part of Central Junior High. (SCHS)

FACING PAGE, LEFT
In 1905, when St. Mary's Church and grade school faced on St. Germain Street, Lake George reached up to First Street South. The large object on the skyline at the left is the city's water tower. (SCHS)

FACING PAGE, RIGHT
This school was known by three different names: the Independent School, the German School, and finally the Franklin School. The building pictured was replaced in 1898 by a new one, which was razed in 1956. The location was between Tenth and Eleventh avenues and Second and Third streets north. (SCHS)

and all the amenities of a contemporary high school.

With the opening of Technical High School, the old Union School was converted to Central Grammar School, which helped ease the pressure on the crowded primary schools in the city. The Catholic school system, though now outdistanced by the public schools in the number of students, kept up with the times by erecting Cathedral High School in 1914.

By the early 1920s Tech was educating 100 more students than it was designed to hold. To relieve the pressure, a junior high was added to the old Union School in 1929, and Central Grammar School became known as Central Junior High; seventh, eighth, and ninth grade students were sent there.

We have mentioned so far only primary and secondary education as it matured in St. Cloud. The area had been particularly enriched educationally by being selected in the 1860s as the site for a normal school. The "normal school" concept represented an effort to upgrade education by requiring formal (normal) training for teachers.

As this Eastern idea spread following the westward migration of pioneers, states began to demand better trained teachers, and Minnesota joined the trend by establishing the Third State Normal School in the former Stearns House hotel in Lower Town in September 1869. Seventy students, all from St. Cloud (whose population was then only 2,100) made up the first class.

In spite of this show of confidence by the community, the Normal School idea was not universally welcomed in its first years. Many parents were not certain that that much education was necessary for their children in order to get a job; others thought teachers needed no special training; still others opposed the idea of free education at that level.

That the school survived in the face of these and other objections, as well as legislative measures which cut the school's appropriations, is due to the various principals and board members who fought an almost daily battle to keep the school open and growing. By 1886 the curriculum list had grown from a three-paragraph description to a 10-page catalog. The public complaint against free tuition was answered by asking Minnesota students to promise to teach in Minnesota public schools for two years; those not willing to promise that dedication were asked to pay $30 in tuition per year—to be paid quarterly—in advance.

The school's name was changed from Third State Normal School to State Normal School at St. Cloud in 1894; but five years later the school faced a greater problem than the name-changing which

awaited it in the years ahead. The State Supreme Court ruled in 1899 that high school teachers had to have a degree. The normal schools were not then degree-granting institutions, which meant their graduates would be limited to elementary school teaching. But the state legislature's new ruling requiring statewide elementary school attendance somewhat compensated the teachers for the court's increased requirements, since compulsory elementary school attendance created larger classes, and thus an increased demand for teachers. But three years later the normal schools were struck yet another blow when a state-aided program was enacted that would train elementary school teachers while still in high school for teaching jobs in rural areas. This program minimized the need for normal school training.

FACING PAGE, TOP
The Stearns House, once a temperance hotel for Southern vacationers, became the Ladies Hall for the Normal School. (SCHS)

FACING PAGE, BOTTOM
When Old Main was gutted by fire, it was rebuilt and wings were added. It has since been replaced by Stewart Hall. (SCHS)

BELOW
Lawrence Hall at the Normal School was named for Isabel Lawrence, who came to the school in 1879 as director of training. (SCHS)

By 1925, however, normal school administrators achieved a three-part goal: the education students' pledge to teach in Minnesota was abolished; the normal schools were authorized to confer bachelor of education degrees; and the normal schools were now officially designated Teachers Colleges. The legislature had given in, but not the state's private colleges or the University of Minnesota, which felt it was better prepared to train high school teachers. It was 1929 before the teachers colleges in the state were allowed to train secondary school teachers.

For the entire St. Cloud School District, the years from 1930 to 1960 were marked by a dramatic increase in the size of the district and a massive building program required to handle the continuing influx of students. As, one by one, the small one-room country schools closed, erasing a nostalgic but outmoded picture, the urban schools were again crowded beyond capacity. Eight outlying districts in the three-county area elected to close and become part of what is now District 742, further burdening the already teeming schools.

When the population bulge known as the baby boom began to enter the system additions had to be made to Lincoln, Jefferson, and Madison schools, and a new Westwood Elementary School was built to accommodate the westward expansion of the city. Desperately needed junior high and high school space was constructed in the form of North and South junior highs, Apollo High School, and additions at Technical High School. Part of the reason for the physical plant expansion was the state legislature's call for consolidation of school districts, a move that later left the district with surplus, empty school facilities in the wake of the passing of the baby boom. Only the population growth of the city itself has allowed for the orderly conversion of school facilities to other uses by slowing the tide of increasingly empty classrooms. Central Junior High School, for example, has been sold to the city and is being converted to municipal office space.

Over the years the campus of the Teachers College had grown from the original five and one-half acres to spread across the river—including the Beaver Islands of Zebulon Pike. Enrollment at the college, which had dropped to less than 400 (with only 13 men) during World War II, rebounded following the war.

The increased enrollment had a desirable side effect. The college had failed in its first attempt at seeking accreditation from the North Central Association of Colleges and Secondary Schools in 1941. But the affluence brought about by the increased enrollment allowed the college to upgrade its staff and facilities, and it gained accreditation in 1947. Once the hurdle of accreditation had been cleared, the college quickly made up for lost time. By 1953 it was allowed to grant a master of science degree in education.

The expansion of Teachers College facilities now made it the major occupant of the city's south side. Although dormitory space was being added almost continuously, students still had to fan out into rental residences in the south and southeast sections of the city.

In 1957 the legislature finally recognized that the additional classes had changed the character of the college, and its name was changed from Teachers College to State College. Within a short time the state colleges were seeking permission to be called universities. And many were, in fact, what they sought to be called: they had separate colleges offering a variety of degrees in many subjects; they could grant graduate degrees; and they did extensive research in several fields—all hallmarks of a university. St. Cloud's Teachers College fulfilled these requirements, and in August 1975 the final name change was made to St. Cloud State University. As evidence of its changing status, the 1973-74 graduating class, for the first time in the school's history, represented more four-year degrees in non-educational fields than in educational fields.

St. Cloud's interest in education was sparked by the interests of the people who had settled in the area. Their interests included the desire to be well informed and this spawned a proliferation of early newspapers, unusual for a small pioneer settlement.

George Brott, founder of Lower Town, owned the first newspaper in St. Cloud, which he called, with some bravado, the *Minnesota Advertiser*. The

A NASA space module may be viewed on the campus of Apollo High School. The school, which opened in 1970, features a team teaching approach to instruction.

first issue was published January 1857; the paper's existence, under publisher Caleb West, was short. The *Advertiser* ceased publication in the fall and its equipment was purchased and used to start the *St. Cloud Visiter* on December 10, 1857, with James Mowatt as publisher and Mrs. Jane Grey Swisshelm as editor. Where the *Advertiser* had called itself "Neutral—but Independent," and had Democratic leanings (its editor James Shepley was Sylvanus Lowry's friend and attorney), the *Visiter* quickly reflected its new editor's stand on slavery and women's rights: she was forever against the former and firmly for the latter.

The *Visiter*'s motto was "Speak unto the Children of Israel that they go forward," and Mrs. Swisshelm wrote with such vigor and righteous anger against slavery and those who supported it that some felt a reply was called for. It came in the form of a public lecture on "Women" by James Shepley on March 10, 1858. Shepley, in his lecture, described four kinds of women: the flirt, the coquette, the old maid, and "the strong-minded

ABOVE
Jane Grey Swisshelm's rather delicate appearance masked a will of iron and the heart of a lioness. Her circumstances, combined with her temperament, placed her in a position few women in her time would have sought. That she succeeded admirably attests not only to her intelligence, but also to her courage. Self-portrait, circa 1855. (SCHS)

FACING PAGE
Pictured in 1860 is the *Democrat* office with the Swisshelm home attached in the rear. The office was on Fifth Avenue between Second Street South and Third Street South. (SCHS)

woman who dabbles in politics." He found redeeming qualities in all but the last who, he said, "unsex themselves by seeking to vote, by shrieking for niggers' rights and women's rights," and "whose highest ambition is to fill the columns of a newspaper."

Mrs. Swisshelm reported his lecture—the above quotes are from her paper. But she thought his lecture presented nothing new, "except that high flavoring of double distilled extract of gall one might expect from a bilious man." She added that Shepley had overlooked a fifth kind of woman: "a large, thick-skinned, coarse, sensual featured loud-mouthed double-fisted dame," a

"frontier belle who sat up all night playing poker with men."

The description bore a resemblance to Shepley's wife, and although Mrs. Swisshelm denied that her caricature was of Mrs. Shepley, the townsfolk knew better. It was enough for Shepley; on the night of March 24, he and a group of friends broke into the *Visiter*'s office, damaged the press, scattered some of the type and cast other type into the nearby Mississippi.

The deed backfired. Instead of abandoning her, many residents who might have been lukewarm about her causes now came to her aid and defense. Money was raised to buy new equipment, and Mrs. Swisshelm resumed publication on May 13, 1858.

Jane Grey Swisshelm was no stranger to controversy; she had carried on a long and ultimately successful struggle for women's rights to hold property in Pennsylvania, and she had written on abolition for Horace Greeley's newspaper. But now she faced a new challenge. Shepley, in a letter to the *Pioneer and Democrat*, a St. Paul newspaper, on April 2 admitted his involvement in the break-

in, but he said he had feared a further attack on his wife by Mrs. Swisshelm in her paper. He had intended paying for damages to the office and equipment, but he also instituted a suit against Mrs. Swisshelm for $10,000 for libeling his wife's name.

While the people might have been with her, Mrs. Swisshelm feared the courts, controlled by Lowry, might favor Shepley, so she agreed to an out-of-court settlement. She would publish a notice in her paper exonerating Shepley from blame in the incident and she promised to never again mention the event . . . in the *Visiter*.

Early in August the promised notice appeared in the *Visiter*, the whole issue printed on a half sheet. On August 5 a new newspaper appeared, under the title *St. Cloud Democrat*, with Mrs. Swisshelm as sole editor and publisher.

She continued to publish the *Democrat*, striking out wherever and whenever she saw fit—which is to say, frequently—until June 1863 when she sold the paper to her nephew, William Bell Mitchell, the son of early settler Henry Zehring Mitchell. In September 1866 Mitchell changed the name of the paper to the *St. Cloud Journal,* and combined it 10 years later with the *St. Cloud Press* to form the *Journal-Press.*

In 1893 Mitchell sold the paper to a stock company, which immediately began publishing the paper as a daily under the editorship of Alvah Eastman. The *Daily Journal-Press* entered a field that the *St. Cloud Daily Times* had for six years had to itself.

The *St. Cloud Daily Times* had grown from a newspaper called the *St. Cloud Union,* started by Upper Town founder Sylvanus B. Lowry in July 1861, probably as a vehicle to answer Mrs. Swisshelm. The ubiquitous Christopher C. Andrews was the paper's first editor. The paper changed publishers again before being bought by the firm of Spofford & Simonton, which, in 1864, placed it under the editorial management of R. Chaning Moore and changed the name to the *St. Cloud Times.* The paper changed ownership a number of times and in November 1872 the offices, presses, files, and all other equipment were lost in a fire. Soon back in circulation, the *Times* was bought in January 1875 by Colin F. Macdonald, who also assumed the editorial duties. In September 1887 Macdonald established the *Daily Times* and it has been published continuously since. St. Cloud's inveterate newspaperman Fred

Schilplin bought an interest in the *Times* in 1903 and became its sole owner and publisher in 1920. Schilplin's ownership was marked by innovation in a number of areas. Schilplin was a founder, and the *Times* a charter member, of the Associated Press; his interest in politics led him to run (unsuccessfully) for the Democratic nomination for governor; he was a founder and first president of the Northwest Daily Press Association; and he began the first commercial radio station, KFAM, in St. Cloud.

The *Daily Times* and the *Journal-Press* merged in August 1929 when Schilplin bought the latter paper and made Alvah Eastman the editor of the new *Daily Times Journal-Press.* The unwieldy name was eventually shortened to the *Daily Times.* With the death of Fred Schilplin in 1949, his son, Frederick C. Schilplin, assumed management duties. A program of expansion followed during which the *Times* acquired the *Little Falls Transcript* and the *Royalton Banner* and prepared to move into a new plant. But Schilplin died before the move could be made and his heirs sold the paper to Speidel Newspapers, Inc., a national syndicate, in May 1974. Two years later, Speidel merged with the Gannett Company, the *Times'* present publishers.

The pervasive influence of the German settlers

in the area extended into publishing as well as other facets of business and cultural life. In 1872 an attorney and an educator discerned a need for a German language newspaper in the area. The attorney, Peter Brick, and the educator, Peter Kaiser, tested the idea by sending the first two issues free to every household named on the county tax lists. In one month *Der Nordstern* (The Northstar) had 800 paying subscribers. Despite early changes in ownership and editors (Peter Brick was editor for one year, then sold his

ABOVE
Colin F. Macdonald, publisher of the *St. Cloud Daily Times,* is pictured about 1910 with reporter William Boerger. (SCHS)

FACING PAGE
This group of St. Cloud pioneers included (left to right): Dan Freeman, Bernard Reinhard, Josiah Elam West, Henry Chester Waite, Hanford Lennox Gordon, Charles A. Gilman, Colin F. Macdonald, William Bell Mitchell, and John Coates. (SCHS)

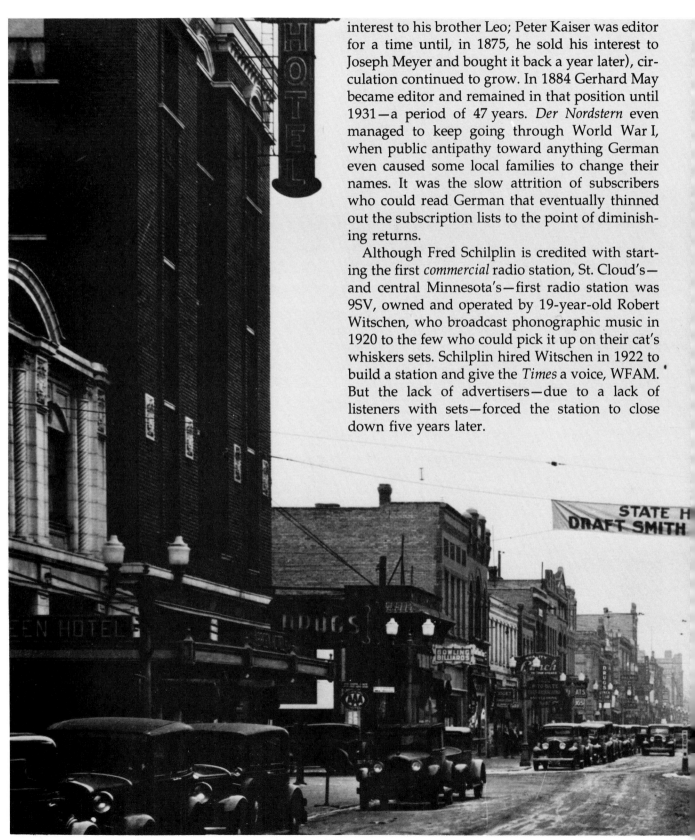

interest to his brother Leo; Peter Kaiser was editor for a time until, in 1875, he sold his interest to Joseph Meyer and bought it back a year later), circulation continued to grow. In 1884 Gerhard May became editor and remained in that position until 1931—a period of 47 years. *Der Nordstern* even managed to keep going through World War I, when public antipathy toward anything German even caused some local families to change their names. It was the slow attrition of subscribers who could read German that eventually thinned out the subscription lists to the point of diminishing returns.

Although Fred Schilplin is credited with starting the first *commercial* radio station, St. Cloud's—and central Minnesota's—first radio station was 9SV, owned and operated by 19-year-old Robert Witschen, who broadcast phonographic music in 1920 to the few who could pick it up on their cat's whiskers sets. Schilplin hired Witschen in 1922 to build a station and give the *Times* a voice, WFAM. But the lack of advertisers—due to a lack of listeners with sets—forced the station to close down five years later.

When Schilplin decided to try again in 1938, Witschen became chief engineer for KFAM. (The original call letters had been taken over by another station, and Schilplin's second choice, KSTC, was, according to the FCC, too similar to St. Paul's KSTP.) The station was sold in 1975 by the Schilplin heirs to Al Leighton, who changed the call letters to KCLD for the FM mode and KNSI for AM programming.

A second St. Cloud station, WJON, entered the market in September 1950. FM facilities were added in 1970. WJON started a cable TV facility in 1968, but sold it in 1971 to General Television.

St. Cloud's UHF station, KXLI, (Channel 41), went on the air in 1982, completing the city's communications network. St. Cloud is now served by every modern communications medium.

Pictured here is St. Germain Street in the late 1920s, when the hotel was still the Breen, when the St. Mary's building housed the St. Cloud Clinic and the Green Lantern Cafe, when streetcars still ran down the center of the street and the stop and go signs were offset for them, and when Al Smith ran for President against Herbert Hoover and lost. (SCHS)

6

Expansion and Maturity

Growth in Size and Spirit

St. Cloud is something of an anomaly. While presenting the appearance and earning the reputation of a rather stolid, conservative city, it has experimented—almost toyed with—a number of forms of government. Each of the changes, except perhaps the first few, was preceded by a long study by appropriate committees.

St. Cloud moved from its first simple charter, provided by the Territorial Legislature in 1856, to a new one six years later that provided for a mayor, a recorder, and four aldermen, all elected at large. Five years later the city was divided into four wards, each electing an alderman of its own. The following year the council was expanded to 15 and the charter provided for the first strong mayor in the city's short history. (The idea of having a strong mayor was one that would recur at frequent intervals and for extended periods.) Only the mayor, in the form of government established in 1868, was elected at large, and his duties

included hiring and firing city officials, recommending legislation to the council, and heading the police and fire departments.

The concept of a strong mayor lasted until 1908. Its susceptibility to abuse and to the aggrandizement of political power had led the Minnesota legislature, in 1896, to require all cities to adopt their own home-rule charters through charter commissions and submit them to local referendum. While the proposed new form of government was not a complete change, it abolished the mayor's broad appointive powers and established a financial committee which separated public funds so that the council couldn't raid one fund for another's purposes.

No sooner was the new form of government installed than 600 citizens, in 1910, petitioned the courts to revive the charter commission in order to study yet another type of municipal administration, the commissioner form, in which a three-man commission would control the city. The commissioners would make the laws, assess the taxes, and hire and fire the officials. The three commissioners would each head a city department: Public Affairs and Safety, Finance and Accounts, and Streets and Public Improvements.

The first of the Beaver Islands shows in the foreground of this aerial view of the south end of St. Cloud taken around the time the sewage disposal plant was being constructed (lower left). (SCHS)

TOP
The Little Giant Fire Brigade (1875) was one of the first organized efforts to combat the hazard of fire. Until this unit was formed, a frequent solution to fires was to tear down the buildings on either side of a burning structure in order to contain the fire. (SCHS)

ABOVE
By 1884 a fire barn in the downtown area housed wagons, horses, and a dog who got the only chair in the picture. (SCHS)

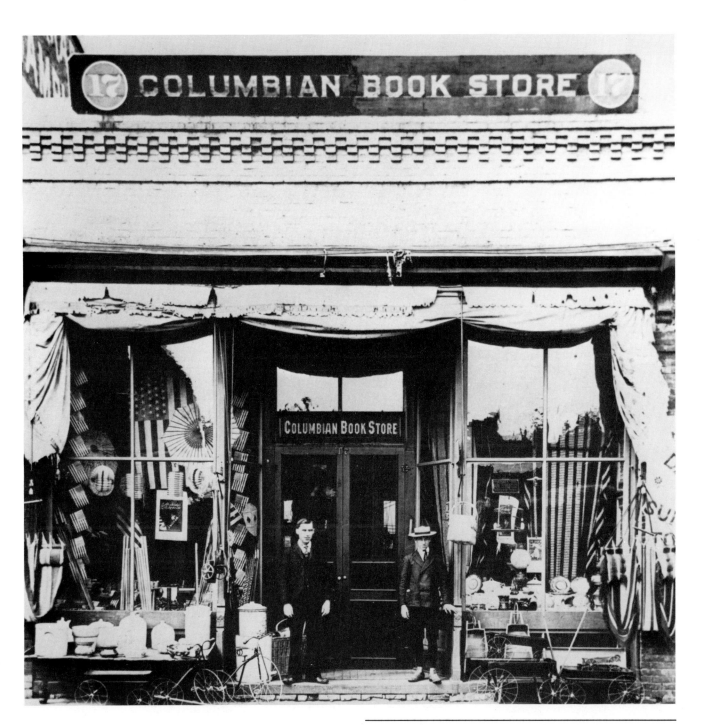

Peter (left) and Robert Schaefer stand in the doorway of the Columbian Book Store on Sixth Avenue South. The name was later changed to Schaefer's Book Store, and the place became a St. Cloud institution until it was demolished early in the second half of this century. (SCHS)

The petition touched off one of the most bitter contests in the city's governmental history. Labor opposed it as a "businessman's government," claiming that three men would find greater opportunity for graft than 15. (Graft was often evident in the administrations of larger cities and the citizens of smaller communities were quick to suspect it on a local level.) But the petitioners claimed the new government would be more efficient and more economical. The mayor/council form, they argued, was not suited to local government, since it did not leave the checks and balances where they properly belonged—between the people and government.

ABOVE
In 1920 a new courthouse was erected on the site of the 1863 courthouse, and county business was moved during construction to the Institute building across from St. Mary's Cathedral. In this picture the original spire of Holy Angels Cathedral can be seen on the left, and Ervin's mill is seen over the corner of the courthouse on the right. Neither the steeple nor the mill exists today. (SCHS)

FACING PAGE
The Stearns County Courthouse was built in 1863 by John W. Tenvoorde on land given by John L. Wilson. Wings were added in 1899. (SCHS)

When the matter was put to city-wide vote on September 20, 1910, it received a majority but fell short of the 60 percent needed for passage. An analysis of the tally indicated that labor's labelling of the reform as a "businessmen's government" had proved successful; most of the opposition to it had come from the city's laboring sections.

In July of 1911 the charter commission again proposed the new charter, but made a few changes in the form of the new government, adding a five-man council elected at large, and designating one of the commissioners as "mayor" with veto power. The new charter was adopted, with some trepidation, on November 28, 1911, and St. Cloud stayed with this hybrid commis-

sioner/council administration for more than 35 years.

By 1947 the city's growth had made the commissioner/council government unanswerable to the electorate in any real sense. The city's growth had resulted in a confusion of powers and some jurisdictional bickering between commissioners. The size of the city and the complexity of the issues facing it demanded a trained, knowledgeable, and experienced administration. A city manager was suggested by the commissioners.

A new charter commission tackled the issues and suggested a compromise: a council/manager government that would allow for six councilmen and a mayor, elected for four years, who had the right to appoint a city manager. Included in the proposal was a planning commission which would look at long-range goals and veto council actions running counter to those goals.

On February 20, 1948, the proposal suffered the second worst defeat ever given a proposed charter change in St. Cloud. But the city voters traditionally took two looks at any proposal before adopting it. A new commission went to work on

FACING PAGE, TOP
Automobiles lined up on Fifth Avenue South for a sociability run in 1913. (SCHS)

FACING PAGE, BOTTOM
This house belonged to Charles A. Gilman, who, in addition to many years in the state legislature, served as lieutenant governor of the state for nine years beginning in 1879. His home stood at the south end of Hester Park, named for his wife, and for which he donated the land. (SCHS)

BELOW
Seventh Avenue South was still unpaved in 1915 when this sprinkling truck wet the dirt to keep the dust down. (SCHS)

ABOVE
In 1894 St. Cloud's library was moved into three rooms in the West Hotel. In 1901 the hotel burned down, and many volumes were destroyed. Appeals to James J. Hill and Andrew Carnegie resulted in funds for a site and a library building. Photo by Mike Knaak. (SCHS)

FACING PAGE
The St. Cloud Public Library building opened for use October 13, 1902. Eighty years later, following completion of the new library, the Carnegie-donated building was demolished. Photo by Mike Knaak. (SCHS)

a revision in 1951 that was designed to bring St. Cloud kicking and screaming into the 20th century.

Taking a cue from the first proposal's opponents, who cited as a negative factor possible lack of responsiveness from a manager who did not have to submit to an election, the new commission went back to a strong mayor/council form of government but added a new idea: an aide, appointed by the mayor, who would devote full time to municipal duties. This was tacit recognition of the fact that, while St. Cloud may not like the idea of a full-time "professional" mayor, it was long past the point where it could successful-

ly operate with a part-time mayor without governmental expertise.

The plan was immediately branded a "city manager in disguise," and the battle was on. A well-orchestrated campaign explaining the new system was begun and the plan passed the voters' examination in 1951.

For a time St. Cloud was the focus of municipal study as a result of its new charter. Only two other Minnesota cities had a strong mayoral system, but none had the added fillip of an administrative assistant. The city now had both: elected officials, in close contact with citizen reprisal through the ballot box, and skilled professional help in city management. The seven-member planning commission, appointed by the mayor with council concurrence, had responsibility for zoning, land-use, and development, as well as the maintenance of a comprehensive, long-range plan of development and expansion for the city. How well they would be able to hold to that plan in the face of the demands of rapid population growth would soon be seen.

Proponents of the city manager idea had not given up completely. In 1964, 1967, and 1969 they attempted to revive interest in the council/manager form but were met in the polling booth by an electorate numb with fatigue from hearing new "plans."

Perhaps to forestall stronger effort to promote the city manager idea, the city decided to bow in that direction by giving the mayor's aide some needed status in city hall by officially titling the position "administrative assistant." The mayor selected his aide with council assent, and the role and functional range of that position was almost totally contingent on the mayor's disposition to personally exercise or delegate his own functions. Like many of St. Cloud's prior systems, this governmental form was a hybrid seemingly well-suited to the city and its electorate... for the moment.

The slow but steady growth of St. Cloud eventually exhausted most of the vacant land within the city limits. Residential development had begun, at first along the banks of the Mississippi, both north and south of the city. Curiously, several other "population bulges" were triggered by golf courses.

Just prior to World War II, the city had leased a tract of farmland southwest of the city limits where it prepared and operated a municipal golf course. When Highway 152, passing the course, was completed to Minneapolis, the land was sold to private owners and was operated as Hillside Golf Club. But with the demand for homesites following the war, the golf course was converted into St. Cloud's first residential suburban area, Fernwood.

The loss of Hillside convinced members of the much older St. Cloud Country Club, south of the city, to expand their course; besides adding another nine holes, much of the land was converted into a high-quality residential community.

The city's eastward movement was sparked by the construction of a golf course along Highway 23. The first development near the city, Woodland Hills, initiated a spate of home construction along the highway that resulted in a small community named for the golf course itself; Wapicada Village.

The westward fringes of the city lacked quick access to a golf course for only a short time. Starting as a short, low-par course, Angushire golf course became the nucleus of a development called Angus Acres.

The suddenly rapid growth of the city was so pronounced that by 1970 the St. Cloud Metropolitan Area was classified as the fastest-growing area in the five contiguous states. In 1974

the Bureau of Census officially designated the St. Cloud district as a Standard Metropolitan Statistical Area, meaning that its economical and demographic data was nationally significant. A contributing reason for the classification was the Department of Commerce's ranking of St. Cloud as one of the foremost cities in the country in per capita retail sales.

With prominence came the inevitable pitfalls. The urban sprawl now made obvious a problem other growing communities had contended with, although few had contended with the same traps that awaited St. Cloud. Few, if any, had the limited tax resources of St. Cloud. The state reformatory, university, veterans hospital, municipal parks, church-owned property, and various government buildings and properties were all tax exempt—confining the taxable property within the city limits to less than 45 percent of the land.

In addition, outward residential development meant that fewer people were living within the city limits while more were using the city's facilities. The prospect of additional urban growth, while advantageous for the businessmen of St. Cloud, presented nightmares to the municipal government. How those problems have been dealt with can perhaps best be seen by taking a look at the administrations of three of St. Cloud's recent mayors: George Byers, Edward L. Henry, and Alcuin G. Loehr.

George Byers (who was elected in 1953 and again in 1956) ran for mayor at a time when the city needed drastic rebuilding of its water plant

RIGHT
The oldest remaining building in the city was removed to Riverside Park in 1916. It was built around 1855 by Balthasar Rosenberger on Sixth Avenue South and later was owned by Barney Overbeck, who used it as a home, hotel, fort, jail, courthouse, and claim office; the building served several of these functions at the same time. Prisoners were put in the cellar and hotel guests got the loft. (SCHS)

FACING PAGE
The Water Treatment Plant, constructed in the late 1950s, was one of the first municipal improvements the city undertook following World War II. (SCHS)

and a sewage disposal plant. The city's sewage disposal system had been the Mississippi River, as it had been for a number of other cities both upstream and downstream. Many cities had also been using the "self-cleaning" river—upstream, of course—as the source of their drinking water, trusting to filtration to remove what its upstream neighbor had added.

Byers, the youngest mayor St. Cloud had ever elected, spent the major portion of his two terms shepherding a new water treatment plant and a sewage plant into existence.

During the latter part of Byers second term, he, along with the city council, provided what municipal help they could to a group of Chamber of Commerce members who organized a nonprofit industrial development group called St. Cloud Opportunities, Inc. (Although St. Cloud's industrial base enjoyed a healthy diversification, the rapid population growth of the late 1950s expanded the need for employment opportunities.) The group successfully bid on 180 acres of surplus land being sold by the Veterans' Administration on the western edge of the city, selling individual bonds in the amount of $250 to pay the selling price of several hundred thousand

dollars. The area, which was annexed to the city and zoned as an industrial park, was soon providing jobs for over 3,000 people and bringing in half a million dollars annually in tax revenues for the city. And the entire St. Cloud Industrial Park complex was managed without government grants, local tax writeoffs, or subsidies of any kind.

Mayor George Byers' policy of limited intervention in the economic life of the city can be contrasted sharply with Mayor Ed Henry's more aggressive approach. Though his family had long been connected with Democratic politics, Henry's only elective office, prior to being elected as mayor in 1964, had been a school board position. His doctorate in government led many to hold him suspect as an idealist or philosophical dreamer (his victory margin in his first mayoral campaign was only 43 votes), but the notion was quickly dispelled when he took office.

Philosophical, yes; a dreamer, emphatically no. Henry immediately made a number of proposals that caught some of the more conservative council members by surprise. He quickly realized that, strong mayor or not, he would need full council backing if his plans for community improvement were to succeed. His willingness to work as a full-time mayor ("on half-time salary," as one of his supporters said), in addition to maintaining his position as a professor of government at St. John's University, soon won over many of the council members. They also discovered that his growing stature and knowledge of the theory and practice of government had earned him—and the city—a ready ear and a good deal of respect on the state level. Henry already had excellent rapport with the state's two Democratic senators and the Democratic Vice-President Hubert Humphrey. These entrées into higher levels of government frequently gained grant money and other financial aid. They also led Henry to explain that whatever recent state or federal monies the city had received "would not cost the citizens of St. Cloud one red cent!" (to which one exasperated councilman was quoted to have mumbled, "Just where does he think that tax money comes from? The Vatican?")

Henry's terms as mayor (1964 and 1968) were marked by a number of confrontations with the business community, not to mention the more conservative members of the council. During his mayoral campaign Henry had frequently promised that property taxes would not be raised if he was elected. But in the face of rising municipal costs and expansion, he began casting about for a source of additional revenue. Fortuitously, the Northern States Power franchise for the city's electric service was due to be renewed in 1966. (It's previous contract had run for 20 years.) Henry selected NSP as the most appropriate candidate to bear some of the city's tax burden.

The utility was informally advised of Henry's intentions. Henry advised the council of his plan to tax the utility for its use of city land for its utility poles. Henry expected strong opposition; not only were there two public utility men— George Reasbeck of Northwestern Bell and Dick Statz of NSP—on the council, but many of the other councilmen were business oriented and, he felt, would look on the franchise fee as an increase in the cost of doing business in St. Cloud.

To convince some of the uncommitted members of the council, Henry sent each member a copy of *Overcharge*, an anti-utility company book written by U.S. Senator Lee Metcalf. As a precedent for his

proposal, Henry cited the street rental fee of six percent on revenues the city had levied on WJON Cable TV for its use of public land in running its cable on utility poles. (The cable company also paid NSP a rental fee for use of the poles or underground facilities.) NSP, Henry was sure, would pass the fee on to consumers in its rate structure, thus broadening the tax base of the city in addition to getting something back from those nonresidents who worked in the city but did not directly contribute to its support with their taxes.

NSP, through its district manager Vincent Forrest, replied that Henry's proposed franchise fee was "a selective tax on one of the necessities of life," and that it would drive the cost of electrical service up. NSP, its representatives pointed out, was already paying a property tax on its poles and wires—a tax which, they claimed, was really a disguised property tax on the utility's users, since the company's higher costs would eventually be passed on to consumers.

Henry countered that residents could either pay for their government in one lump, as with a property tax, or in small installments in the form of higher costs which would be added to their electric bills.

During the ensuing debates—sometimes at public meetings, sometimes in the newspaper editorials and replies—Henry occasionally used homely examples to explain the principal to residents. When NSP noted the personal property tax it paid, the mayor replied that all businesses paid taxes on their equipment, but not all businesses stationed their equipment permanently on city property. "Who of you," Henry asked, "can put up an apple stand in Hester Park without paying rent?"

In mid-December 1966 the council—by a 5-to-1 vote with Statz of NSP abstaining—approved a 25-year electric franchise with a five percent fee. NSP announced that it could not accept the franchise in that form, but nonetheless continued its operations.

The city was now receiving its power from a disenfranchised utility; and NSP was operating illegally. Neither Henry nor NSP wanted to press the matter, although privately Henry made in-

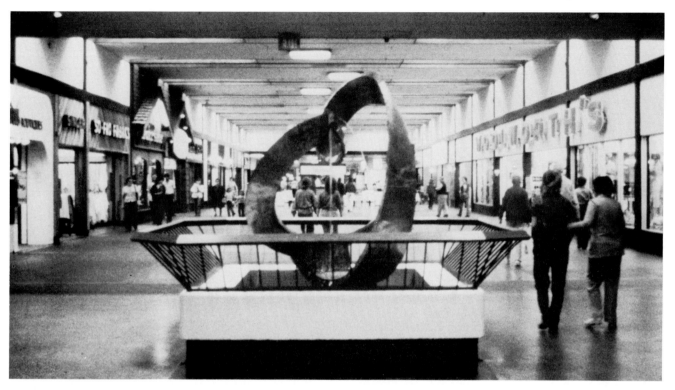

quiries. REA was approached as an alternate utility but was prevented by law from entering the city, and the private utilities that were contacted didn't care to enter the impasse.

Also privately, the mayor contemplated harassing NSP by such tactics as arresting repair-truck drivers for blocking alleys, not granting permission for streets to be torn up for service work, or refusing to inspect gas and electric installations, thus slowing down NSP's "connects." But he quickly discarded this approach as unfairly injurious to the consumer.

When, after several months, state legislation was introduced to replace the property tax on utilities with a state gross earnings charge and to prohibit municipalities from levying any charge against utilities, the mayor decided a compromise was in order. When it was learned that the legislation was unlikely to be reported out of committee, NSP also agreed that a compromise was in order and suggested a three percent fee on gross earnings on both gas and electricity. In July 1967 NSP signed the franchise agreement and shortly thereafter gas and electric rates went up three percent.

The annexation of the Crossroads Shopping Center provides another example of Henry's methods as mayor. When Crossroads opened in 1965 on the western border of the city it was one of the largest shopping centers in the state, containing over 400,000 square feet of space. The city's attempts at urban renewal had failed to provide more space in the loop area for two of its largest retailers, Sears and Penneys, who both chose to move to Crossroads while other merchants either closed their downtown locations and moved to the shopping center or opened a second outlet there, postponing the remodeling of their downtown facilities. This added to the slightly distressed look of the loop area.

Located on West Division Street, Crossroads Shopping Center was one of the largest enclosed-mall shopping centers north of Minneapolis-St. Paul. It was opened in 1965 and annexed to the city after a lengthy legal battle.

Crossroads, it was obvious, was depending on the city's population base but was avoiding municipal taxes. St. Cloud township taxes were about $7,500, but city taxes, if the shopping center were annexed, would have been 10 times that much. Crossroads had already entered into an agreement with the city whereby municipal water and sewage lines were extended to the shopping center (which would pay double rates for its water and contribute $50,000 toward the construction of the lines, recoverable for the most part in case of later annexation).

Located downtown, the three-block Mall Germain provided convenient shopping and an area where residents could partake of leisure activities. The pedestrian mall contained decorative benches, flowers, trees, modern sculpture, and numerous stores. The Mall was reopened to two-way traffic and parking in 1997–1998.

While the city was pondering the possibility of annexation, the state's attorney general rendered an opinion in a similar situation. Where no voters resided in an area to be annexed, he ruled, no referendum was necessary for annexation if the annexing power could show cause. Henry suggested to the council—in executive session—that if the residents in the area around the shopping center were left out of the annexation for the moment, Crossroads could be annexed.

The mayor's office quietly began researching the law and collecting data on tax rates, property ownership, and layout of sewer lines. The work was done in strict secrecy because any advance information, Henry felt, might prompt Waite Park to submit an annexation petition of its own, or permit Crossroads to establish a resident on their property, thereby forcing a referendum which would surely turn down annexation. Once the petition had been filed, any such moves could be considered *ex post facto* and therefore would have little or no effect on a decision.

The filing of the petition with the Municipal Commission in December 1967 precipitated a three-year legal battle. It ended when Crossroads

agreed not to take its fight to the state supreme court in return for being granted an off-sale liquor license by the city.

Before the end of his second term, Mayor Ed Henry resigned to accept an educational position. Alcuin Loehr was elected to fill Henry's unexpired term in November 1970, and served St. Cloud until 1980, when he was defeated in his attempt at a fourth full term. Second only to Phil Collignon, who served from 1932 to 1945, Loehr has had the longest continual mayoral reign in St. Cloud's history.

By design or not, Loehr's mayoralty seemed to calm the disquiet that prevailed during the previous administration. It was characterized by a consolidation of the city's prominent role in area government as opposed to the more local role it had been used to. As the largest municipality in central Minnesota, St. Cloud was expected to provide leadership and cohesion in area planning without ignoring the rights and needs of smaller governmental units.

Early in Loehr's term the completion of the Mall Germain and the fruition of other developments in and around the city firmed a decision to seek

The ring road around St. Cloud's "Loop" was an attempt to lure pedestrian traffic back to the business district by eliminating car traffic in the core area. The ring road was converted to two-way traffic in 1995. (SCHS)

the All-America City award, granted by the National Municipal League to cities throughout the nation. The League, in granting the awards, required a demonstration that a community had taken steps to improve itself and its quality of life by upgrading its physical structure, its business future, and the liveability of its environment. All

new industrial park; sports and recreation facilities; and its sharing of services and facilities with neighboring communities.

The Mall Germain had been the city's answer to the Crossroads Shopping Center. The city had realized that its loop area was in danger of dying when several downtown retailers moved to the Crossroads. Expansion to the south was blocked by Highway 23, and the number of residences, schools, and large businesses on the northern edge limited expansion in that direction. The river blocked easterly expansion. Only in the west was any growth possible, and it was happening so fast that land values seemed to increase from morning to afternoon.

The decision was made that the loop would be served best by limiting traffic in the core area. The much-maligned ring road, which routed traffic around the loop, was an attempt to increase pedestrian traffic in the mall, which resembled an open air shopping center.

The first industrial park proved to be such a success that a second was opened in 1978 and rapidly developed the same track record. As the city used its municipal facilities to anchor large businesses in the vicinity through industrial parks, their payrolls and tax revenues were a vital factor in contributing to the economic health of the entire area.

The city's solution to another problem was a significant part of its award application to the National Municipal League. The baseball stadium on Division Street had become valuable commercial property due to the westward expansion of the trade area. But, in addition to its sentimental value—something that old baseball parks seem to generate regardless of condition—the park was still in fairly decent shape, adding to citizens' objections to its demolition.

A representative citizens' committee proposed an alternative that answered all but the most sentimental objections. Forty acres of parkland had been acquired by the city from construction of the first industrial park. With the income derived from the sale of the baseball park property to a developer, the city constructed a new recreation complex, including a ballpark, an ice arena

of these attributes had to be demonstrated in more than good intentions or governmental action. In fact, a major consideration was the amount of citizen input and the leadership of community volunteers.

St. Cloud, in its application for the award, cited four areas of development: the Mall Germain; the

(actually a multi-use meeting facility), and playground and park facilities. No taxes had to be raised to pay for the complex and the old ballpark site was now reaping tax revenues for the city.

The final item in the city's application might have been labeled "neighborliness." All core cities surrounded by rapidly developing suburban communities find themselves forced to provide more and more services for fewer and fewer taxpaying residents. Expansion, if it is possible, is one answer. But the surrounding municipalities tended to be jealous of their prerogatives, quick to demand what they felt was theirs by right, and loathe to surrender one iota of "sovereignty." St. Cloud has had the advantage of municipal neighbors willing to work to achieve common goals and ready to sacrifice for the common good. This sense of cooperation extended to the Metro Transit

The Rox Ball Park, built following World War II, was on valuable property the city could well use for tax purposes. Surplus land from the city's first Industrial Park was the site of a new Municipal Arena complex, and the Rox Park became Westgate. (SCHS)

Commission, which served St. Cloud and the adjacent area; to the St. Cloud Water Pollution Control System, which handled waste treatment for neighboring populations; and to the Metropolitan Planning Commission (now the St. Cloud Area Planning Organization), which managed area-wide traffic and thoroughfare control.

The city submitted its application to the National Municipal League in 1973. The result was announced on April 15, 1974: St. Cloud was one of 10 cities out of 500 applicants to be awarded the title of All America City.

In the years since, those qualities that were the hallmark of that award have intensified. Growth was not sought for its own sake. In many ways St. Cloud in the 1970s was still a small pioneer town, caring first for its citizens and neighbors and their welfare, and only secondarily for its place in the harmony of cities and towns that comprised the state.

But its outlook was, as it had been over the years, to seek the growth of its community spirit in the physical growth that attended success.

No less than it looked forward the city searched its past, not in empty regret at the passing of golden days and years, but fully aware of the commitment of the Wilsons, the Lowrys, the Brotts, the Swisshelms, the Burbanks — even the Pandolfos — and the thousands of others whose contribution to their present still marked St. Cloud's past and future.

A view of Lake George and downtown St. Cloud.
Courtesy, St. Cloud Area Convention and Visitors
Bureau

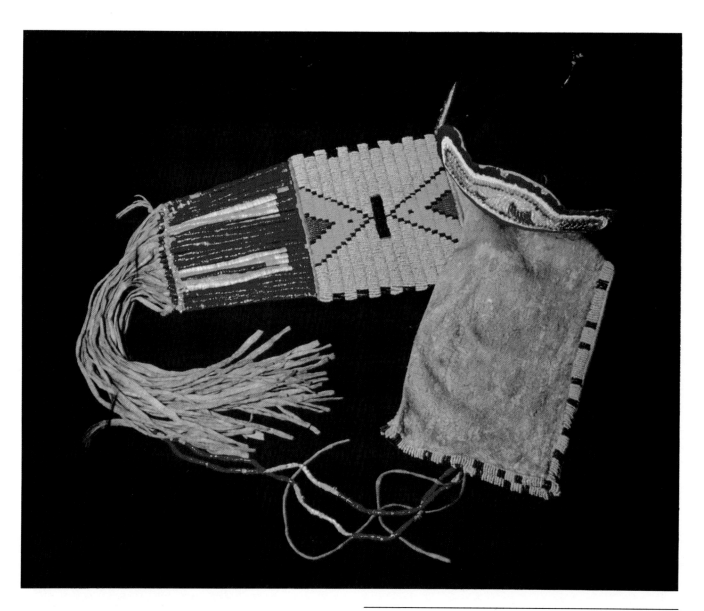

ABOVE
Although the St. Cloud area was primarily inhabited by Sioux, Ojibway, and Winnebago Indians, this Dakotah pipe (or tobacco) bag, decorated with intricate beadwork, was not an uncommon item in the area during the 1850s. (SCHS)

LEFT
This Ojibway cap (dated about 1860) was found along the Sauk River. It is typical of the kind of item that was obtained from the Indians through trading. (SCHS)

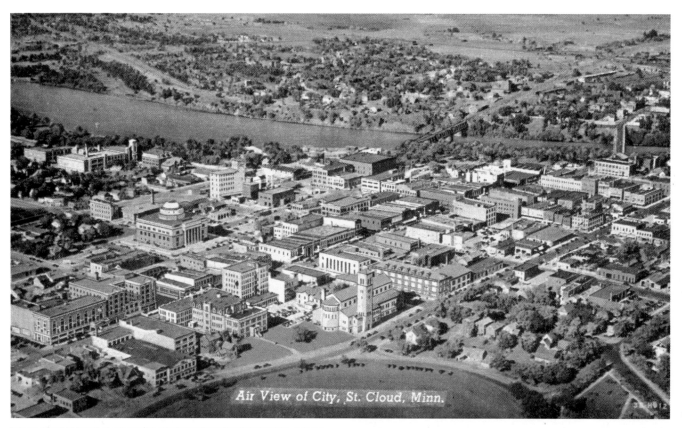

Air View of City, St. Cloud, Minn.

Mississippi River, St. Cloud, Minn.

ABOVE
Aerial view of St. Cloud, circa 1940. MS6.9/SC1/r3, courtesy, Minnesota Historical Society

RIGHT
A view of the Mississippi River, circa 1915. MS6.9/SC4/r32, courtesy, Minnesota Historical Society

FACING PAGE, TOP
Immaculate Conception Church and St. Mary's School faced north on St. Germain Street at Ninth Avenue until the church burned down on August 25, 1920. A basement church, renamed St. Mary's, was completed on the present site by Christmas 1921. The upper church was completed 10 years later and was made the cathedral in 1937. (SCHS)

FACING PAGE, BOTTOM LEFT
Holy Angels Procathedral was built in 1883. The main steeple was 183 feet high and was a favorite perch of agile photographers wanting a "bird's-eye view." The church was gutted by fire in the fall of 1933, and in the reconstruction the steeples were lowered to become towers. (SCHS)

The two and one-half story St. Raphael's Hospital, constructed originally in 1900 and rebuilt after fire destroyed its upper floor, served as the city's hospital until 1928. (SCHS)

St. Cloud Hospital, St. Cloud, Minn.

ABOVE
Looking down St. Germain Street, circa 1957. MS6.9/SC2/r16, courtesy, Minnesota Historical Society

LEFT
View of St. Cloud Hospital, circa 1940. MS6.9/SC7.1/r10, courtesy, Minnesota Historical Society

FACING PAGE, TOP
The Stearns County Courthouse in St. Cloud was the seat of county government, but was also important to the city. By the time this view was taken in 1917, the wings had been added and the building of a new courthouse was only a few years away. Courtesy, Minnesota Historical Society

FACING PAGE, BOTTOM
The St. Cloud Public Library pictured here was made possible by monetary gifts from James J. Hill and Andrew Carnegie. The building was razed in 1982. (SCHS)

FACING PAGE, TOP
Garrison Keillor (second rider from the front) rode the
Stearns County Lake Wobegon Regional Trail as part
of its Grand Opening ceremonies on September 30,
1998. The original, 10-foot-wide surfaced trail extends
from Avon to Sauk Center along the former Great
Northern railroad track. A spur was added on the
abandoned Soo Railroad track from Albany to
Holdingford. Courtesy, Chuck Wocken, director,
Stearns County Parks Department.

FACING PAGE, BOTTOM
St. Cloud all city High School Marching Band
drummers. They marched in the cities 1999 annual
Wheels. Wings & Water Festival parade. Photo by
Jason Wachter, *St. Cloud Times*.

ABOVE
Enjoying a Central Minnesota summer day at one of
the 25 quarries designated as a swimming area in
Quarry Park & Nature Preserve in Waite Park. This
Stearns County 553-acre-park was opened on January
1, 1998. Its quarries provided the exterior stone of
many of the State's Capitol buildings. Natural features
include scenic woodlands, open prairie, wetlands and
unquarried bedrock areas. Courtesy, Chuck Wocken,
director, Stearns County Parks Department.

RIGHT
Narcisse Necklace of Yankton, South Dakota, provided Margaret Ripplinger of Hayward, Wisconsin, a little relief from the sun during the St. Cloud Area Unity Powwow. The 1997 powwow was added to the Wings, Waters, Wheel, beginning the annual tradition of an event focused on ethnic heritage. About 500 people attended. Photo by Paul Middlestaedit, *St. Cloud Times*.

BELOW
St. Cloud State University. Courtesy, St. Cloud Area Convention and Visitors Bureau

FACING PAGE, TOP
The 10th Street Bridge spans the Mississippi River just above the dam. It was replaced with a new concrete bridge in 1985. Photo by Jerry Currey

FACING PAGE, BOTTOM
St. Cloud State University in the winter. Courtesy, St. Cloud Area Convention and Visitors Bureau

124

FACING PAGE, TOP
Playing hockey on Lake George during Winterfest. Courtesy, St. Cloud Area Convention and Visitors Bureau

FACING PAGE, BOTTOM
Canoeing on the Mississippi River. Courtesy, St. Cloud Area Convention and Visitors Bureau

ABOVE
The Whitney Center Complex was constructed on the 140-plus acre Whitney Memorial Park land. Shown here is the Whitney Recreation Center, which provides the community and its citizens with a wide array of programs and activities, and the Whitney Senior Center, which offers opportunities for individuals 55 years and older to socialize, maintain their wellness, and have access to a variety of services. Photo by Dennis Hemme, courtesy, City of St. Cloud

RIGHT
Molitors Trout Heaven Park. Courtesy, St. Cloud Area Convention and Visitors Bureau

ABOVE
The view from the Balustrades offers vistas of both the Perennial and White Gardens of Munsinger Clemens Gardens. Photo by Bob Firth, courtesy, St. Cloud Park and Recreation Department

FACING PAGE
A view of the fountain at Munsinger Clemens Gardens. Courtesy, St. Cloud Area Convention and Visitors Bureau

The Virginia Clemens Rose Garden, centered around the Janey Crane Fountain, features 1,100 roses. Near the iron trellis is a memorial to Virginia, the Garden's generous benefactor. Photo by Bob Firth, courtesy, St. Cloud Park and Recreation Department

7

Continuity, Change and Challenge

1980-2002

In the 1970s public radio personality and author, Garrison Keillor, invented the mythical town of Lake Wobegon—"a small town where the women are strong and the men good-looking and the children all above average . . . ." When fans seemed disappointed that it was fictional he started saying that it was located "in central Minnesota, near Stearns County, up around Holdingford, not far from St. Rosa and Albany and Freeport, northwest of St. Cloud . . . ." St. Cloud's Division Street "a five mile strip of commerce in full riot . . ." is its eastern approach. His humorous, but sensitive and understanding portrayal of a homogeneous rural Christian community has intrigued many Americans.

While elements of his portrayal remain, continued rapid growth has resulted in more diverse and less "rural" communities by 2000. In the post-2000 reapportionment, St. Cloud and the neighboring cities were moved from the largely rural Seventh to a reconfigured suburban-exurban Sixth Congressional district. Lawrence Schumacher, *St. Cloud Times* reporter, described it as "a rude reminder that the rest of Minnesota already considers the area a Twin Cities suburb, or expects it to become so in

the next decade." The mayor of Freeport, Rodney Atkinson, (near where Keillor lived some three decades earlier and from where he drew much of his fictional community portrayal) was quoted: "We're becoming a suburb of St. Cloud, which is becoming a suburb of the Twin Cities." St. Cloud's Mayor John Ellenbecker noted the potential impact of the shift: "Now, we're going to be more in competition for transportation dollars with the north metro area than we were with anybody in the old Seventh." The mayor also pointed out that the area had "lots in common with the north metro in terms of growth issues . . . the population growth between Minneapolis and St. Cloud is significant and we have to deal with it."

Renee Lundgren, executive director of the Great River Interfaith Partnership (GRIP), wrote in a recent grant request that "Less than a generation ago, the region's core city of St. Cloud was a homogeneous town (80 percent German Catholic) . . . surrounded by rural farm based communities . . . ." She also pointed out that the "region is experiencing a rate of social and economic change greater than that of any [other] area in Minnesota" and that "civic, religious, and political institutions are struggling to respond, and forces beyond their control are setting much of the course of the future."

St. Cloud had grown to a community of over 59,000 by the end of the 20th century, including population in three counties—Benton, Sherburne and most, in Stearns—and two metropolitan statistical areas. All three counties exceeded Minnesota's growth rate of 20.7 percent in the closing decades of the 20th century. Stearns County grew by 23.1 percent, Benton by 35.9 percent and Sherburne by 115.4 percent. Following the 1990 Census, Sherburne County was moved from the St. Cloud Metropolitan Statistical Area to the Minneapolis-St. Paul Metropolitan Statistical Area. All of St. Cloud Township, following the 1995 merger agreement, became part of either St. Cloud or Waite Park.

Like many other rapidly growing and changing communities, the area's cities, faced the challenges of: increasing urban sprawl; growing ethnic and religious diversity; the challenges of intra-gov-

FACING PAGE
Community and church leaders (from top left), State Representatives Jim Knoblach and Joe Opatz, St. Cloud Mayor Larry Meyer and Clarence White clapped and sang a song about justice after signing the Great River Interfaith Partnership covenant at St. Mary's Cathedral. Photo by Kimm Anderson, *St. Cloud Times*

BELOW
Aerial view of St. Cloud and the Mississippi River. Courtesy, St. Cloud Area Convention and Visitor's Bureau

ernmental cooperation and planning on issues ranging from transportation and land use to affordable housing and public services; and heightened ethnic and racial tensions.

In 1978, "seven townships, five cities and three counties," entered a joint powers agreement making the St. Cloud Area Planning Organization the area's cooperative planning unit.

In Stearns county, the city shares boundaries, with Waite Park and St. Joseph Township on the west; Sartell, including areas covered in its orderly annexation agreement with Le Sauk Township, to the north and the newly incorporated city of St. Augusta to the south. On the east side of the Mississippi River, it shares its northern border with Sauk Rapids and to the east with Minden Township in Benton County and to the east and south with Haven Township in Sherburne County.

Minnesota's population growth of 12.4 percent, during the 1990s, led the Midwest and Northeast regions of the United States but "was slightly slower than the national average of 13.2 percent." The five area cities were part of the fastest growing part of the state. Their growth accelerated from 12,069 (20.7 percent) during the 1980s to 19,865 (28.2 percent) during the 1990s. They grew by 32,200 or 54.8 percent during the last two decades of the 20th century. (See Table 1 following page).

While St. Cloud grew by 38.8 percent overall from 1980 to 2000, the rate of growth decreased in both Sauk Rapids (35.8 percent in the 1980s to 29.9 percent in 1990s) and Waite Park (43.6 percent in the 1980s to 30.8 percent in the 1990s), but still higher than the state growth rate. St. Cloud's lower rate of growth than the region, reflects the dispersal of area growth.

The challenges of growing urbanization and the need for regional cooperation and planning became more obvious by the late 1990s and early 2000s. St. Augusta Township, incorporated as the city of St. Augusta in 2001, had a 2000 population of 3,065. A seventh area city was added in 2002 with the decision by the towns of Rockville and Pleasant Lake, the fastest growing Minnesota community in the 1990s, and Rockville Township's 2,507 residents to incorporate.

Sue Halena, reporter for the *Times*, in reviewing the 2000 census, wrote "Welcome to the new Lake Wobegon," where "home construction is strong, families have a different look and the median age is below average." Central Minnesota followed both state and national trends towards an aging

Table 1

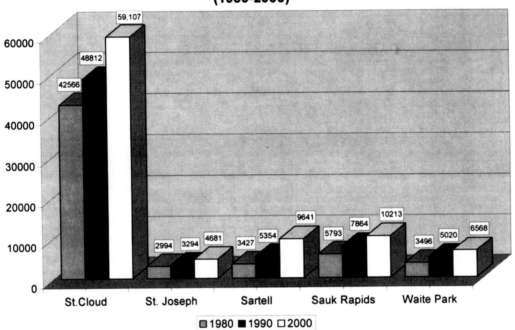

**Population Growth
St. Cloud Region
(1980-2000)**

Table 2

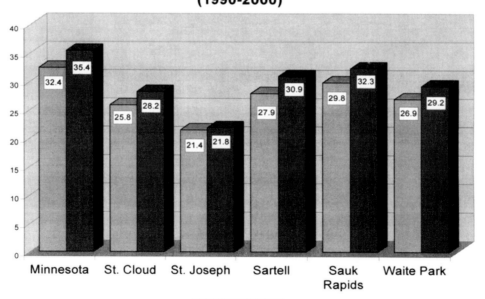

**Median Age
St. Cloud Region
(1990-2000)**

population during the closing decades of the 20th century. But the median age in all five cities remained lower than both the state and national median ages, as illustrated by Table 2, and the area remained one of the youngest in Minnesota.

The presence of St. Benedict's College and St. John's University had a greater influence on the smaller St. Joseph with its relatively youthful image, than St. Cloud State University's and St. Cloud Technical College's student populations had on the median age of St. Cloud, in both 1990 and 2000. St. Cloud had the second youngest population of area cities in both census years.

Sartell's median age increased the most from 1990 to 2000. Its population growth was strongly influenced by the growth in the number of "traditional" families. The addition of the predominantly family suburban population of St. Cloud Township along with the baby boom generational impact were the key factor in the dramatic increase in the 35–54 age group.

Times staff writer, John Molene, in analyzing the 2000 Census concluded that "the traditional family model is changing. There are an increasing number of cohabiting couples, single mothers, single fathers, roommates and people living alone." The majority of individuals in central Minnesota lived in what the census termed "family households (families)." The census definition of family household included any household in which one or more members were related, to the first person listed, by marriage, birth or adoption. This included both traditional married couples and single parent households.

Fewer than half of the family households were "married-couple families." In St. Joseph, St. Cloud and Waite Park the percentage was somewhat less. All three of these communities have a large number of college students and other young adults living in apartments. The average central Minnesota family followed the trend towards declining size. Among area cities Waite Park had the smallest average family size at 2.8 people and Sartell with the largest family size at 3.23.

Of the three area counties, Benton, had the lowest percent, 4.3 percent, ethnic or racial minorities, including Hispanic. Sherburne County had 6.6 percent and Stearns 6.7 percent at the close of the 20th century.

David Unze, *Times* writer, examined the influence of the dramatic increase in, and growing impact of, the area's Asian population during the late 20th century. While the state's Vietnamese population doubled during the closing decade of the 20th century, St. Cloud's grew by 234 percent. By 2000, Vietnamese made up 20 percent of the city's Asians. They were also the largest subgroup, 23 percent, of all Asians in the five area cities.

Unze interviewed Vy and Long Lam as he examined the impact of Asian settlement on the area. Vy Lam came to St. Cloud from Vietnam in 1990. After she had moved from the area she married Long Lam in Texas, in 1994. They returned to St. Cloud where they opened an Asian market in 1997. Three years later, as the area's Asian population grew, they expanded their Viet-Tien Market, by relocating to a former neighborhood pizzeria. Vy and Long Lam saw many of the area's Asians in their market. Vy commented that she sees "new people a lot, almost every day . . . I ask them where

Devon Grant talking with players during halftime on the Central Minnesota Youth Soccer Association field. Photo by Kimm Anderson, *St. Cloud Times*

ABOVE
Mayor Larry Meyer opened a diversity discussion of community leaders and decision makers. At left were Paula Engdahl, St. Cloud Human Rights Director and Les Green a professor at St. Cloud State University. Photo by Mike Knaak, *St. Cloud Times*

BELOW
Owen Long Lam sorts through a basket of sticky rice at Viet-Tien-Asian Market. Photo by Marsha Haberman, *St. Cloud Times*

they come from. Many of them say they come from the Fargo area. Some also are coming from California and Texas."

Unze commented that "If the census numbers don't tell the tale of the Asian population boom, take a look at the area's ethnic food offerings. In 1990, five restaurants served primarily Asian cuisine in the five-city St. Cloud area. Today there are more than a dozen such eateries and double the number of Asian markets." He quotes Vy Lam describing why she thinks so many Asians are coming to this area "because they have a good choice of schools and for the jobs. In Texas, the wages are much lower, and here there are good jobs and lots of job openings."

Unze points out that "St. Cloud State University, in a 1998 estimate, had as many as 250 students from Asian countries such as Japan, Malaysia, China and Indonesia. Vietnamese refugees, released from communist work camps, also have relocated to the St. Cloud area."

Hispanic or Latino were the next largest group in the three counties. Hispanic or Latino comprised 1.3 percent of St. Cloud's population in 2000. Unze,

headlined "Hispanic boom reshapes Stearns," in the *Times*, noting that "Hispanic growth is mirroring that of the Asian population in the St. Cloud area. Their population is stabilizing and moving into middle-class jobs, neighborhoods and business ownership." Their largest concentrations, outside of St. Cloud, are in the Cold Spring and Melrose school districts.

In another column he observed that the influence of the "burgeoning Hispanic population . . . perhaps best resonates on Sundays at St. Boniface Catholic Church. It's not the twice-monthly Spanish Mass that highlights the evolution of a community, originally inhabited in the 1850s by Arcenaults, Jacobys, Fuchses and Maselters. The Hispanic influx also springs to life at the Catholic Mass, still attended regularly by descendants of . . . European settlers." He quotes parishioner Tom Westerhaus "The parish sings in Spanish at the regular Mass . . . . And it's in a heavy German accent from a parish that still sings 'Stille Nacht' at Christmastime."

Ramon Querales, who came to Stearns County from Barquisimeto, Venzuala, was hired as an English as a Second Language (ESL) teacher by Rocori Area Schools in Cold Spring. He said that other Hispanics in areas like south Texas, California and Mexico hear "from the people who are already here, that they can come to central Minnesota and know that within two to three weeks they are going to have a job. And not a job where they're making just $3 to $4 an hour. They can make probably $7 to $8 an hour."

Unze discovered "anecdotal evidence" in doing research for his *St. Cloud Times* articles of continued growth of the minority population. Mari Walker, ESL coordinator and a teacher in the St. Cloud Area School District 742, told him that there has been "a rapid increase in just the last few months in the Somalian population . . . the district has hired the equivalent of one and a half ESL teachers this year to work with new Somalian students." By 2001, individuals of Somali background became the fourth largest minority group in the St. Cloud public schools "when it passed Cambodian." Walker believes that growth in minority population will continue, especially if "the jobs go well, I

think more families will be coming in."

The St. Cloud Public School District number 742's K-12 English as a Second Language (ESL) program had grown to serve over 300 students, representing 23 native languages other than English, by the 2001–2002 school year.

SCSU continued growth in students made it the state's second largest post-secondary institution during the closing decades of the 20th century. By Fall 2001, it had a record enrollment of 15,650 students. The student population of color had increased gradually to make up 5 percent of the student population. The stories of Kiyoko Yokota and Nishta Rao are part of the growing impact of the University's international studies programs and foreign student enrollment during the last quarter of the 20th century. Nine hundred and fifty students from 84 countries attended classes during the 2001–2002 academic year.

Yokota, a Japanese native, started her pursuit of a bachelor of science degree in biology in 1991. She graduated summa cum laude four years later. After returning to work in her field in Japan she decided to come back to Minnesota, this time to pursue a doctorate degree at the University of Minnesota. Yokota chose SCSU through her contact with a SCSU professor who was teaching English at a junior high lab school in Japan and could not find any university programs in Japan targeted to her interest in environmental sciences. Her initial impression of SCSU when she arrived for orientation in June 1991 was a small, quaint and quiet place. Yokota changed her perspective as students arrived to "wow, this is an American university." She found that the "faculty members especially were very sensitive" and she met some great students.

Rao, born and raised in India, began her journey to a degree at SCSU during the winter of 1997. She described her 3½ years at SCSU as a journey "and an experience that I will cherish and treasure for the rest of my life." Professors, staff and students at SCSU impressed her. As part of her participation in the Honors program she was able to study at Oxford. "SCSU," Rao said, "has instilled in me the confidence to reach higher for my goals and achieve them. It has given me an education in the classroom, but more importantly, it has given me an education outside the classroom as well, something that has helped me become a more complete, compassionate and confident individual . . . ."

SCSU offers international study opportunities involving its faculty and students in China, Costa Rica, Czech Republic, England, France, Germany and Poland. Christopher Ernest, a 1992 graduate in Computer Science and German participated in the program in. Ernest found "most memorable" the opportunity to be "a part of the local culture—making friends with the locals and just blending in."

The area's excellent K-12 public and private schools and four post-secondary institutions help provide a well-educated labor force and a strong economic base for the area's economy. For example, the St. Cloud Public Schools with its 10,000 plus diverse student population (4 percent Asian, 2 percent Hispanic, 6 percent black non-Hispanic and 1 percent American Indian during 2001–2002 school year) added about 2,000 to the area's employment base. SCSU, large student population served as a source for workers in local industries ranging from new technology to telemarketing and service or retail to factory workers. They also were a significant influence in the area's growing retail trade. SCSU added about 1,500 employees to the local economy. St. Cloud Technical College part- and full-time student enrollment and 300 faculty and staff added workers as well as specialized training to the area's economy. One example of the role played by the area's strong educational structure is the tripling of employment in computer and data-processing services during the 1990s.

While still small, when compared to national averages, the dramatic growth in St. Cloud's racial and ethnic minorities focused renewed attention on cultural diversity. Ethnic and racial minorities had grown by nearly 250 percent in St. Cloud, during the 1990s. The 9.97 percent of the city's population identifying themselves as nonwhite or Hispanic was coming closer to those who identified themselves in the state—11.8 percent in 2000. Comparisons to earlier censuses present some problems since the racial and ethnic classifications

ABOVE
Paula Engdahl (left), St. Cloud Human Rights Director, Mayor Larry Meyer and Betsy Mahowald, assistant director, Office of Cultural Education, College of Education, St. Cloud State University planning ways to address diversity issues, January 28, 1998. Photo by Les Green

FACING PAGE, TOP
Mayor John D. Ellenbecker presenting Special Life Saving Award to Christopher Donte Davis, January 28, 2002. From left to right: Police Chief Dennis Ballantine, Officer Thomas Schlieman, Christopher Donte Davis (and his sister whose life he saved), Mayor Ellenbecker. Courtesy, City of St. Cloud

FACING PAGE, BOTTOM
Audience of area leaders and community members listening to residents express their concerns about racism and tell their personal experiences. The Wednesday meeting was scheduled by then St. Cloud Mayor Larry Meyer. Photo by Jason Wachter, *St. Cloud Times*

varied. But, the degree of change is very obvious. In 1980 the minority population of St. Cloud was 2.3 percent, in 1990 it grew to 3.2 percent and by 2000 it was over 8 percent, or just under 10 percent depending on the census definition used.

Like many communities undergoing rapid growth and changing religious and ethnic complexion, the community faced tensions and challenges to change. City government, schools, St. Cloud State University, churches and businesses all faced new pressures to adapt. Some worked to respond, not always successfully, to charges ranging from indifference to racial discrimination to religious bigotry.

The city formed the Human Rights Office in 1973 to "respond to housing and other complaints of discrimination." Four years later it adopted a Human Rights Ordinance and established the St.

Cloud Human Rights Commission for the purpose of securing "for all citizens and visitors equal opportunity in education, employment, housing, public accommodations, and public services, and full participation for all citizens in the affairs of this community." In June 2000 Paula Van Avery's part-time position as Human Rights Director was increased to full-time. In her Human Rights Division annual report for 2000–2001 she notes that "Unfortunately, discrimination has continued and offenders have become more sophisticated."

Council member Larry Meyer, in his position paper "Into the Third Millennium," during his campaign for reelection in 1993, addressed the challenge of cultural diversity. Meyer recognized that "In the minority community, both in the Twin Cities, and locally, St. Cloud is often termed 'White Cloud'—a reference not only to its 97 percent white community, but also a reference to a feeling by many minorities that they are not welcome here and are viewed as 'outsiders.'" Meyer points out that many skeptics consider any "problem" primarily the result of St. Cloud State University's recruitment of minority staff and students who "have higher expectations, and demands, of St. Cloud's white community, and that this is not a symptom of community-wide racism. That," he continues, "response is a bit too simple."

Earlier in 1993 Mayor Charles (Chuck) Winkleman invited the CEOs of the area's largest employers to a kick-off meeting on cultural diversity. The featured speaker was Dr. Edward Nichols, an expert in the area. Winkleman and Meyer made persuasive calls to those who had not responded, encouraging them to become involved in this project to initiate cultural diversity programs within these businesses and institutions. Meyer concluded that: "The issue indeed is one of persuasion, leadership, example and education. It is my goal that my grandchildren not know the terminology 'White Cloud' and that it becomes a trivia footnote in St. Cloud history."

Two months after being elected mayor in 1997, Meyer brought together a group of community policy makers committed to the promotion of cultural diversity and the building of respectful relationships. They represented individuals from 12 segments of the community. Meetings are held quarterly to exchange information and their experiences of inclusion within their areas. In an effort to allow the mayor, city staff and resource people to reach out into communities and begin the process of relationship building, Meyer started "community conversations." Response in the ethnic and racial minority communities was strong. Informal gatherings were hosted in homes and neighborhoods by members of the Vietnamese, Cambodian, Laotian, African American, Somali, American Indian, and Spanish speaking groups as well as other community members. The city has dual language "interpreter cards" and "legal fact sheets" in English and Cambodian, Hmong, Laotian, Russian, Spanish and Vietnamese. The later provide information on rental rights and responsibilities, housing discrimination, conciliation court, becoming a U.S. citizen, protection orders and child custody issues.

Although considerable progress had been made, problems remain. The St. Cloud Human Rights Office received 88 complaints involving race between June 1, 2000 and May 31, 2001. Half of the complaints were related to housing. The remainder was divided among employment — education, public service and business.

In December 1995 a group of area pastors and community leaders, from a broad spectrum of denominations, met to discuss their concerns over the lack of an effective vehicle with which to voice the concerns of people of low and moderate incomes in shaping public policy and the communities social economic structure. This led to the organizing of a broad interdenominational group, GRIP. After extensive discussions with their parishioners and examination of challenges facing the community, an assembly of representatives from member parishes and organizations met to develop an action plan. Two issues emerged: the lack of adequate affordable housing and housing discrimination. GRIP task forces started working on both issues.

The work and encouragement of GRIP was an important factor in the 2000 adoption of anti-discrimination language in the St. Cloud housing ordinance. The ordinance includes a program for landlord education, investigation of complaints, reviewing of test compliance with anti-discrimination and litigation, when necessary.

During 2001, the city's Human Rights Division distributed nearly 2000 free fair-housing publications to rental licensees; offered fair housing training sessions to licensees and staff; the Human Rights Director was authorized to certify two hours Continuing Education Real Estate Credit to participants; joined in a cooperative program with the police department and the Crime-Free Multi housing program with over 200 Crime-Free Multi housing participants; developed brochures on fair housing and landlord/tenant laws, and distributed over 4,000 to local human service agencies. The first housing tests were conducted in the areas of disability and family status discrimination during 2000–2001. Three of the most egregious audits were selected for litigation. . . all were resolved through mediation. A five-year program of testing of race-based housing practices in St. Cloud was started in 2001.

Some challenged whether any significant progress had been made in changing the perspective or acceptance by local citizens of cultural diversity. Three members of St. Cloud State University's faculty wrote a lengthy letter on February 15, 2002, to approximately 40 Twin Cities area high school guidance counselors asking them to advise their students not to attend SCSU as "residency in St. Cloud can be hazardous for black people." They had also sent a letter to Twin Cities area community colleges the preceding year advising against transfer to SCSU by black students. The 2001 letter presented a lengthy history

ABOVE
From left to right: Reverend David Potter, Salem Evangelical Lutheran Church; Les Green, St. Cloud State University professor and Reverend David Reiter of First Presbyterian Church closing a meeting with about 60 community and church leaders at First Presbyterian Church in St. Cloud to address ways churches can help foster racial unity. Photo by Kimm Anderson, *St. Cloud Times*

FACING PAGE
About 200 members of Catholic, Lutheran, Methodist, Episcopal, Unitarian, and other denominations gathered Sunday, May 17, 1998 to affirm the Great River Interfaith Partnership at St. Mary's Cathedral. Photo by Kimm Anderson, *St. Cloud Times*

of minority-white relations at SCSU and in the local community. Included were brief accounts of a *St. Cloud Times* story headlined "Minority recruitment unpopular." It charged that in 1990 Dr. Josephine Davis, vice-president of Academic Affairs received death threats and her son was "harassed more by St. Cloud police than those in rural Georgia where he grew up;" an article in the SCSU *Chronicle*, headlined "College not dealing with abuse of minorities;" stated that "police invaded, beat and maced several black students for absolutely no reason" at a "university sanctioned gathering at the SCSU Cultural Center" on October 16, 1988; and a March 1990 threatening letter from a Ku Klux Klan leader. The writers state that more recently St. Cloud "Police Chief Dennis O'Keefe told the St. Cloud chapter of the National Association for the Advancement of Black People (NAACP) that 90 percent of all arrestees are minorities.'" Their analysis: "either St. Cloud has the nation's most prolific Black criminals or police racism has been raised to new heights."

SCSU President, Roy Sago, who was a member

An aerial view of St. Cloud State University, "home of the Huskies." Photo by David J. Nordgren

of the community's cultural diversity program, met with St. Cloud Mayor John Ellenbecker to discuss the issues raised in the letter and how to address them. Sago had already requested a federal investigation of charges of racism and anti-Semitism on campus. The Equal Employment Opportunity Commission report was released on February 11, 2002. It found that SCSU "suffers from a severe lack of credibility" on diversity issues due to "many years of complacency."

St. Cloud was part of the "Golden Corridor" which stretched northwest along I94 from Minneapolis. This area of Minnesota experienced a "continuing acceleration of business and residential development . . . (and) sustained, robust growth" during the closing decades of the 20th century with rate of growth accelerating during the 1990s," said the report.

By 2000 the St. Cloud area had solidified its role as a thriving regional hub for healthcare, post secondary education, government and retail. It boasted a diverse economy, including a solid mix of manufacturers, professional services, a rapidly growing printing industry, tech industries with employment in computer and data-processing services tripling during the 1990s.

Health services experienced the largest growth in the number of employees in the area, (for example, 970 were added between 1994 and 1998) during the closing decades of the 20th century. The largest area health care provider, CentraCare Health Systems, "an integrated health care delivery system," was formed in 1995. Included were the St. Cloud Hospital, specialized (such as, the Central Minnesota Heart and Emergency Trauma centers) and general practice clinics and senior housing. By the end of the decade it had grown to be the area's largest single employer with a staff of over 4,000 doctors, nurses, other health care providers and support staff. The Trauma Center was verified as a level II Trauma Center in 1998. At the time it had nine trauma surgeons. Three years later it had 13. The Central Minnesota Heart Center had its roots in the late 1980s when the first open heart surgeries were performed at the St. Cloud Hospital. During the next decade it expanded rapidly. By the opening of the new century St. Cloud was ranked among the nations top 100 heart care providers. CentraCare continued regular expansion and remodeling at its major campus on the Mississippi River. It added a new facility along the Sauk River in northwest St. Cloud. It includes the Coborn Cancer Center.

There are also numerous other medical service and physicians groups not affiliated with CentraCare in the area. HealthPartners, formed as Central Minnesota Group Health, is a local health maintenance organization. St. Cloud Medical Group, an "independent, family-oriented, multi-specialty healthcare group," added a second clinic in northwest St. Cloud with a medical staff of over 20 during the 1990s. Abbott Northwestern Hospital, Minneapolis, opened a "Specialty Care Center" in Sartell. The Veterans Administration Medical Center was the second largest medical staff employer with 800.

Printing and publishing had the largest percentage increase—46.1 percent during the late 1990s. The October 2000 Minnesota Department of Trade and Economic Development "Community Profiles" reported that Bankers Systems, Inc., a national provider of products and services to financial institutions, had 875 employees. Commercial products printers Merrill Corporation had 800, and Nahan Printing had 553 employees.

Business services, bars and restaurants, construction industries, trucking were other areas of growth as were retail and food sales. However, the "relative importance of retail sales seems to be shifting from the city of St. Cloud to the nearby communities of Sauk Rapids and Waite Park." For example, major home improvement centers like Home Depot and Menards joined Mills Farm Fleet in building their regional outlets in Waite Park during the 1990s. Coborns, a regional food retailer located in Sauk Rapids, built its Super Store in Waite Park.

The number of business establishments in the St. Cloud area grew 3 percent faster than for the state and the employment growth rate exceeded Minnesota's by 8 percent in the 1990s. All area industries included in the Minnesota Department of Economic Security Research and Statistics Office data at the turn of the century were expanding except agriculture, forestry and fishing.

Many 19th and 20th century merchants like Metzroth and Fandel had disappeared. Others, like Herbergers, had been bought out and their headquarters moved from St. Cloud. Some, like Tenvoorde Motor Co., now Tenvoorde Ford, have grown and prospered through adaptation from its humble 19th century roots as a bicycle shop, to be the oldest Ford franchise in the nation.

Area per capita income continue to be "approximately 75 percent of the state's average. In 1999 Sherburne County ranked 38th, Stearns 40th, and Benton 53rd, among Minnesota's 87 counties percapita personal income. St. Cloud had a higher ratio of lower-income households than the larger urban area: 14 percent in St. Cloud and 11 percent of household with an income less than $10,000.

Citizens of St. Cloud feel great sense of pride in the beauty and bounties of nature and in the resourcefulness of their friends and neighbors. In the 2001 SCSU survey, conducted as part of the comprehensive plan update, community residents gave the city a positive rating above 80 percent in "overall quality of life," police protection, fire protection, "the availability and quality of park facilities," and the "overall quality of life in your neighborhood."

Citizens organized to save and bring into productive use one of the area's man-made landmarks, the Paramount Theater. Through a joint private and public venture the building was restored and renovated. It reopened in September 1998 as the area's cultural center. Included were a 700-seat Paramount Theater, visual arts studios and classrooms, as well as administrative office space for several arts organizations. The theater supports events presented by the Central Minnesota Children's Theater, County Stearns Theatrical Company and the Troupe Theater. The Paramount, which originally opened on Christmas Eve, 1921 as the Sherman Theater, is one of seven downtown Historic Places.

When rapid growth and sprawl threatened the extinction of many of the region's last natural areas, citizens working through and with Mayor Meyer and the city planning office crafted the St. Cloud Environmentally Sensitive Areas Ordinance. The city council adopted the Ordinance of August 24, 1998. When the last remnant of the "Big Woods," a hardwood forest that originally stretched between the Minnesota River and the Sauk River running through St. Cloud, faced destruction for housing development people, joined together to raise funds to purchase the half not already owned by the city.

Successful founder of Bankers Systems and local businessman, Bill Clemens donated land between Munsinger Gardens and Kilian Boulevard to establish a rose garden in honor of his wife, Virginia Rose Clemens, in 1990. Through further financial contributions more land was added and a fund for maintenance and development was established. By the end of the decade the garden had grown to six gardens, covering seven acres. The gardens are modeled after the classical formal European gardens.

In 1994 the Municipal Athletic Complex (MAC), located on the northwestern side of St. Cloud, went through an extensive renovation. Two years later MAC broke ground for a second sheet of ice. The second arena opened in December 1997. On July 23, 1998 the original arena was named and dedicated as Dave Torrey Arena and the second sheet was named and dedicated as Ritsche Arena. The city also renovated and expanded Whitney Senior Center, and added the Whitney Recreation Center in the 1990s.

During the early 1990s, St. Cloud experienced trauma and fear over the incursion of gangs from large cities like Minneapolis and Chicago, eroding the community's sense of safety. Small cities, like St. Cloud, are becoming the new haven for gangs, as they search for new areas and untapped money sources—bringing with them drive-by shootings, graffiti scrawled on downtown businesses and increased gun thefts. The SCSU surveys indicated a change in attitudes towards crime in the community. Individuals who expressed concern about crime in "your neighborhood" increased by 6 percent in 2001.

The erosion of a sense of security, reflected in the shifting attitudes towards crime, is just one indicator of the erosion of the homogeneous community envisioned by most individuals as typical of Central Minnesota. Half of the individuals surveyed in 2001 felt the area lacked adequate quality, living-wage job opportunities. Traffic was also considered a major problem by 73 percent of the population, up from 51 percent 20 years earlier.

However, by and large, survey responses reflected a broad satisfaction with the quality of life from parks to police and fire protection as well as the quality of the area's educational opportunities. Overall, the quality of life in the city of St. Cloud received an 86 percent positive rating.

While Lake Wobegon country had undergone significant changes during the closing decades of the 20th century, the community's citizens, governmental agencies and the business community responded positively toward meeting the challenges of a rapidly growing and changing population.

RIGHT
The tranquil Lily Pond in Munsinger Gardens has been a part of the gardens since the 1930s. Courtesy, St. Cloud Park and Recreation Department

BELOW
The Mississippi River with SCSU in the background. Courtesy, St. Cloud Area Convention and Visitors Bureau

The Stearns County Courthouse, circa 1920. Courtesy,
St. Cloud Area Convention and Visitors Bureau

8

Chronicles of Leadership

St. Cloud's location was identifiable. Early traders and trappers knew it as the site of fords over the Mississippi and Sauk rivers, a place to cross with their ox carts on journeys north and west. Steamboat travelers knew it as the end of the line, for the shallow water that provided the Mississippi River ford also halted further travel by steamboat. And when the railroad was extended north from the Twin Cities it stopped. Many travelers, weary from weeks and hundreds of miles of travel, looked at the abundant forests and rich farmland and went no farther.

Nature had done its part.

Whether the city would grow and prosper was up to the people — farmers, lumbermen, and a handful of businessmen. The latter were gamblers really, willing to bet lives and fortunes on their ability to provide needed goods and services. Initially these goods and services didn't amount to much, only the basic necessities required by the pioneering families who had settled the area. What industry there was, mostly granite, consisted of widely scattered small firms. There were no industry giants whose failure might bring a town's demise.

The nearly 50 years since the beginning of St. Cloud's second century has been a period of rapid change and growth. By the 1980s the area lay at the northwestern tip of the fastest growing corri-

dor in Minnesota. New businesses flourished under active public and private cooperation. By the close of the 20th century the city had emerged as the heart of a thriving diversified regional education, medical and business center.

Area governments, although sometimes hesitantly, learned to cooperate in addressing common challenges. Intra-governmental efforts evolved into the Area Planning Organization to address traffic planning issues. Gradually its work expanded to include tentative steps into other areas such as land-use planning and how to address urban sprawl. The multi-city Metropolitan Transit Commission provided a public transportation system to serve St. Cloud, Sauk Rapids and Waite Park. Sartell was added in 2001. The St. Cloud Regional Airport provided regular air connections to other Minnesota cities. The St. Cloud Housing and Redevelopment Commission was active in a wide ranging program to expand business development and new housing.

Private organizations such as the Chamber of Commerce, Business Partnership and Convention and Visitors Bureau often worked in partnership with public agencies to enhance the area's business climate. The following accounts tell the story of some individual businesses and private agencies in greater detail.

THE ANTIOCH COMPANY/CREATIVE MEMORIES

Founded in 1926 by a man with an eye for reducing waste and a belief in human potential, The Antioch Company has since grown into an international organization. The company's highest priority is to serve human needs and to make a difference in the way people remember, celebrate and connect.

As of 2002 The Antioch Company has operating facilities in Minnesota, Nevada, Ohio and Virginia.

With headquarters in St. Cloud, Minnesota, the direct-sales arm of the company, Creative Memories, provides scrapbook photo albums, album-making accessories and education in the United States, Canada, Australia, New Zealand, Germany, Japan and the United Kingdom. Plans call for expansion into other European countries.

The company employs approximately 1,000 people and manufactures, packages and markets more than 3,000 products to tens of thousands of independent sales consultants and retailers. Most important, throughout its continual, successful growth, The Antioch Company has always kept its founder's focus on people.

The company was founded by Ernest Morgan and Walter Kahoe, students at Antioch College in Yellow Springs, Ohio. Ernest and Walter worked at the campus print shop as part of a work/study program offered by the college.

Distressed by the volume of paper cut-offs generated by the printing

In the 1930s, Wilbur Whipple Holes ran this small printing business in St. Cloud, Minnesota.

The visionaries of The Antioch Company and Creative Memories include (from left): Wilbur Whipple Holes, founder of the Holes Webway Company; Ernest Morgan, founder of The Antioch Company; and Cheryl Lightle and Rhonda Anderson, co-founders of Creative Memories.

process, the two decided to find ways to turn waste into an opportunity. Scrounging printing supplies and using the shop's press after hours, they printed a trial run of decorative bookplates.

With permission from the college, the students named their venture The Antioch Bookplate Company. Eventually, Walter sold his interest to Ernest for $200. Ernest continued his education by day and printed bookplates and bookmarks by night.

As Ernest neared the end of his college education, an attractive employment opportunity with McGraw-Hill presented itself. He had to decide between a promising future with an established publishing firm or continuing the struggle to make his own business grow.

After much thought, Ernest decided to follow his own course because his dreams included much more than simply earning a living. His goal was to create a community of work, based on the Quaker values with which he was raised. These values included honesty, mutual respect, tolerance, and recognition of the dignity of people and their ideas as well as corporate and individual responsibility.

Far ahead of his time, Ernest looked upon the workplace as a community of equals, sharing in the process of meaningful work and its rewards. As early as 1929 profit sharing was practiced at The Antioch Bookplate Company. When the company incorporated after World War II, employees were allowed to nominate two of their own board members. Both practices continue to this day.

The company grew and its business and people prospered. Antioch's products included: bookplates, bookmarks, calendars and commercial printing.

In 1985 Antioch purchased the Holes Webway Company in St. Cloud, a manufacturer of photo al-

bums and social books. Antioch thought it had found a good facility and avenue with which to expand its line of gift products. What it had actually found turned out to be much more.

The Holes Webway Company was founded in 1926, the same year Ernest Morgan started the Antioch Bookplate Company. Like Ernest, its founder, Wilbur Whipple Holes, nicknamed Web, was a commercial printer and an innovative entrepreneur. In 1938 he invented and patented a unique "flex-hinge" binding method for scrapbooks. He also engineered and built the binding machinery needed to produce his invention. The company soon became a leading manufacturer of scrapbooks and photo albums. His binding was originally known as Web's Way, which led to the name Webway.

Like Antioch, the Holes Webway Company grew and prospered through the decades, but by the late 1970s, the company's strategy was adrift and desperately needed change.

In 1985 Cheryl Lightle, a longtime Antioch employee, was sent to Minnesota to oversee the transition. The name was changed to Webway Incorporated. Management structure was flattened and employees were given freedom to contribute ideas and participate. Webway, like Antioch, became employee-owned. At Webway, Antioch found a workforce similar to its own—dedicated and skilled—many with decades of experience. They returned to what Webway did best. Their album lines were reengineered, repackaged and marketed to meet the demand for durable, attractive long-term photo storage.

Antioch's respect for the potential of new ideas provided a receptive environment when Cheryl Lightle answered an after-hours telephone call in 1987. Rhonda Anderson, a Montana homemaker, was on the

Creative Memories' staff, offices and manufacturing and distribution facilities have grown rapidly, and plans are being developed to expand to a new location in the furture.

other end. She had recently spoken to a women's group about her tradition of creating family scrapbook albums. Her presentation generated an astonishing amount of interest. Determined to satisfy the needs of her group, Rhonda called to place an order for 40 scrapbook albums.

From that phone call evolved their vision—Creative Memories. Their vision held that one day there would be thousands of people giving presentations, selling albums and spreading their photo-preservation message on a global scale.

Cheryl started putting together the first sales brochure and consulted with Antioch executives to set up a business plan. She provided momentum for the program and is now president and co-founder of Creative Memories. Meanwhile, Rhonda started building the field organization, selling albums and introducing the program to others. She and her family packed a van and traveled throughout the United States to share the Creative Memories message.

In 1992 Rhonda moved to St. Cloud to work at the Creative Memories Home Office. Today, as co-founder of Creative Memories, she travels throughout the country to inspire, teach and motivate consultants.

Now 15 years old, Creative Memories celebrated its anniversary in 2002. More than 60,000 consultants now represent the company and its products and the photo-preservation tradition is being taught throughout the world.

In its eighth decade, The Antioch Company continues to grow and prosper. Following the credo of its founder, the company continues the tradition of giving back to the community and its employees.

Ernest Morgan's dreams of 70 years ago have been realized. His vision of a community of work dedicated to making quality products marketed honestly and fairly to meet the consumers' needs have been achieved. His hope for an enthusiastic workforce, where diverse ideas are represented and profits shared has been actualized. His desire to be a good corporate citizen, working with the community for the betterment of everyone, has been accomplished.

The Antioch Company, with its employee-owners and independent sales force, truly makes a difference in the way people remember, celebrate and connect.

BANKERS SYSTEMS, INC.

Banking is a complex business. For every loan that's approved and every account that's opened, there are hundreds of laws that require financial institutions (such as banks and credit unions) to collect and disclose specific information. To make things even more complicated, regulations can vary from state-to-state and change from year-to-year.

Bankers Systems helps institutions navigate through that maze of regulations. The company follows legislative and judicial changes in state and federal law. Then, it creates solutions ranging from software applications to printed documents to training tools that are used by over 80 percent of all banks and one-third of all credit unions in the nation.

By the time it celebrated its 50th anniversary in 2002, Bankers Systems (which is an operating company of Wolters Kluwer) had grown to more

Left to right: William Clemens, founder and former president and CEO of Bankers Systems; John Weitzel, former president and CEO; and Bob White, current president and CEO.

than 1,000 employees, developed more than 6,000 compliance products, and established itself as the leading national provider of compliance solutions—serving more than 12,000 financial institutions across the country.

Not bad for a company that, in 1952, started out selling binders, journals, and ledger sheets from a one-room office in downtown St. Cloud.

"In our early days, most of the rural banks that were our clients did pen-and-ink entries for everything," said founder and former owner William Clemens. "To imagine how the industry and Bankers Systems would change would have been like a person in the 1800s thinking we'd put a man on the moon."

The biggest change came just 17 years after Bankers Systems opened its doors, when Congress passed the Truth-in-Lending Act in 1969. It was the first major federal law regulating consumer transactions—and the industry would never be the same.

To help consumers make informed decisions, the act requires institutions

to disclose the costs, terms, and conditions of a loan up front. The new act meant every lending form in use at the time was obsolete.

"It pretty much took the printers out of the forms business. Bankers Systems made the decision to stay in and become a new kind of company," said John Weitzel, president and chief executive of Bankers Systems from 1987 to 1997.

"The community banks we served at that time didn't have the resources to set up legal departments, track and analyze the laws, or draft documents that complied with those laws," said Weitzel. "We realized we could develop the documents and provide them to each customer for less than it may cost them to do their own."

Based on that foresight, Bankers Systems evolved from a forms company to a compliance company.

In the years that followed, compliance became more and more complex. With each new federal regulation came a number of state laws and variations. In addition, the financial industry was growing at a rapid pace. Banks were adding

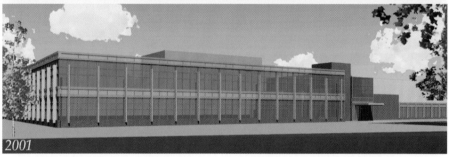

Bankers Systems has moved and expanded several times since 1952 when it opened its first doors in downtown St. Cloud.
1971–With 13 in-house employees, Bankers Systems moves into its fourth office space, the newly constructed corporate offices on North 37th Avenue.
1982–A new corporate complex is completed on Saukview Drive. Over the next 20 years, the facility would undergo three major renovations and numerous remodels.
2001–Bankers Systems breaks ground on a three-phase renovation that will expand its Saukview facility and bring the employees from the company's two St. Cloud locations under one roof.

branches and expanding across state lines, which made it even more difficult for them to manage compliance issues.

Once again, Bankers Systems was determined to change with the industry and stay at the forefront of solutions.

In 1979 the company started a Legal Development Department.

Beginning with one attorney, the department grew to 75 attorneys, legal assistants, and compliance specialists by 2002. From Bankers Systems' corporate office in St. Cloud, they track literally thousands of regulatory developments each year in the federal government, state legislatures, and the court system. Then, they help create products that can be used across the country.

"Compliance is very complicated and there are a lot of choices that financial institutions have to make about the policies they're implementing," said Bob White, president and CEO of Bankers Systems since 1997. "We do not practice law for our customers, but we can help them understand their options and make informed decisions about their com-

pliance documentation."

While Bankers Systems was expanding its Legal Development Department, another change was taking place in the financial industry—technology.

By 1983 the need for faster, more efficient solutions prompted Bankers Systems to create a Software Products Division. Over the next two decades, it continued to grow as software became a vital part of Bankers Systems' product line. By 2002 the software department employed 180 programmers, business analysts, quality-assurance testers, and support staff in St. Cloud. Today, technology is a major factor in how the company makes complying with regulations more convenient for the industry.

In 1994 Bankers Systems was purchased by the investment firm Goldner Hawn Johnson & Morrison in Minneapolis, and then sold in 1999 to Wolters Kluwer, a provider of business law information and software that operates in 26 countries. With the support of its new parent company, Bankers Systems acquired two market leading companies in 2001: TSoft Financial Software, Inc. and CBF Systems, Inc. The acquisitions helped Bankers Systems grow its software line and expand even more into the market of larger financial institutions and mortgage companies.

As the financial industry continues to change and expand, Bankers Systems will invest in new technology, solutions, and even more acquisitions to meet the most complex challenges of its customers. But, one thing that will never change is the value of its employees.

"Our employees are the real strength of our company," explained White. "From the beginning, we've benefited from the dedication and talents of the people who live here, and we're proud to be a part of the community's growth."

BAUERLY BROS, INC.

Building better communities is something Bauerly Brothers employees do with pride. Rocks are mined, crushed and mixed with other products to make concrete or asphalt; producing roads, parking lots, bike paths, building foundations, sidewalks and driveways. Bauerly Brothers employees know that what they do is essential to America—essential to this nation's stability and its growth. They build the infrastructure that keeps America moving.

One of the key requirements of a vibrant and healthy economy is an efficient transportation system. The ability to move people and products quickly and safely across our nation is a major contributor to our country's success. Aggregates are the critical ingredient for our nation's infrastructure.

The business that began with a couple of dump trucks and four employees has evolved into a company that is known statewide as a high-tech producer and placer of asphalt, ready mix and concrete. By the beginning of 2002 Bauerly Brothers

A Bauerly designed aggregate crusher.

employed more than 750 employees in Central Minnesota. Based in the St. Cloud area, the company has 21 ready-mix plants; five asphalt plants; 19 aggregate crushing, screening and washing plants; a state-of-the-art quality control lab; and numerous aggregate mining pits.

The Bauerly family, which includes six sons and three daughters, grew up on a dairy farm outside of Sauk Rapids, Minnesota. Their father, Leo Bauerly, possessed an entrepreneurial spirit and passed this trait along to his sons. Leo began hauling aggregates early on as one of many ways to supplement the farm income. The two oldest boys, Dave and Jerry, earned their way through college by working for their father doing construction and driving trucks. They were headed into different careers when Leo was killed in a car accident on July 10, 1968. That day, the lives of all the Bauerly's abruptly changed. Upon their father's death, Dave and Jerry took on the respon-

Leo Bauerly in 1968 with granddaughter Shelly.

sibility of providing for the family by starting Bauerly Brothers. With several dump trucks and four employees, they began renting out trucks and driving for other contractors, as well as crushing gravel. By the mid-1970s, the other four brothers, Mike, Brian, Mark and Jake—oldest to youngest—all joined as partners as they completed their education. From day one, their mother, Agnes, worked side-by-side with her sons providing the necessary administrative support. Today, at 85-years-old, Agnes still works part-time in the office, keeping a watchful eye on her family.

The business has changed since the early days. Technological advancements require a scientific precision in asphalt and concrete mix designs. An in-house, state-of-the-art laboratory, located at the Sauk Rapids-St. Cloud office, ensures that the technical requirements for ready-mix and asphalt mix meet required specifications. In addition, portable labs may be set up at job sites for quality and efficiency purposes. Mining and moving rock and sand, cement, concrete and asphalt requires a lot of equipment, materials and supplies. Bauerly Brothers is a team of innovators, paralleling technical skills with an ever-present goal of building better communities. Believing that innovation is key to success, the company

The Bauerly Brothers (from left to right) A. Jake, Mike, Dave, Brian, Jerry and Mark.

designs and builds its own plants and equipment, including ready-mix plants, asphalt plants, and aggregate crushing and washing machines.

The company is very serious about its environmental initiatives. Bauerly Brothers is an active recycler. Aggregate is a finite resource and it is in everyone's best interest to preserve it. Everything is recycled—used oil, concrete, and asphalt. Bauerly Brothers has taken an industry-leading role in the reclamation of its mined aggregate sites. These sites have been reclaimed as wildlife haST. CLOUDbitat, agricultural-use areas, wetlands, prairies, or housing sub-divisions. Since approximately 1993, Bauerly Brothers has conducted a granite-recycling program with Cold Spring Granite company. Bauerly Brothers takes Cold Spring Granite's waste granite and recycles it into a high-quality aggregate product for use in concrete and asphalt. This benefits the environment by conserving resources. Bauerly Brothers is one of the few companies that are successful at recycling granite.

All of this is why Bauerly Brothers is on the cutting edge of training and education. Through its corporate objective "Improve Employee Development," Bauerly Brothers provides development opportunities to its employees throughout the organization. It is a learning organization committed to continuous growth and development in technical, leadership, interpersonal, safety, environmental, and technology enhancement of its employees.

Bauerly Brothers implements a team-based management structure and a principle-based leadership. The company is organized through five divisions: asphalt, concrete, central operations and aggregates, equipment, and central services. Each of the Bauerly brothers is responsible for a specific area. Jerry is president, Dave is the engineer, Mike is in charge of the equipment division, Brian oversees the concrete division, Mark is responsible for central services and the aggregate division and Jake runs the asphalt division and is in charge of the finances. With the brothers' guidance, the company is led by division management teams.

The company is active in the community. Its Partners for Parks program has been well recognized in the community, as well as in the industry, as being a premier environmental and community stewardship program. Through this program Bauerly Brothers partners with government, schools and neighborhoods to provide funds, materials and/or labor for building "green" areas.

The company has received numerous awards and recognition for excellence—receiving many National Asphalt Paving Association, Minnesota Asphalt Paving, Department of Transportation, Minnesota Association of Ready-Mix, and National Sand and Gravel Awards. Locally, Bauerly Brothers received the 2001 Entrepreneur of the Year Award from the St. Cloud Area Chamber of Commerce.

Bauerly Brothers' reverse-triangular merger in 2001 with Knife River Corporation added to its capabilities to handle future growth. Within Knife River Corporation, Bauerly Brothers remains a separate legal entity. Synergies from Knife River have given Bauerly Brothers additional strength. National purchasing power, resources and efficiencies for growth will benefit Bauerly Brothers long into the future.

A Bauerly designed "Super-Truck."

CONTINENTAL PRESS

When Louis Rothstein decided to open a print shop on the city's south side it did not take him long to discover that his World War II experience in the medical field was not much of a qualification to put ink on paper. Neither were his pre-war occupations as a city bus driver nor a plumber. So instead of the one-man shop he had envisioned, he quickly found himself looking for a press operator.

That first pressman, hired in 1948 shortly after the shop opened in a garage behind the family home, became the first employee of Continental Press. That one-stall garage has evolved into a modern printing facility on St. Cloud's greater East Side. The current large array of equipment is in sharp contrast to the one letterpress, the hand paper cutter and the single typeface with which Rothstein started. The original business was so small; in fact, the paper companies were not interested in taking his minuscule orders for 500 envelopes or two reams of paper. A friendly paper salesman came to the rescue by

The family garage served as the first home of Continental Press, located on the city's south side.

buying the products himself and re-selling in small quantities to Rothstein.

The printing firm was not Rothstein's first business venture. In 1946 he and a friend had set up the L & L Photo Service to process pictures in the basement of the Rothstein home. The friend soon found his way into the salted peanut business and later became one of Rothstein's printing customers when he began buying labels for his peanut bags.

By 1950 Continental Press outgrew the garage and moved to the basement of the Clepper building at the

east end of the old St. Germain Street bridge. A few years later it took over the main floor as well. When a former furniture store on Northeast Riverside Drive became available in 1960, the business was soon moving again. This move almost doubled the company's space allowing for the addition of new equipment, employees and services. At this time the business began offering a complete line of office and school supplies to its central Minnesota customers.

In 1965 Rothstein's son, Terry, came home from military service and took over the production end of the operation. Two building additions were quickly added and more employees were hired. Following the elder Rothstein's death in 1971, Terry moved into the front office. He faced a major challenge three years later when a fire destroyed most of the buildings and its equipment. A new structure was up and running four months later with new equipment and even more space. The supply business was soon eliminated to make room for a new duplicating process labeled "The Copy Monster." The name became so popular Terry acquired an official U.S. copyright for it.

Most high school students in the 1970s probably hadn't heard of Continental Press, yet thousands of them have had an association with the firm. One mainstay of the business was the production of buttons, primarily for high school homecoming celebrations, which sold in all 50 states.

The business that started in the family garage in 1948 is still a family operation. In 1990 Terry's older children started working with the company. After graduating from the College of St. Benedict, Kristin

A move to its current location on Riverside Drive in 1960 doubled the size of Continental Press.

Continental Press, now in its third generation, is family owned. Left to right: Kurt, Terry, Judy, Kristin and Erich Rothstein.

North Dakota State University in 1995, Erich Rothstein came on board as a customer service representative. He has since moved into pre-press operations where he keeps the company on the cutting edge of technology with computer-to-plate equipment and computerized typeset and design.

This family printing business has evolved dramatically since 1948. The first year sales of $600 have grown to over $2.5 million. The single employee now has 18 co-workers and the 240-square-foot shop now measures 15,000-square-feet. The original press is still in operation, but used only for special jobs. No longer is type hand set, paper folded by hand or cut by brute force. The presses print four colors with one pass; an unlimited number of typefaces are accessed with a simple key stroke; 1,000 sheets of paper are cut with the touch of a button; and the presses run at 12,000-sheets per hour. All of this was impossible in 1948.

Rothstein took over the pre-press/composition department and mastered computerized typesetting well ahead of the competition. She moved into outside sales and quickly took over as sales manager. Kurt Rothstein joined the company with a position in production after graduating from St. John's University. He later became production manager, a position he holds today. After graduating from

Buttons and supplies are no longer the mainstay of Continental's business. They were replaced with high-quality four-color printing, high-speed document reproduction on the "Copy Monster," computerized typesetting and design with complete bindery equipment to cut, fold, pad, collate, staple and finish. These, along with a dedicated sales staff who follow up on the details, continue to make Continental Press "easy to do business with."

The present home of Continental Press, still located on Riverside Drive, was rebuilt in 1974 following a devastating fire that destroyed the previous building.

The family business continues to move forward. Kristin became president in 2001 upon Terry's retirement, and Katie Rothstein joined the company as a customer service representative after her graduation from The College St. Benedict that same year.

GOLD'N PLUMP POULTRY

More Than 75 Years of Innovation—that is the proud slogan of Gold'n Plump Poultry which began as a small hatchery and evolved into the largest producer of premium chicken products in the upper Midwest. By 2002 it operated three production plants processing more than seven million pounds of chicken per week with annual sales of $200 million.

When the company first incorporated in 1926 it was called St. Cloud Hatchery and was located in downtown St. Cloud on Seventh Avenue South. E.M. Helgeson, the company founder, wasn't satisfied with that name. He wanted something to make his chicks stand out as the hardiest and healthiest on the market. In the early 1930s he purchased the name Jack Frost from an "idea man" for $25.

Under the Jack Frost name, the company sold day-old chicks to farmers throughout the Midwest, primarily through direct-mail catalogs and delivered by road, rail and air. Helgeson founded the company at a time when an independent hatchery was a relatively new idea. It prospered, even during the Great Depression, because it offered financing, first independently and then through Liberty Loan and Thrift Corporation.

Company founder E.M. Helgeson incorporated St. Cloud Hatcheries in 1926. The company eventually became Gold'n Plump. This photo shows Helgeson with a new grower barn built in the 1960s.

Don Helgeson (right) managed the company's transition from a hatchery into a fully integrated poultry producer. In 1993, his son Mike Helgeson (left), became the third generation to lead the company and continue its growth.

When Helgeson's sons Don and Jerry bought the hatchery in the early 1950s, they diversified into meat production to keep the business viable. The company entered into a joint venture with Armour Meat Company in 1955 to grow and process chickens. At the same time, it established long-term contracts with local farmers to raise chickens in barns specially designed for efficient poultry production and added a production farm, breeder facilities and a feed mill.

In 1964 the company opened a new hatchery on Lincoln Avenue. While Jack Frost continued to sell chicks from the hatchery, its shift toward broiler meat production, processing and marketing was clearly underway.

The Gold'n Plump name was born in the late 1970s when the company began branding its fresh, tray-packed chicken. In 1983 Gold'n Plump acquired Armour's processing plant in Cold Spring, Minnesota and became a fully integrated processor, controlling all aspects of production. Today, the company oversees the breeding and growing operations of its contract farmers, hatches chicks, mills the feed, processes the chickens and markets finished products.

Gold'n Plump quickly built name recognition with memorable, award-winning advertising campaigns. The company's ad campaigns have featured parachuting chickens, a fox and hen, exercising chickens and a chicken popping up inside a suburban home. These ads helped make Gold'n Plump a household name in Minnesota and Wisconsin. Nine out of 10 consumers in Minnesota recognize the Gold'n Plump brand and more than eight out of 10 prefer it to other brands.

In 1993 a decade after it acquired the Cold Spring plant, Gold'n Plump purchased the Arcadia Fryers production complex in Arcadia, Wisconsin. It expanded the facility, investing in a new state-of-the-art feed mill and adding more contract growers. This increased capacity helped drive sales and new product development.

The company suffered a fire in August 1998 that destroyed part of its Cold Spring processing plant. A cooperative effort between the company, its customers and vendors kept production going even as reconstruction and expansion of the Cold Spring plant continued into 1999.

Later in 1998 Gold'n Plump further increased its value-added processing capabilities by acquiring a plant in Luverne, Minnesota. This made it possible to sell a plant that had operated in Sauk Rapids for nine years, consolidate production and boost operational efficiency.

Throughout its history, Gold'n Plump has been innovative in production methods and product development. It was one of the first poultry companies to remove fat from fresh tray pack products; voluntarily provide nutritional labeling; use an automated chicken catching machine; and offer a full line of certified organic products under the North Country Farms label.

In 1999 Gold'n Plump became the first company in the industry to package an entire line of fresh chicken by

Gold'n Plump processes more than seven million pounds of chicken into a variety of products sold to supermarkets, grocery delis and restaurants.

fixed weight. This means that each package in a product category is produced to weigh the same amount. When it arrives at the store it receives a unit price, not a price based on a per-pound random weight. This provides advantages for both the retailer and the consumer. Retailers save time and money getting the product from the warehouse to their shelves. Consumers gain the added convenience of buying standard-size packages that make recipe preparation easier, as well as enjoying special marketing promotions, such as two-for-one sales, that aren't feasible with random-weight meat products.

Gold'n Plump chicken is found in supermarkets, grocery delis and restaurants in more than 20 states. It remains a family- and employee-owned company in its third generation of family leadership. Michael Helgeson, grandson of the founder, became the chief executive officer in 1993. He presides over a company that has grown tenfold since 1982 and has greatly expanded its market area.

Gold'n Plump sees the future in ready-to-cook and fully cooked convenience products that appeal to time-starved consumers.

More than half of the company's 1,600 employees work in and around St. Cloud. Gold'n Plump also contracts with nearly 300 growers in Minnesota and Wisconsin, and buys millions of bushels of corn from area farmers for feed.

Gold'n Plump is expanding its product line to include fully cooked products and continues to look for new ways to package and market its products. The company is also gaining a following on the Internet with a consumer website that provides meal ideas and recipes that are nutritious and easy to make. Its website is www.goldnplump.com.

At Gold'n Plump there is never a debate about whether the chicken or the egg came first. For this company, it all started with the egg. But the company's future is now very much dependent upon the chicken, and the many ways it can be marketed to satisfy the next generation's desire for easy, nutritious meals.

GREAT STEPS ORTHOTIC & PROSTHETIC SOLUTIONS

Great Steps Orthotic & Prosthetic Solutions was founded and incorporated by John Held in spring 2000. John had spent the previous 11 years working as a certified orthotist (designer, fitter and fabricator of orthopedic braces) in Minneapolis, Fargo and St. Cloud. After incorporation of the business, John was joined in September 2000 by Dan Tysver, certified prosthetist/orthotist and Warren Hagen, C.Ped to develop the new practice. The company opened for business in the Centrasota Centre, a new medical building conveniently located on the corner of Highway 15 and Veterans Drive (8th Street) in St. Cloud. Great Steps O&P provides prostheses (artificial limbs) and orthoses (orthopedic braces) to the residents of Central Minnesota. It designs and fits a wide variety of items which include: arch supports, custom and off-the-shelf shoes, diabetic shoes and inserts, short and long leg braces, back braces, arm braces,

Great Step's home office is located on Highway 15 in the Centrasota Centre.

spinal braces, custom helmets as well as prostheses for feet, legs and arms. These products which are prescribed by a physician are designed and fit by the staff.

With a complete laboratory on the premises, Great Steps fabricates the majority of the thermoplastic appliances that they fit. The lab includes an equipment room; plaster modification center; sewing area; general

Dan Tysver, C.P.O., adjusting a computer controlled lower extremity prosthesis.

technical space; and vacuum-forming stations. The clinic area has private examination areas that are designed for their clientele. These include rooms designed specifically for pediatrics and amputees.

Great Steps goal is to give the highest attainable level of care to all of their patients. They strongly believe that their clients are not merely numbers but are unique individuals that require thought and dedication. Great Steps goals are met by the personal attention that they give to their customers, assuring them that they will receive sufficient time with their practitioners so that the appropriate products will be manufactured for their use. Using cutting edge technologies and materials in the designs of its products, the final devices are as unique as the clients that receive them.

Great Steps is committed to giving the St.Cloud area a locally owned and managed orthotic and prosthetic company that will grow with the community yet retain a personal level of attention to its clients. The company views itself as a partner of the community. Great Steps O&P has actively supported community organizations such as United Cerebral Palsy of Central Minnesota. Its owners believe that they have a personal, as well as a company responsibility to the community, dedicating time and resources to a number of nonprofit organizations. Great Steps is committed to keeping much of its resources in the local economy and plans to positively impact the St. Cloud area as it continues to grow.

While Great Steps O&P is still in its infancy, its professional recognition has become national. Prior to founding Great Steps O&P, Held was involved with Dr. James Johnson, an orthopedic surgeon from Fargo, North Dakota, in the research and design of a new and unique ankle brace. Over a several year period of time the product was designed and reworked and finally used in clinical studies. In 1996 Held and Johnson teamed up with Bledsoe Brace, an internationally renowned manufacturer of orthopedic braces, in the final designing and manufacturing of the product. The brace is now being sold by Bledsoe Brace worldwide. These experiences in research and design have allowed Held to develop impor-

John Held, C.O., left and Dan Tysver, C.P.O., owners of Great Steps.

John Held, C.O., casting a client for a custom lower extremity brace.

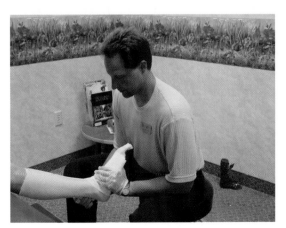

tant relationships with the orthotic and prosthetic leaders of the United States. These relationships have allowed Great Steps O&P to maintain its leadership in the field of orthotics and prosthetics.

In 1999 Held met with the training staff of the Minnesota Vikings. At that time he presented them with his ankle design. The Vikings used the brace that year in situations where other products weren't achieving the desired results. Held then became a consultant for the Vikings and Great Steps O&P now provides the custom designing and manufacturing of specialty products for the team. Great Steps O&P has also worked with the Minnesota Timberwolves in a slightly lesser role.

Dedicated to cutting edge prosthetic care, Great Steps staff members are fully trained and experienced in the latest technologies available to amputees. Some exciting breakthroughs include computer-controlled joints for both upper extremity and lower extremity amputees. Great Steps prosthetic staff maintains close relations

with industry leaders in the prosthetic field. These relationships afford the company access to nationally known prosthetists when new technologies hit the market.

Great Steps' diligence to quality care and leadership has triggered tremendous growth for the company. Their staff has more than tripled in the first 24 months and Great Steps opened a second full-time clinic/laboratory in Willmar, Minnesota in 2002. Plans are underway for another clinic opening in summer/fall 2003. The quality of its core employees has enabled them to hire other quality staff members. Great Steps leadership will continue in the coming years through its dedication to quality care and service. The company persists in its use of cutting edge technology and materials and sets the highest standards for the field of Orthotics and Prosthetics. Great Steps has forged other relationships, which will give them an active roll in research and development. This will support continued improvements in the quality of care received by patients around the globe.

LIBERTY SAVINGS BANK, fsb
LIBERTY LOAN AND THRIFT CORPORATION

The location of the headquarters for Liberty Savings Bank, fsb in a former hatchery building on Seventh Avenue South is appropriate, for it was baby chicks that really gave Liberty its start in 1934.

E.M. "Mike" Helgeson, who had operated a hatchery business at the location, found that during the Depression many farmers had a need for credit to purchase his baby chicks. Initially using his own funds to provide that credit, a need for additional funding caused the firm to progress to bank borrowing, funded by notes from individuals who placed their money with Helgeson as an investment.

Initially the company was known as Liberty Finance and in 1939 was chartered as Liberty Loan and Thrift Corporation. By that time other forms of credit were being offered including loans for automobiles,

Don Helgeson, chairman.

furniture and appliances. In 1954 Liberty was granted authority to accept public deposits. With this new funding source, lending activity expanded rapidly including financing for broiler barn operations, mobile homes and other investments.

E.M. Helgeson remained active in the banking business until 1975, three years prior to his death.

In 1995 Liberty converted to a Federal Savings Bank, charter and became Liberty Savings Bank, fsb. As Liberty entered the new millennium led by Chairman Donald Helgeson, son of the founder, Liberty found itself to be the last remaining original bank charter in St. Cloud. The distinction of being St. Cloud's "Oldest Name in Banking" creates a special bond between Liberty, its customers and the community.

Today Liberty is a leading provider of retail banking products in the Central Minnesota area. Liberty is also a recognized leader in the mortgage industry. During the mid 1990s Liberty pioneered the use of computer generated decision technology for mortgage loans in the state of Minnesota. Today Liberty offers a wide array of mortgage products for Conventional, FHA, VA and first-time homebuyers. Liberty also services the Conventional loans it provides, giving customers the comfort and convenience of knowing who they will be dealing with for many years to come.

Customers have access to a wide array of checking, savings and certificate of deposit products. It has designed specific checking accounts for groups such as homeowners, seniors, nonprofit organizations and many others. These products are the result of Liberty's continuous and extensive research into the requirements of today's consumers.

While Liberty Savings Bank has emerged as the leading home loan provider in the Central Minnesota area, and has greatly expanded its deposit account relationships with its customers, Liberty has never abandoned its original purpose of providing consumer credit to area residents. Its home equity loan products have attractive features and flexibility along with desirable rates. The development of credit card products and consumer loans tailored to the needs of customers continue to be signature products offered by Liberty.

The Internet has provided Liberty Savings Bank with a new and creative way to provide better service to its customers. Today bank customers can order checks online, pre-qualify for home loans and do all their personal banking from the convenience of their personal computer. As the growth of the internet continues, Liberty Savings Bank looks forward

Original headquarters, circa 1950s.

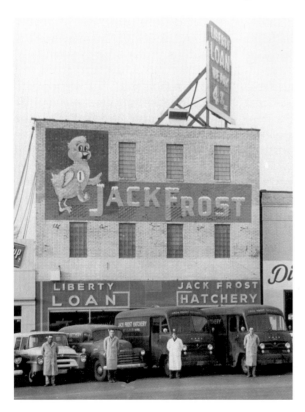

to continually adding to the attractive features at www.libertysavings.com.

Liberty Savings Bank has been an acknowledged leader in giving back to the community it serves. Community festivals have benefited from Liberty's direct, hands-on involvement. Many nonprofit organizations have been the recipient of the hard work and input of Liberty employees. Building and other trade groups have also experienced Liberty's deep commitment to the industry it serves. All of these organizations, events and community landmarks have benefited from Liberty's philosophy of continued support and hands-on involvement. It is all part of a continued philosophy of contributing to the good life here in the "Land of Liberty."

Above: Downtown Liberty Savings Bank, fsb, located on Seventh Avenue South, St. Cloud.

Left: Westwood Liberty Savings Bank, fsb, located at 5801 Ridgewood Road, St. Cloud.

Below: The annual Liberty Savings Bank block party is always well attended.

LUMBER ONE, AVON INC.
AND LUMBER ONE, COLD SPRING INC.

When Frank Schmid, an area resident of the tiny town of Avon Minnesota, hauled a load of cordwood to his first customer, he may never have dreamed in what direction his descendants would take his fledgling business. It is equally doubtful that Frank's sons Ben and Roman, who purchased Schmid Lumber from their father in the 1950s, could have envisioned the enormous success the company would eventually enjoy.

Roman's son Terry purchased Schmid Lumber from his father and uncle in 1962. At that time the lumberyard, still located in Avon, supplied building materials to area residents and local farmers. Terry, a recent graduate of St. John's University, saw a way to create a larger market for the newly renamed Avon Lumber Yard, Inc. There were no professional contractors in the Avon area, so Terry expanded to include general contracting services through Avon Lumber. A similar sense of creative enterprise eventually led to Lumber One becoming involved in land development.

Ted Schmid, Terry's son and current chief operating officer of Lumber One, Avon Inc., credits his father with the company's phenomenal growth. With the purchase of a second lumber yard in Cold Spring,

Inside the lumber shed, 1930s—Ed Schmid and customer note the "ship lap" at right. Once used extensively for roofing and now replaced with oxboard.

Early 1920s, Ed Schmid (one of Frank's sons and the father of Lee Schmid, who is still employed at Lumber One).

Minnesota, his father began branching out in the 1970s into the construction of apartment buildings. Ted characterizes those years as a time of significant growth in the company's history. By the early 1980s Avon Lumber Yard Inc. and Cold Spring Lumber Yard Inc. had grown to become established, respected businesses in central Minnesota. Terry recognizing the growth renamed his companies in 1987, Lumber One, Avon Inc. and Lumber One, Cold Spring Inc.

Company trends throughout Lumber One's history have kept pace with national trends and industry trends. The construction of multi-unit complexes constituted a large part of company sales until the mid 1980s, when the tax code regarding capital gains made investment in bigger projects less attractive. Terry, recognized the advantages of land development, (the purchase of large tracts of land subdivided into single-family lots), during this economic climate and quickly capitalized on the idea. Land development as a service to builders and their custom-

ers, merged with Terry's original business plan of supplying building materials to local contractors. Lumber One now handled all phases of the home building process from land purchase, marketing, road construction, financing, and home construction.

Lumber One, Avon's and Lumber One, Cold Spring's land development business is a significant benefit to small area general contractors, allowing them to purchase one or two lots in a large development, without the necessity of needing a large amount of capital or staff to create their own development. Lumber One benefits by the sale of the lots and the building materials for all the homes in the developments. This strategy, again, is based on Terry Schmid's philosophy: it is better to work with many smaller customers than one or two larger ones. Lumber One's commitment to the smaller contractor extends to offering drafting, blueprinting, and other technical services.

In addition to its success in the areas of retail building supply and land development, Lumber One maintains a strong presence as a general con-

Past, present and future principals at Lumber One, Avon Inc.

tractor and materials supplier for multi-unit housing projects throughout the state. Ted's sister, Barbara J. Brandes, serves as C.E.O. of Lumber One, Avon Inc. and concentrates her talents on the development of senior housing and apartment projects. Ted and Barbara's mother, Terry's widow Judith C. Schmid, serves as the company's C.F.O. and is especially active in loan closings.

Lumber One can also handle the details as illustrated in a spring 1996 article in *Home & Outdoor Living*. A St. Cloud couple contracted Lumber One to build their new home, situated in a "quaint old neighborhood" on the city's north side. The project presented Lumber One with a formidable challenge: the construction of a tall narrow structure in keeping with big-city row-housing, combined with the new owner's desire for Victorian styling and some of the features of an old fashioned farmhouse. The care and expertise of the Lumber One crew delighted the buyers, as did

their capable handling of many of the home's unusual features: counter-weighted windows, window sills large enough to accommodate the family cats and even the erection in the small backyard of an old fashioned set-in clothesline. The owners, thrilled with the inclusion of so much that was reminiscent of older days, noted, "If my grandparents were living, they'd love this house."

The company that was started by one man now employs over 100 people, many of them carpenters and job supervisors. The Schmids evince a sense of community pride and continuity through their employment of talented and loyal area residents as Judith Schmid indicates, from "Avon, Albany, St. Joseph, St. Cloud, Spring Hill, Cold Spring, Rockville, Richmond, and throughout central Minnesota." Carpentry crews are kept on payroll even through the long midwestern winters.

Ted Schmid, although understated when discussing his company's expansion, notes that its revenues have increased 35 percent the past year. His mother Judith, understandably proud of this successful family business, attributes growth within the company to the expertise of a new generation in relation to "the new direction the business has grown," and to the dedication of every Lumber One employee.

Ted Schmid of Lumber One and Governor Jesse Ventura tour their affordable housing community in Rochester, Minnesota.

RESOURCE TRAINING & SOLUTIONS

Since 1985 Resource Training & Solutions has become the most recognized professional training provider in Central Minnesota. Under the leadership of Dr. Robert C. Cavanna, executive director, Resource Training & Solutions has seen tremendous growth and greater community outreach. As a result the organization changed its name in 2000, from Central Minnesota Service Cooperative to Resource Training & Solutions, to more accurately reflect what the organization does. The new name, along with the mission, relationship building and demonstrating the benefits of collaboration, were among Cavanna's major objectives in growing the organization to meet the needs of the community.

Resource Training & Solutions started as a small two-person office in south St. Cloud. In 1985 Dr. Robert C. Cavanna became its first full-time executive director. Hired to build the organization into a viable and successful one, Cavanna worked on hiring quality people and emphasizing "outrageous customer service." The organization began by

Since 1985 Dr. Robert C. Cavanna, has been the executive director of Resource Training & Solutions, the most recognized professional training provider in Central Minnesota. Ever the visionary, he was named Entrepreneur of the Year in 1997.

serving school districts and has since expanded its outreach to cities, counties, government, businesses, non-profits and families. Under his leadership, the organization promotes growth through educational seminars, student events, family education and software courses.

Taking an entrepreneurial approach, Cavanna saw the need in

1989 to establish a discounted health insurance pool for school districts. It has grown to be the second largest health pooled plan in the state serving 9,000 employees from over 40 organizations in Central Minnesota. In 1996, seeing a need again, another insurance pool was formed for cities, counties and other governmental agencies, now serving 1,300 employees.

In 1995 his vision led him to initiate a community Technology Training Center for the general public. There are so many successful parts to this program. Its enrollment has increased almost twofold (98 percent) since its opening. The custom sessions have doubled and a new laptop-training lab was introduced, which has gone on the road to numerous cities as far away as Chicago, Illinois. The newest venture, online software training, is for those who need convenient, affordable training. Whether at the organization's site, the customer's site or online, there is a broad range of courses to choose from for all levels of users. Microsoft Office, Microsoft Project and Publisher, Group Wise, Photoshop, Quark, Illustrator and Dreamweaver, and HTML are just a few of the many that are offered. However, training does not stop with software. Leadership development and parenting education are also part of the organization's community outreach.

Resource Training & Solutions has always been committed to strengthening families and youth. Cavanna, recognizing a need for strengthening families, collaborated with many partners to put on a free event. In October 2000 over 6,000 people came from all over Central Minnesota to see and hear Dr. Stephen Covey, the famous author of the *7 Habits of Highly Effective People* and the *7 Habits of*

Resource Training & Solutions' state-of-the-art community software lab provides hands-on training for all community members.

Highly Effective Families. Covey spoke on the need to strengthen families. Writing a family mission statement and making time for children were part of his message. Due to this event, Resource Training & Solutions started a Strengthening Families Fund. Training is now offered by the organization in both "7 Habits of Highly Effective People and Families" as well as the "What Matters Most" time management course, all of which follow the Covey philosophy.

Since its inception, Resource has continually designed new workshops to train educators in the most state-of-the-art curriculum as well as academic enrichment opportunities for students. One of the organization's commitments to youth and families is to celebrate their successes. A Students of Excellence Banquet is held for about 150 seniors, their families and teachers to celebrate both the youth's success and their families.

Resource Training & Solutions brings Dr. Stephen Covey to speak to over 6,000 families in Central Minnesota in October 2000.

Students are chosen by their school to attend and receive an award, and a motivational speaker is always a highlight of the evening. Famous speakers such as Garrison Keillor, *The Lake Woebegon* author, are among the wonderful people who have spoken to the students.

Cavanna has created a very positive and affirming work environment for his employees. He dedicates an Employee Appreciation Week to thank them for their hard work and dedication. He also encourages them to be involved in their

own communities. Leading by example, he is an active member of the St. Cloud Area Chamber of Commerce, serves on the Partnership Board, the North Central Regional Educational Laboratory Board and the Board of Trustees of the Central Minnesota Community Foundation. The organization collaborates with many non-profit organizations such as St. Cloud Area United Way, Girl Scouts, The Community Foundation, arts organizations and universities in the surrounding area.

Resource Training & Solutions, in Dr. Cavanna's own words, "is a premiere training center for educators, businesses and families. The future looks very promising and exciting as we move into the millennium. We build personal and organizational success through effective training and innovative solutions."

Garrison Keillor signs autographs for students attending Resource Training & Solutions' Students of Excellence Banquet for over 600 students and family members.

ST. CLOUD REGIONAL AIRPORT

Not many airports can boast of having three locations in their histories. St. Cloud Regional Airport has that distinction and, with a still-new 7,000-foot, heavy-duty runway to its credit and an 85-foot control tower in the wings—chances are a fourth is not in the distant future.

Organized aviation came to this part of central Minnesota in March 1929 when Alice Wheelock Whitney donated 143 acres to construct a municipal airport four miles east of St. Cloud in an area known as Cable.

Two months later, the Whitney-Cable Airport went into service, a phase that was destined to last only four years when the same benefactor traded the parcel for a larger tract north of the city. Whitney Memorial Airport sent its first plane airborne in June 1935. The Cable acreage reverted to farmland.

By the mid-1960s urban sprawl had reached the perimeters of the airport. Hospital projects, school constructions and the spread of resi-

The Airline Terminal, which opened in 1995, was a much-needed addition to the St. Cloud Regional Airport after scheduled air service commenced in 1993.

Passengers boarding the Mesaba Airlines/ Northwest Airlink departing St. Cloud to the Minneapolis/St. Paul International Airport.

dential areas had red-flagged the 30-year-old general-aviation airport for replacement because of unlighted runways and the lack of safety zones.

The city of St. Cloud purchased a 1,400-acre site east of downtown in 1967 and began developing what is now the two-runway, St. Cloud Regional Airport on 45th Avenue Southeast. Complete with a fixed-base operator, it went into service two years later, ending safety-zone, lighting and runway-strength/length problems.

Guided by a 1975 master plan and an airport advisory board formed in 1983, it continued to evolve as a general-aviation facility catering to limited air-charter service and corporate/leisure flights.

By the early 1990s the operation began taking the steps that now make it the fastest-growing airport in Minnesota in terms of passengers. Mesaba Airlines, operating as Northwest Airlink, began service to St. Cloud Regional Airport in July 1993— 11 arrivals/departures on weekdays; nine on weekends.

"Prior to then," said airport director Brian Ryks, "people hopped whatever private flights they could or drove to the Twin Cities airports to make connections because this was still a general-aviation facility."

Airlink's arrival was great news, but also brought some not-so-good news, especially when the Northwest affiliate upgraded its fleet to boost the number of passengers—from 19 to more than 30.

"Suddenly," said Ryks, who came to St. Cloud as its first full-time air-

The recently reconstructed runway, taxiway, and air carrier apron, positions the airport for long-term growth and expansion.

port director in October 1997, "our mile-long runway was not long enough for the larger planes. That restricted service because some flights could not take full loads."

Community leaders began lobbying at the state capital and with the Minnesota congressional delegation in Washington.

"One of our hurdles," said Ryks, who is an alumnus of St. Cloud State University where he dual-majored in criminal justice and aeronautics, "was the Federal Aviation Administration. FAA guidelines state you can receive federal funding to build runways to serve your current air-traffic mix. Beyond that, local funds are required.

"That wasn't our vision," he said. "We didn't want a runway to meet our current needs. We wanted one for the long-term, a 7,000-footer to handle the big carriers. We wanted

to build it right the first time. That took a lot of talking to convince the FAA. All that lobbying paid off, and our part of the state is the winner."

Ryks, who spent more than five years at the Denver International Airport and worked at the Metropolitan Airports Commission, came home with a $16.1 million project that offers the ability for the airport to now accomodate regional jet and future air-cargo operations. The FAA forked over $12.6 million; the Minnesota Office of Aeronautics $1.4 million; and the city of St. Cloud $2.1 million—recognizing that it is such an important factor in the region's economic vitality.

The primary runway was extended from 5,280 feet to 7,000 and widened from 100 to 150 feet. Instead of an asphalt surface, it is 12-inch thick concrete. All that was celebrated at a ribbon-cutting ceremony on October 29, 2001.

The crosswind landing strip, which is 3,000 feet long continues to serve general-aviation traffic.

Next will be an 85-foot control tower, funded by a $1.1 million federal grant; $1.2 million in state money; and $300,000 from the city of St. Cloud. It should be ready to scan the air space by the end of 2003. Also blueprinted are additional instrument-landing systems and in-pavement runway lighting.

"We are positioning ourselves to accommodate larger cargo carriers, bigger business jets and airlines offering service to new destinations," Ryks said.

If passenger growth (from 10,000 to 50,000 annually over the last four years) is any indication, the airport will continue to serve a significant role in the states aviation system.

"Demographics show the St. Cloud region is a growth area," Ryks said. "Before the runway improvements, we couldn't accommodate the 50-passenger jets. Now we can, and it's the key to additional service. Next will be direct service to Chicago. I can see that happening within five years."

The population within the airport's service area is 350,000 with passengers attracted from a 60-mile radius. Smaller airports are becoming more popular for business travelers because of their convenience and reliability.

"We see our mission as being one of the major economic forces in this region," Ryks said. "The airport has a $20-million impact on the economy here annually. With more service, we see nothing but growth in that figure."

On the horizon are two projects that might land in the St. Cloud environs, and spur growth even more. One involves establishing a major air-cargo facility within a 70-mile radius of the Twin Cities; the other deals with moving an Army National Guard helicopter base from its current location in downtown St. Paul.

THE ST. CLOUD SURGICAL CENTER

The St. Cloud Surgical Center staff has a long history of listening—listening to the needs of their customers and their community. It all started in the early 1970s when Doctor Joseph C. Belshe, an anesthesiologist, listened to the plea of local physicians and dentists who said they needed a more cost effective, more efficient and less confining alternative for procedures performed under general anesthesia. Today, going home after surgery with general anesthesia is commonplace; not so in the 1970s. Having general anesthesia meant you had to stay in the hospital for several nights.

Listening to the customers during changing times brought many "firsts" to the St. Cloud Surgical Center. In 1972, under the pioneering leadership of Dr. Belshe, the St. Cloud Surgical Center became the first outpatient surgery facility in Minnesota and the second in the nation. At that time, all surgical patients were hospitalized. With increasing demand, the original facility at 1401 West St. Germain Street grew from one operating room to six.

In 1983, Medical 21 purchased the Surgical Center from Dr. Belshe and

Joseph C. Belshe M.D., founder of St. Cloud Surgical Center.

associates. The focus was to strengthen the positions of surgical centers nationally by combining forces, which significantly impacted lobbying efforts, purchasing leverage for equipment and supplies and overall bench-marking between centers. When acquisitions developed internationally, Medical 21 became Medical Care International to better incorpo-

rate their mission. A merger followed with Critical Care America, which resulted in Medical Care America, the nations largest surgical center company. In September 1994, Medical Care America was acquired by Columbia/Healthcare Corporation of America (HCA), creating a Hospital Division and an Ambulatory Surgery Division. In July 1998, all of the surgical centers in Columbia/HCA which did not have a hospital and surgical center in their market (the non-aligned centers) were sold to Alabama-based HEALTHSOUTH, the nation's largest outpatient healthcare company—located in all 50 states. HEALTHSOUTH started primarily as a physical therapy company and, at present, consists of four divisions: Physical Therapy, Diagnostic, Inpatient Rehabilitation and Surgery. In spite of various corporate ownerships over the years, the St. Cloud Surgical Center's mission remains the same: "To create and sustain a standard of excellence whereby our patients, physicians and employees consistently perceive St. Cloud Surgical Center as being uniquely qualified and able to deliver quality patient services in a manner which clearly differentiates our center as the preferred alternative when surgery is necessary."

After 21 years, customer demand exceeded building capacity. The employees and physicians created building plans with the assistance of an architectural firm leading to the opening of the current facility at 1526 Northway Drive in May 1993. The opening gave Minnesota its first outpatient surgery center with an Overnight Recovery Care Unit. Today, the Surgical Center performs over 10,000 surgeries each year, and continues to expand to better serve the needs of the community. Another expansion in 2002 created more patient support rooms and two

Original Center founded in 1972.

additional operating rooms, resulting in a total of 11 operating rooms and almost 37,000 square-feet of space.

The St. Cloud Surgical Center serves patients from across the state, a little over half of whom live in the Stearns and Benton communities. The employees of the Center care for patients during all stages of their lives. Listening to parents is important since over a quarter of the patients are children. Responding to their needs, the St. Cloud Surgical Center became the first in the area to allow parents to accompany their children in the operating room for the induction of anesthesia.

Feeling better faster is a priority for today's patient. The St. Cloud Surgical Center physicians and staff utilize advances in technology to initiate new procedures with shorter recovery times. Patients of the St. Cloud Surgical Center are back to work, back to play, and back to living, sooner than ever before. In the traditional pioneering spirit, the center continues to be on the cutting edge of the healthcare industry. The fol-

Parent accompanying their child in the operating room.

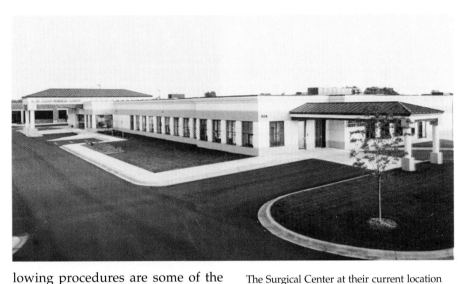

lowing procedures are some of the firsts performed not only at the Surgical Center, but also in the St. Cloud area: laparoscopic gallbladder surgery (1990); endometrial ablation (1992); laparoscopic assisted vaginal hysterectomy (1992); endoscopic breast augmentations (1993); ultrasonic liposuction (1997); and LASIK procedures (1997). Advanced surgeries as well as minor procedures are performed at the Center. Surgeries performed include: colonoscopy, lump removal, ear tubes, cataract extractions, knee surgery, laparoscopic cholecystectomy or hysterectomy,

The Surgical Center at their current location (1993).

laminectomy, mastoidectomy and advanced shoulder surgery (to name a few)—are all performed in the Center.

The St. Cloud Surgical Center administration considers its employees its most valuable asset—and it shows. Employees find the environment family-friendly and staff turnover is low. The patients notice and frequently make comments about the happy employees. Employees feel the ownership and go above and beyond their expected duties for surgeons and patients alike. In 1995, employees had a chance to put their customer service ideas to a test by participating in the prestigious Malcolm Baldridge Health Care Pilot Program. They pooled resources with their corporate owner, the Ambulatory Surgery Division of Columbia/ HCA, to discover the best practices possible for their customer-patients. This resulted in national recognition.

Customer driven quality care has always been, and will always be the primary focus of the St. Cloud Surgical Center team of employees. Listening to the customer, whether it is the patient, the surgeon, or the employee, is second nature. Working together means continued success in meeting the healthcare needs of the community.

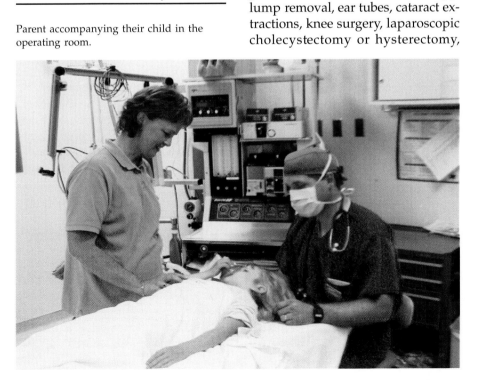

SISTERS OF THE ORDER OF SAINT BENEDICT
SAINT BENEDICT'S MONASTERY

On July 4, 1857 six women from Saint Joseph Convent, St. Marys, Pennsylvania, stepped off a boat on the Mississippi River and climbed the riverbank to the frontier settlement of St. Cloud, Minnesota—Mother Willibalda Scherbauer, superior, Sisters Evangelista Kremmeter, Gregoria Moser, Gertrude Kapser and candidates Prisca Meyer and Marianne Wolters. Each had come in response to a call to teach the children of German settlers and to establish a Benedictine community of women on the Minnesota frontier.

Six years later, in 1863 the new community relocated seven miles west of St. Cloud in the village of Clinton (later renamed St. Joseph), where the community has had an unbroken existence for 145 years. For the greater part of its history Saint Benedict's Monastery in St. Joseph, Minnesota, has been the largest

Main entrance to Saint Benedict's Monastery. The college administrative building is in the background on the right.

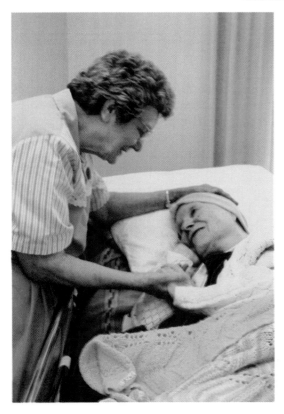

Care of the sick is an important Benedictine ministry.

Benedictine community of women in the world, with a peak membership of 1,278 in 1946.

The Benedictine sisters of Minnesota were pioneers in a variety of ways, establishing elementary schools, high schools, colleges and health care institutions, while maintaining their dedication to prayer and living in community. From 1930 until recently the community has been integrally involved in mission work in several countries outside the United States.

Between 1857 and 1957 Saint Benedict's Monastery established: the College of Saint Benedict; four high schools (among them, Cathedral High School in St. Cloud); 51 grade schools (eight of them in St. Cloud); three hospitals (most notably the St. Cloud Hospital); two schools of nursing (one of them in St. Cloud); a school of x-ray technology; a school of anesthesia; four missions abroad; and three Native American missions.

During the past 45 years, educational and health care ministries have continued alongside new and more diverse ministries, such as pastoral ministry, spiritual ministries (retreats, spiritual direction, adult formation workshops and programs) social justice ministries, research and writing, the arts and liturgical renewal.

A key development in the history of Saint Benedict's Monastery has been its role in the founding of other independent houses of Benedictine women in the United States and abroad. Its earliest foundations were made in Atchison, Kansas in 1863 and Duluth, Minnesota in 1892.

When its membership reached its highest peak in 1946, Saint Benedict's Monastery, under the leadership of Mother Rosamond Pratschner, petitioned Rome for pontifical status and the authorization to establish a third federation of Benedictine women in North America. On March 24, 1947 the "Decree of Praise" was given from the Roman Secretariat of the Congregation of Religious.

Since 1947 the following independent monasteries have been established by Saint Benedict's Monastery: Annunciation Monastery, Bismarck, North Dakota (1947); Saint Bede Monastery, Eau Claire, Wisconsin (1948); Saint Paul's Monastery, St. Paul, Minnesota (1948); Saint Placid Priory, Lacey, Washington (1952); Saint Benedict's Monastery, Sapporo, Hokkaido, Japan (1985); Saint Benedict Monastery, Tanshui, Taipei, Taiwan (1988); Saint Martin Monastery, Nassau, Bahamas (1994); Mount Benedict Monastery, Ogden, Utah (1994); and Monasterio Santa Escolastica, Humacao, Puerto Rico (2000).

According to current records 2,446 women have entered Saint Benedict's Monastery throughout its history and 1,025 professed members have died. Currently, the community numbers 369 perpetually professed members, two members in first profession and one novice. Oblates living in North America and abroad, numbering 725, form the extended Benedictine community of Saint Benedict's Monastery.

Over the years the Benedictine sisters have made a positive impact on the people of St. Cloud and Central Minnesota. The members of Saint Benedict's Monastery continue today as a monastic community of women who seek God in their daily lives according to the Gospel and the *Rule of Benedict*. Through their ministry of prayer, work and community living they listen and respond to the needs of the church and the world. A strategic focus of the community at this time in history is the commitment of themselves and their resources to enrich the spiritual lives of the people to whom and with whom they minister, particularly women.

The wisdom resulting from years of living in community, celebrating liturgy, welcoming others in hospitality, stewarding the earth, valuing education, practicing the arts and healing the sick and suffering, is the foundation of the service the members give today at the Monastery itself, and in other locations of ministry.

Spiritual direction is offered at the Monastery's Spirituality Center.

Education has been a vital work throughout the Monastery's 145-year history.

TENVOORDE FORD

The invention of the automobile was many years in the future—when John W. Tenvoorde, born in Grundle, Holland in 1823, came to America with in his parents in 1842 and settled in Evansville, Indiana—but it is the automobile that has perpetuated the family name. In 1855 Tenvoorde led a group of 50 families of German/Dutch settlers from Indiana to St. Cloud.

The roots of the Tenvoorde family were planted when John W. Tenvoorde opened his first business on the corner of Fifth and St. Germain Street. He later moved his mercantile business to the corner of St. Germain and Ninth Avenue. He was one of three local settlers elected to the State Constitutional Convention in 1857.

Steve Tenvoorde, son of the early settler engaged in several occupations; working for a carriage builder; opening a blacksmith shop; and invented several items that were patented. He developed an interest in bicycles and opened a bicycle shop on Fifth Avenue South where he achieved fame as a bicycle racer. In 1899 his career took an abrupt turn

In 1932 Tenvoorde Motor Co. showed off the first Ford V-8 in its Fifth Avenue showroom; to demonstrate the smoothness of the new engine, salesmen placed a glass of water on the fender of the idling car.

Tenvoorde Garage, Fifth Avenue South, circa 1910.

when the opportunity arose to purchase a Milwaukee Steamer. Steve Tenvoorde and his buddy P.R. Thielman drove from Minneapolis to St. Cloud over a rough oxen trail, bringing the first automobile to Stearns County. Steve was hooked on this new invention and in 1901 he began selling cars from his bicycle shop in downtown St. Cloud.

On March 21, 1903, when Henry Ford incorporated the Ford Motor Company, Tenvoorde was granted a franchise to sell Ford cars. The franchise has remained in the Tenvoorde family since that date. For the first few years Tenvoorde also handled the sales of other models, including the Milwaukee Steamer, Saxon, Oakland, Chandler, and Oldsmobile, but by 1915 most of these lines were discontinued and the dealership was devoted exclusively to Fords. The first generation!

In 1910 a brick building, later enlarged, was constructed on Fifth Avenue South. The firm remained at that location for nearly 70 years

until a new facility was constructed on Roosevelt Road in 1978.

Three of Steve Tenvoorde's sons, Cy, Lloyd and Walter, grew up in the business, with each having ample opportunity to learn everything there was to know about a car. In the early days automobiles were shipped unassembled in boxcars. It meant unloading and partially assembling the vehicles at the railroad depot, mounting the wheels and towing them to the garage on Fifth Avenue for final assembly.

At age 12 Cy Tenvoorde started working at the dealership and helped with the unloading and assembly process. By 1921 he was keeping the company's books and was instrumental in the company's survival of the Great Depression. Cy and his two brothers became the second generation to take ownership of the dealership when Steve Tenvoorde died in 1943. It was not an opportune time. The dealership, like those across the nation, had no new cars to sell because factories were converted to producing military equipment for World War II. The dealership was forced to lay off all of its salespeople, except

The Tenvoorde family, left to right: Rob, Paul, Dave, Debbie, Brian, Jack and Mike.

one. Concentrating on repairing car-buretors, fuel pumps, generators, ignitions, distributors, transmissions, crankshafts, and rebuilding engines— used cars were repaired and put on sale. They sold service by encouraging, through advertising, the need to keep cars in good repair. The purchase of a crankshaft grinder that cost a shocking $8,000 at the time, eventually paid for itself through the business of repairs.

Against all odds the business grew. The company reached a point where it was rebuilding an average of 125 engines a month for retail customers and several competitive dealerships.

In 1951 the dealership built a new facility on the original three-quarter-acre site at Fifth Avenue South in downtown St. Cloud. It remained at that site for the next 25 years. A transition in ownership occurred in 1966 when Cy Tenvoorde purchased the interests of the other family members. Cy was honored in 1976 to drive the four millionth Minnesota-built Ford out of the Twin Cities assembly plant in St. Paul. The plant now builds Ranger pickups, but at that time it

built the LTD, which carried a sticker price of $6,455.

Sales kept growing, and another expansion was in the works. On June 16, 1977 ground was broken for a new facility on the same 10 acres of farm-land that Cy had plowed when he was 12-years-old to demonstrate the versatility of Fords on tractors sold at the dealership. The new dealership opened in March 1978, the year Ford Motor Co. and Tenvoorde Motor Co. each celebrated their 75th anniversaries.

Active in the dealership daily until 1992, Cy Tenvoorde died in 1995, two days shy of his 90th birthday. The second generation!

Today, the dealership is operated by Cy's sons Jack, Dave and Paul. The third generation!

Tenvoorde Ford acquired Abra Auto Body and Glass in 1993 moving their body shop to an off-site facility. Abra enables body and glass repair to Tenvoorde Ford customers, as well as other makes. The dealership also built an off-site light repair and maintenance facility on the east side of St. Cloud in 1999. The Quality Care Service Center, the seventh in the nation, is a new concept in customer service.

Three of Jack's four children are in the business and making their mark. Son Michael, a graduate of National Automobile Dealers Association Academy is currently general manager; daughter Debbie is the customer relations manager; and son Brian works in after-market sales. Dave's son Robert is involved in the parts department. The fourth generation!

Debbie's son Eric is in high school, but works part-time during the summer, the fifth generation!

Tenvoorde Ford and Ford Motor Company will celebrate its 100th anniversaries in 2003 with both a Tenvoorde and a Ford at the helm!

Since Steve Tenvoorde was granted a Ford franchise on March 21, 1903, until the present, Tenvoorde Ford remains the "Oldest Family-held Ford Dealership in the World."

Tenvoorde Ford, present site, 2002.

NAHAN PRINTING, INC.

Forty years ago, in 1962, Jim Nahan founded Nahan Printing, Inc. Originating as a one-person operation he acquired the equipment of a small and failing single-room basement print shop at 14th Avenue and St. Germain. Unfortunately, all of the equipment was for offset printing, a new method of printing, which at the time was fast replacing the letterpress method he had worked with in the past. Jim acquired his letterpress knowledge during his apprenticeship and had served another eight years as a newspaper compositor. After just one year in the basement, the first move was made to a half-basement building on 16th Avenue and St. Germain. With the support and encouragement of his wife, Helen, this would be only one of many moves for Nahan Printing.

By 1965 Nahan Printing, consisting of three employees, relocated to its own building in the 1800 block of Third Street North. Nahan served a local market; acquired a large bank forms customer in 1968; increased their employees to six; and added 5,200 square-feet to their existing building.

In 1979 Jim moved his 23 employees into a new 20,000-square-foot

Above: James D. Nahan, founder of Nahan Printing, Inc.

Below: The 20,000-square-foot facility of Nahan Printing, Inc. was constructed in 1979 at Industrial Center West.

facility on a four-acre parcel of land available in the new Industrial Center West. It was believed this parcel would allow sufficient space for future growth. By 1985 the company outgrew its original building and constructed a 23,000-square-foot addition. This expansion made room for a new Heidelberg 5-unit half-web press and a Heidelberg 6-color sheet-fed press. Over the next few years Nahan Printing began diversifying their capabilities by adding new equipment, more employees, and serving customers nationwide.

Jim attributes the steady growth of Nahan Printing to his philosophy of providing craftsmanship and quality with friendly, dependable service, reasonable prices, and a close-knit group of experienced, dependable employees. This same philosophy had been handed down to his children, who in 1989, purchased the company from their parents and continued to direct the future of the company.

Jim and Helen's four children, Michael, Linda, Daniel and Tracy continue to be involved in the company. Michael, the eldest son, is the president/CEO, responsible for production and marketing. Linda, the eldest daughter, is executive vice president, responsible for financial and administrative functions. Daniel is in charge of major corporate accounts in sales and business development and Tracy is responsible for the information systems of the company.

By 1990 the original parcel of land proved to be too small for further expansion. The company purchased a 23-acre parcel in the

Helen and Jim Nahan.

same Industrial Center West and built a 120,000-square-foot state-of-the-art facility in 1991. Although the move was only a short distance, the enthusiasm and team effort of 180 employees working through the chaos of construction while maintaining production, was phenomenal. The new facility included the addition of modern and diverse presses to produce products that could be cross-sold to the existing customer base and new customers alike. The road to the future direction of Nahan Printing had just begun.

The guiding principles Jim Nahan set forth when he established his printing business in 1962 continues. His intention was to build a business through uncompromising quality, outstanding customer service and continual improvement.

These guidelines allow Nahan Printing to pro-

gressively grow. The philosophy that better people provide a better product has been demonstrated repeatedly. Continuous improvement through employee involvement is the way of life at Nahan Printing. Each employee receives extensive training in communication, problem solving and team building. Dedicated to the highest standards of quality and service, along with respect and commitment to their employees, explains why Nahan Printing has continued to be a successful and growing business.

By 1995 three more additions were made to the original facility creating a total of 191,000 square-feet for its now 440 employees. This growth was attributable to the creation of the Nahan Printing Mail Center Department and the addition of two Heidelberg full web-presses, which opened the door to many new markets and filled the growing needs of Nahan's existing customer

Aerial view of the current facility in Industrial Center West, totaling 299,000 square-feet.

State-of-the-art print facility was built by 1991.

base. Continuing diversification of printing services was important to the prolonged success of partnering with their customers. Every operation being under one roof was a valuable asset to the quality control of the product, along with the extended services provided.

Another 44,000 square-feet was added in 1998, enhancing the technology of their pre-press department and data center, enlarging their bindery department, and expanding their customer service and training centers.

Michael, Linda, Daniel and Tracy, owners of Nahan Printing, Inc.

The philosophy that better people provide a better product has been demonstrated repeatedly.

Innovations and employee creativity are also contributing factors to its ongoing success. The "can-do" attitude is what customers have come to expect, and appreciate, when their project is out of the ordinary. With an on-site U.S. Postal Office and a separately owned and operated ink company in-house, Nahan has become the printer with the competitive edge. Long before many other printers in the industry, Nahan operated its production with two 12-hour shifts, seven days a week. Adapting to change has not always been an easy task, but Nahan Printing has found that it is essential in an extremely competitive environment. Flexibility and good attitudes allow change to happen with the least amount of difficulty, and Nahan Printing prides itself in knowing that its employees possess these quality traits. Maintaining a strong family commitment to their company and its customers is directly related to the family values instilled in each of the owners.

With a $20 million investment Nahan Printing will complete its sixth improvement to the original 7000 Saukview Drive facility adding another 64,000 square-feet and a new Heidelberg double-pass Sunday 2000 press by April 2002, the month of their 40th anniversary. Today, with work for national and international publications and Fortune 500 companies, the craftsmanship of Nahan commercial printing has been seen by millions of people worldwide. The direct mail division prints, packages and sends more than 285 million custom mail pieces annually. The future for Nahan Printing, Inc. and its 540 dedicated employees is to continue as a nationally recognized leader in commercial printing, direct mail, and to expand into the field of custom publishing.

During the past 40 years Nahan Printing has grown with the St. Cloud area and is proud of its contribution to the growing area economy. It is also very proud of the leadership and participation many of its employees have given to local organizations and civic projects.

Aerial view of St. Cloud. Courtesy, St. Cloud Area Convention and Visitors Bureau

CAPITAL GRANITE AND MARBLE, INC.

Chuck Johannes is president, owner and founder of Capital Granite and Marble, Inc. He grew up around granite. His father worked at Cold Spring Granite for 45 years, as did the rest of his family at one time or another. Chuck worked at Cold Spring Granite himself, while attending college at St. Cloud State University.

In 1987 Chuck worked at Dale Tile in Minneapolis. During that time he built a good reputation, contact sources and a familiarity with contractors. The hard work and dedication Chuck put into building his well-respected reputation, his reliability to contractors and contact sources, put him into position to start his own business. Contractors and other sources in the Minneapolis had worked with Chuck in the years prior to opening Capital Granite and Marble, Inc. and knew what to expect from him. They knew he was capable of performing the job and that they could count on him for quality results.

When Chuck initially started running the business out of the garage of his St. Cloud home; the city did not favor the idea. But, Chuck's work was so appealing that he decided to do himself, and the city, a favor. He started looking for a different location, and ended up in St. Joseph. Not long after that, production demand started growing rapidly. In turn, Chuck purchased a 100-acre homestead along Minnesota Highway 23, five miles west of St. Cloud and two miles east of Rockville. This is where Johannes built the office and production shop in 1996 for his newly founded business, Capital Granite and Marble, Inc.

After only two years, business at Capital Granite and Marble had expanded so quickly that additional space was needed. With an expansion, the building was brought to its current 30,000 square-foot size, and offered a full showroom for the

Clemens Rose Garden Fountain, St. Cloud.

convenience and assurance of his clients.

There are sample display areas filled with rare and extraordinary upgrades, in addition to the standard colors of granite. A second display area is filled with marble samples in unique and exceptional colors. The front desk and the private desks within the office offer excellent examples of the quality work Capital Granite represents—displaying color from around the world.

In the showroom at Capital Granite and Marble, Inc. there is a fireplace wall with a beautiful marble surround. An off-set counter also demonstrates other options for style and design of tailored granite fabrication. There are two bathroom vanities displayed—one of which has the added touch of cream marfil colored marble tile flooring. A corner counter offers samples of the numerous edge details available, and paint and wood stain swatches help clients decide which effect they like best. For those interested in feedback from existing clients, or viewing results from previous jobs, there are photos of completed work available to demonstrate how impressive the company's designs look in various rooms, homes and atmospheres. To accompany the photo album there is a book of correspondence from clients praising the handi-work of Capital Granite and Marble's outstanding employees. High regard is given to everyone from saw operators and hand polishers to the installers. Clients also comment on the friendly and professional customer service provided to them.

Capital Granite currently has 22 full-time employees. These consist of one office administrator/sales associate to calculate estimates and help the client make their choices; a receptionist to introduce the options of design; and a production manager, who also travels to perform accurate field measures. In addition, there is a field measurer located in the Minneapolis area and two supplementary sales associates, one in the Twin Cities area and another in the Little Falls area. Four installers travel to job sites all over the state, and at times even to the neighboring states to install products. The remaining employees make up the company's talented fabricators and production team.

Capital Granite and Marble, Inc. produces: kitchen counter tops, entertainment bars, bathroom vanities, tub decks, and fireplace surrounds. The bulk of its production is geared towards architects, builders, interior designers and residential customers.

As much as the company focuses on production, it also concentrates on

Limestone fireplace surround.

creating satisfied customers by building strong business relationships with its clients and the general public. As a result of the company's friendly services and outstanding productions, a growing percentage of clients are repeat customers—wanting more. Consumers choose granite for several reasons; more often than not they are intrigued after seeing completed work for a previous client. Sometimes customers include Capital Granite's work in their own advertisements, demonstrating their experience with the reliability of Capital's products, as well as an opportunity to see the final results. Granite is appealing because it is nearly indestructible, maintenance free, and lasts no less than a lifetime.

Capital Granite purchases its slabs and stock material from distributors in central Minnesota. Those distributors purchase stock material from around the world. The majority comes from Argen-

tina, Brazil, Canada, Finland, Germany, India, Italy, Saudi Arabia, and even South Africa. Providing "colors that are conducive to designers' demands," Johannes said.

The company finishes an average of 15 kitchens per week with most of its business coming from the "high-end" of the Twin Cities area. Remodeling projects make up about 20 to 25 percent of Capital Granite's business—and that continues to grow.

One piece of the company's work is displayed in a popular location, the Clemens Rose Garden in downtown St. Cloud. "It was a local job, and it was nice to put a little stamp in town. It was a challenge, but we got it!" Chuck said.

Chuck Johannes sees the future market for granite counter tops as strong as stone—especially as incomes increase. "I think we're in the early stages of a product that will be utilized for a long time," Chuck firmly states. The history of Capital Granite and Marble, Inc. is just beginning.

Marble fireplace surround.

CATHOLIC CHARITIES

Catholic Charities of the Diocese of St. Cloud is a nonprofit, human service agency headquartered in St. Cloud, Minnesota. Over 620 employees, 185 foster grandparents, and 2,700 volunteers provide 40 programs of human service across 16 Central Minnesota counties. Catholic Charities touches nearly 40,000 people each year and is committed to building communities, promoting family life, and enhancing human dignity by offering its services to meet the physical, social, emotional, and spiritual need of individuals and families of all faiths and beliefs.

All are welcome at Catholic Charities' door. The organization operates from a foundation based upon Catholic social teaching and a belief in justice and dignity for all human beings. Those individuals and families served by this faith-based organization are not required to believe as it does in order to receive services. "You see, all people have a right to have their basic needs met, regardless of their ability to pay, race or religion, age or gender," explains Executive Director Steven P. Bresnahan. "We provide help and create hope for "all faiths, all people.""

"The services and ministries of Catholic Charities have only come about because of community support and the dedication of parishes in the Diocese," notes Bresnahan.

This dedication to service is rooted in the Catholic faith of the earliest German and French Catholic settlers. In 1875 nuns from the Order of St. Benedict cared for orphans in St. Joseph. By 1895 Bishop Otto Zardetti, St. Cloud's first Bishop, had moved all orphans to the care of the Franciscan Sisters at St. Otto's Orphanage in Little Falls. In 1916 his successor, Bishop Joseph F. Busch, organized a Women's Guild to do educational, charitable and social work in St. Cloud and in 1924 transferred care of the orphans to the St. Cloud Orphanage.

Bishop Busch reads to the children at the St. Cloud Orphanage, which was dedicated in 1924.

This social ministry was being called "Catholic Charities" by 1922 and was under the direct supervision of the Bishop and clergy. Monsignor Edward Mahowald was its first director, followed by Father Austin Kinsella in 1931 and Father Jerome Bielejeski in 1953.

Yearly, Catholic Charities serves 40,000 people across 16 counties of Central Minnesota with 40 programs to meet their needs in the areas of aging services, individual and family counseling, affordable housing, residential care and day treatment, social concerns and parish ministry.

Because of changing needs, Catholic Charities of the Diocese of St. Cloud was incorporated as a 501c(3) agency in the State of Minnesota in 1955. The St. Cloud Children's Home was considered one of its programs. Others included: Adoption, Unmarried Mothers Service, Marriage Relations Council, and counseling. When Father Bielejeski died in 1958, Father Henry Lutgen became the new director, followed by Father Val Klimek, director from 1962 to 1965.

Father Richard J. Leisen, director from 1965 until 1987, shaped Catholic Charities over 22 years. Father Leisen set up a Board of Directors in 1968 at the request of Bishop Peter Bartholome. This significant step gave the 23 lay members of the board executive authority to make policy with the chancellor of the Diocese of St. Cloud and the executive director.

During Father Leisen's tenure, the agency grew into: Caritas Family Services and Women's Guild (counseling and emergency services); St. Cloud Children's Home (residential ser-

Executive Director Steve Bresnahan became the first lay director of Catholic Charities in 1994, a departure from a tradition of administration by members of the clergy.

vices); Nutrition Program and Foster Grandparent Program in 1965 (aging services); Key Row Community (1968); Services for the Mentally Handicapped (1979) at St. Elizabeth's Home; and La Paz Community housing for persons with disabilities in 1982 (housing services). A specialized program for Refugee Resettlement was set up in 1975 to assist Vietnamese war refugees. This program does not operate today.

Father Leisen was also very instrumental in the development of the St. Cloud Area United Way, originally the United Fund of St. Cloud, in 1967. Today the United Way is a major supporter of Catholic Charities programming.

Recognition of the high quality of Catholic Charities' services came under the directorship of Father Timothy Wenzel from 1987 to 1994, when the Council on Accreditation of Services to Families and Children, Inc. accredited the agency. Also during this time, an Intensive Treatment Unit in Fergus Falls opened; the Hope Community Support Program (1989) for adults with mental illness was initiated.

Catholic Charities took a decisive step in 1994 and named its first lay executive director. Under Steven P. Bresnahan, a website was launched, www.ccstcloud.org. The agency organized a Diversity Steering Committee to address the needs of staff and clients of all faiths, creeds, colors, ethnicity, and genders. An Office of Social Concerns was created to help handle social and rural life issues. Catholic Charities assumed management of St. Cloud's La Cruz Community and apartments in Richmond, Holidingford, Belgrade and New Munich. Of great significance was the acquisition of a building in St. Cloud to house Emergency Services (food shelf, clothing program, financial assistance) and the offices of Aging and Housing Services. This facility allows the food shelf to serve individuals in a spacious, grocery store setting.

Today, Catholic Charities is the largest nonprofit provider of human services in Central Minnesota. Eighty percent of its funding comes via federal, state and county government agencies as grant money or fees-for-service. The remainder comes from individuals, businesses, corporations, and other nonprofit foundation supporters. In 2002 Catholic Charities managed an $18 million budget with almost 90 cents of every dollar spent toward client services in five program divisions: Aging Services, Caritas Family Services, Residential and Day Programs, Housing Services, and the Office of Social Concerns.

"Our mission is to serve the Diocese of St. Cloud," said Bresnahan. "Now, that's a challenge since close to half-a-million people live throughout the sixteen counties—from Sherburne County all the way up to Breckenridge, from Lake Mille Lacs out to Brown's Valley and Lake Travis."

Catholic Charities will continue to respond to the needs of individuals and families who live and work across its service area. Plans for the future include: becoming a full mental health clinic; consolidating numerous St. Cloud offices into three campuses; and becoming an employer-of-choice.

"There is still much to do," said Bresnahan. "However, to quote Bishop Joseph F. Busch, 'much can be accomplished by people who are eager to practice their religion as well as to profess it.'"

Catholic Charities is wise to the value of volunteers. In 2001 the agency benefited from the generosity of 2,700 volunteers, many at the emergency food shelf and clothing programs, Senior Dining sites, and as foster grandparents. While all volunteers are unique, they are connected by their willingness to give of themselves to organizations they believe in.

CENTRACARE HEALTH SYSTEM

In 1995 CentraCare Health System, an integrated health care delivery system, was formed in response to the growing needs of Central Minnesota. The system was formed via the merger of St. Cloud Hospital and the St. Cloud Clinic of Internal Medicine. The mission of the CentraCare Health System is to improve the health of every patient, every day.

The CentraCare Health System includes three hospitals, nine clinic sites in seven Central Minnesota communities, plus four long-term care facilities and senior housing.

St. Cloud Hospital serves a population of 560,000 in a 12-county area of Central Minnesota. A medical staff of more than 300 physicians and 3,300 employees dedicate themselves to providing the finest in patient-focused care.

Melrose Area Hospital is a 28-bed community hospital with a full range of healthcare services and convenient access to a variety of specialists. Melrose Area Hospital employs more than 170 people who serve nearly 10,000 residents in and around western Stearns County.

Long Prairie Memorial Hospital is a 34-bed hospital that employs more than 250 people who serve nearly 18,000 residents in and around Todd County.

Primary care clinics with family practitioners, nurse practitioners, physician assistants and midwives provide quality services to patients of all ages with clinics in Becker, St. Joseph, two St. Cloud locations, Melrose and Long Prairie.

Pediatricians and obstetrician-gynecologists along with pediatric and adult nurse practitioners at Centra-Care Clinic provide primary and specialty care services—The Women & Children clinic is located at the CentraCare Health Plaza in St. Cloud.

Primary care internal medicine services are provided in Little Falls and St. Cloud. Multiple specialty services

are provided in St. Cloud including allergy, cardiology, dermatology, endocrinology, gastroenterology, hospitalists, infectious diseases, internal medicine, medical oncology, neonatology, nephrology, neurology, neurosurgery, pulmonology, radiation oncology and rheumatology and surgery.

A collaborative effort between CentraCare Clinic Long Prairie and Lakewood Clinic–Staples created Eagle Valley Clinic, which provides high-quality, cost-effective and caring services to patients of all ages.

A St. Cloud Hospital clinic, Mid-Minnesota Family Practice Center, is

St. Benedict's Senior Community offers a continuum of care including 95 retirement living apartments at Benedict Village.

Since the creation of the CentraCare Health System, St. Cloud Hospital has developed into a regional refer center serving a 12-county area.

dedicated to serving people who have little or no insurance.

In Melrose, Pine Villa Care Center is a 75-bed nursing home made up of two units: Pine Villa, a skilled nursing unit, and Pine Haven, a special care unit for residents with Alzheimer's, memory loss or other behavior conditions. Park View Center is a congregate senior housing building with 42 independent-living apartments.

Long Prairie Memorial Home is a 103-bed, long-term care facility with a neighborhood concept to provide each wing with a distinct, home-like atmosphere and dedicated care team.

St. Benedict's Senior Community–St. Cloud can trace its roots back to 1900 and St. Joseph's Home. Originally a hospital, St. Joseph's was the first nursing home opened by the Benedictine Sisters in the St. Cloud area. In the mid-1970s it became apparent that St. Joseph's and St. Raphael's, the other nursing home operated by the Benedictines, would need to be significantly renovated and upgraded. The decision was made to close both facilities and build St. Benedict's Center, which opened in 1978. In 1999 St. Benedict's Center was renamed St. Benedict's Senior Community (SBSC) to better reflect the wide range

CentraCare Health Plaza opened in November 2001 to enhance the quality and accessibility of care for outpatient services.

of healthcare and housing options available for older adults. Since its opening, St. Benedict's Senior Community has grown from a nursing home serving 222 people to a wide continuum of care offering health care, housing and services to about 600 seniors.

St. Benedict's Senior Community –Monticello opened in 2000 to provide 60 independent-living apartments, 46 assisted-living apartments and 14 memory-care apartments.

CentraCare Health Foundation was created in 1996 to engage the philanthropic community in partnership to improve health and healthcare. CentraCare Health Foundation accepts charitable contributions for all CentraCare Health System entities. These funds may be used to provide resources to staff or patients, purchase equipment or services, award grants or address major health concerns in the region. The Foundation's benefactors have provided generous financial support to many programs and funds that help CentraCare Health System to fulfill its mission.

A multitude of specialty care programs, such as the Central Minnesota Heart Center at St. Cloud Hospital are available. The Heart Center is a collaboration of the cardiologists from CentraCare Clinic, cardiac surgeons from Cardiac Surgical Associates, P.A., and St. Cloud Hospital. In 2001 more than 450 open-heart surgeries and 4,000 cardiac catheterization laboratory procedures were performed at the Heart Center.

As the area's largest employer, CentraCare Health System employs more than 5,000 persons. The system's total additional economic output in the tri-county area is $1 billion. Visitor-related spending impacts the area with more than $47 million.

The vision of the health system is to enhance the strong regional medical center by continuing to focus on the needs of Central Minnesotans. By keeping patients in Central Minnesota, sophisticated resources are kept in the community and are available to serve all people in the region, including those needing programs that struggle financially, and to make all specialty resources available 24 hours a day, seven days a week.

Unlike for-profit organizations, CentraCare Health System does not distribute earnings to shareholders. Instead, operating revenues, investment income and, in some cases, borrowed money, are used to invest in buildings, equipment and people to ensure excellent healthcare. Philanthropy also plays an important role in CentraCare Health System's ability to meet the region's healthcare needs, with donated dollars helping to fill the gaps between revenues and the cost of facilities and services.

St. Cloud Hospital and CentraCare Clinic collaboratively operate the 328,000-square-foot CentraCare Health Plaza. The Health Plaza's mission is to "provide outstanding care and treatment by creating a healing environment and innovative approaches to improve the health and quality of life for the people we serve."

Providers at the Health Plaza offer convenient primary and specialty outpatient care and state-of-the-art

diagnostic and treatment facilities for comprehensive care under one roof. The specialty programs combine hospital and clinic services in a well-coordinated, patient-focused healthcare environment. The services include behavioral health, diabetes, dialysis, digestive, Child and Adolescent Specialty Center, endocrinology, gynecology, pediatrics, obstetrics, oncology and rehabilitation. Coborn Cancer Center at the CentraCare Health Plaza provides chemotherapy and infusion with 22 private rooms, radiation oncology with two linear accelerators and hematology/oncology services.

The CentraCare Health System is expanding to meet the needs of Central Minnesota for the future, providing comprehensive, high-quality care, close to home.

CentraCare Health System has invested more than $12 million in upgrading hospitals in the Long Prairie and Melrose communities to ensure the viability of small-town healthcare.

COBORN'S, INC.

Determination, hard work, pride and a vision—those are the words that best characterize the owners and employees of Coborn's, Incorporated—*a Heritage of excellence through service, quality and price.*

The legacy of Coborn's began in 1912 when Chester Coborn opened a single produce market on Broadway Avenue in Sauk Rapids, Minnesota. Eventually, dry goods and other merchandise were added to the store's offerings as Chester tried to meet the needs of his customers. Duke and Chester, Jr., Chester's sons, continued running the family market after their father's death. In 1936 a walk-in cooler was purchased, launching Coborn's into the meat business. Cattle were bartered for, bought and slaughtered right at the store.

As time passed, the store continued to evolve with the addition of such amenities as shopping carts and checkout lanes. In 1952 after some consternation, the store adopted the "cash and carry" policy, ending the practice of extending credit to friends and neighbors. In 1960 the third generation of Coborn family members

Dan Coborn already knew about buying power back in the 1960s! Today, Coborn's owns its own warehouse, which has been a competitive advantage in buying by the truckload.

Coborn's leadership extends to the fourth generation. Back row: Chester Coborn with sons Duke (Dan and Bill's father) and Chet Coborn. Front row: Mark Coborn, executive vice president (Bill's son); Bill Coborn (deceased); Dan Coborn, chairman; Chris Coborn, president (Dan's Son).

led development of the business when brothers Dan, Bill, Ron and Bob gained ownership. The second Coborn's store opened in 1963 in Foley, Minnesota, a town neighboring St. Cloud and Sauk Rapids. Development continued, bringing 19 Coborn's stores to locations throughout Minnesota and South Dakota.

Recognized for its pioneering spirit, Coborn's, Inc. was the first grocery retailer in the state of Minnesota to implement a scanning process at its front-end checkout system. Coborn's managers also followed developments in European stores known for innovative product displays and convenient store layouts. "Research and planning have always been key to the success of our store developments," said Dan Coborn. "This industry will continually evolve and change. Being open to new ideas and able to incorporate new products and services has always brought benefits to our customers."

Recognizing the potential for the evolving "warehouse" or "discount" grocery store, Coborn's opened its first Cash Wise Foods store in Willmar, Minnesota in 1979. Operating on the premise that price and

quality outweigh the need for certain services, such as bagging, the Cash Wise concept has been very successful and warmly embraced by consumers. By the end of 1995, the Coborn brothers and company owners, Dan and Bill had launched nine Cash Wise Foods stores throughout the upper Midwest.

In 1986 the proliferation of convenience stores led Coborn's to form Little Dukes, which feature gas, groceries, and other services. By the end of 2001 there were 19 Little Dukes convenience stores in Minnesota, South Dakota and North Dakota.

Capitalizing on the opportunity to offer both unique and quality products at a very competitive price, Coborn's began adding a number of "backstage" operations. The Central Bakery, Central Commissary, Central Dry Cleaning and Grocery Distribution Center, all provide the stores with consistent, top-quality product.

Coborn's also sells a full array of premium private-label products, from bakery items to meat, salads, salsas and barbecue sauce. They continue to develop food products for distribution to their stores and other grocery outlets.

Recognized by industry leaders as a "progressive" company, Coborn's remains active in seeking new services and departments to create the ultimate "one-stop shopping" experience. Most stores include pharmacies, video rentals, floral services, natural foods departments, bath & body products, kitchen centers, one-hour photo processing, dry cleaning service and in-store banking. Liquor stores and sit-down delicatessens complement most Coborn's and Cash Wise Foods stores.

Preparing for the new generation of Internet users, Coborn's offers customers an integrated website (www.cobornsinc.com) where they can view services offered at each store and learn about weekly specials. In addition to being an information source, the company's website also features an extensive floral center, where customers can order customized floral designs for a variety of occasions. Incorporation of additional on-line shopping programs will continue.

Original Coborn's store in the 1920s, on Main Street in Sauk Rapids, Minnesota.

The new era of Coborn's Superstores includes a "one-stop shopping" adventure, with deli cafes, pharmacy, natural foods, floral, one-hour photo developing, video, dry cleaning and banks.

Such success and innovation have brought many awards to the Coborn family. In addition to serving as leaders on state and national industry boards, Coborn's has been recognized in *Forbes* magazine as one of the country's top 500 largest privately owned businesses. Bill and Dan Coborn were honored with the Entrepreneurial Success Award, sponsored by the Chamber and U.S. Small Business Administration. In January 2001 Chris Coborn accepted the "Spirit of America" award from the National Grocers Association for industry and community leadership.

In recognition of the Coborn family culture of community service, Coborn's was named one of the 10 most generous companies in America businesses in a recognition program sponsored in 1999 by actor/philanthropist, Paul Newman and the late John F. Kennedy, Jr. and *George* magazine.

"We all share responsibility for the health of our community," Dan Coborn said. "If everyone gave a small amount of time and/or money to help, we would see an erosion of poverty, a proliferation of well-balanced human beings and significant improvement in the quality of life for all persons."

Each generation of Coborn family members carries on the heritage of excellence linked to Coborn's, Inc. through strong corporate citizenship, employee and consumer advocacy and ethical business practices.

The evolution of family ownership continued in 1999 as cousins Chris and Mark Coborn took more significant leadership roles in the business. Ownership is dominated by the fourth generation of Coborn family members, comprised of the nine children of Dan and Mabel Coborn and Bill and Joyce Coborn. Chris serves as company president; Mark is executive vice president, while Dan Coborn remains chairman of the board.

The entrepreneurial spirit remains a hallmark of the Coborn family. By 2001 Coborn's employed 4,700 people in more than 70 grocery, convenience, liquor and related retail stores in Minnesota, Iowa, Illinois, North Dakota and South Dakota.

"This generation is committed to continued growth of the Coborn organization," Chris Coborn said. "We will continue to listen to our customers, take good care of our employees and stay ahead of competition. In doing so, we expect nothing short of continued success."

HANDYMAN'S HARDWARE INC.

Handyman's Incorporated, doing business as Handyman's Hardware, was founded in spring 1965 in St. Cloud, Minnesota. Its origin was the culmination of the dream founder Stanley (Stan) M. Severson had since he was a teenager. Severson was the youngest of 14 children growing up in Forest City, Iowa. As a 14-year-old he went to work in a hardware store doing odd jobs to earn extra money. Ever since that time he dreamed of owning his own hardware store.

After completing high school in 1949, Severson attended college for two years. Next, he enlisted in the U.S. Navy where he served from 1952–1956. While in the service Stan married Deloris C. Nelson. After his discharge the couple settled in Mankato, Minnesota where Stan began working for the plumbing and heating wholesaler, Crane and Ordway. Eventually he was promoted to a sales position with his own territory. Stan traveled around southern Minnesota selling supplies to plumbing and heating contractors.

In 1960 Stan's territory was changed to central Minnesota, so the family, which now included 3-year-

Founder Stanley (Stan) M. Severson.

Handyman's, a retail hardware center at 604 East St. Germain, has completed a major expansion. From left to right; top hatter Doug Madson, Stan Severson, owner, Debbie Backus, office manager, Doug Severson, vice president, and top hatter Gene Storms.

old daughter Debra, moved to St. Cloud. In August 1960, three weeks after the move, their son Douglas was born. Stanley continued to work for Crane and Ordway until late 1964 when he resigned to pursue his own dream.

Severson needed to arrange financing in order to start his new business. He eventually convinced the president of St. Cloud National Bank to override its Board of Directors and grant him a business loan. Stan promised the bank president that Handyman's would be a new, innovative and nontraditional hardware store. The next step was to secure a location for the store, which turned out to be the old Carl's Supermarket at 404 East St.Germain Street, St. Cloud. The supermarket had moved to a larger location across the street, enabling Stan to lease the building from its owner, Carl Kosloske.

In spring 1965, with $30,000 in capital and loans, Stan started buying store fixtures and merchandise. In order to competitively purchase merchandise the new business became affiliated with United Hard-

ware Distributing or "Hardware Hank." United was a co-op buying group owned by the individual hardware stores it served. The business also became incorporated with the outstanding shares of stock being held by Stan and Deloris Severson.

On June 1, 1965, with all of its merchandise on the shelves, Handyman's opened its doors for business. At that time Stan and Deloris were the only employees. There were nine hardware stores operating in St. Cloud, with a Coast-to-Coast store right across the street from Handyman's. The building they were leasing had 3,000 square-feet of sales area with additional storage room and six parking spaces available for customers.

Sales at Handyman's were slow at first, so to help promote his business, Stan installed plumbing and heating systems for customers. His background in plumbing and heating sales proved invaluable to the new business. In July 1965 a grand opening was held to attract new customers. Jerry Billig, a salesperson for the *St. Cloud Daily Times*, developed Handyman's first advertisement announcing its grand opening. Ironically, 20 years later in 1985, Mr. Billig would become Douglas Severson's father-in-law.

The original business plan for Handyman's was to reach first year's sales of $100,000. They only reached $89,000, but Stan and Deloris were not discouraged. It wasn't until late 1967 that the growing business justified hiring LeRoy Winter—its third full-time employee. LeRoy continued to work for the company until his retirement in 1992. With sales continuing to grow, part-time students were hired to help stock shelves and run errands.

By spring 1975 the Severson's realized the company needed more space for additional merchandise. A larger facility was located a few blocks away at 604 East St. Germain

Handyman's in 1995.

Street. Formerly an old furniture store, the building offered 5,000 square-feet of sales area and another 5,000 square-feet of storage and office space. In addition, there were now 12 parking spaces available for customers.

This location allowed Handyman's to offer many new and unusual products to its customers. Severson's plan was to stock hard to find items that other stores weren't willing to carry. He also used his background in direct sales to encourage other businesses to purchase their supplies from Handyman's. Stan practiced the philosophy that if a business bought from Handyman's, it would support that company and purchase what it could from them in return.

Severson also realized that in order to compete with other suppliers, customer service would need to be a high priority. Knowledgeable, long-time employees would give customers personal one-on-one attention. It soon developed a reputation with customers in the St. Cloud area. They knew that "Handyman's will

have it in stock or be able to locate it."

By 1978 Handyman's employed five part-time students in addition to its three full-time employees. In order to encourage these students to stay with the company full-time, a profit-sharing plan was established. In 1979 Paul Wesenberg became Handyman's next full-time employee. He would later become Handyman's first outside salesperson and eventually its manager.

Business continued to prosper for Handyman's and in 1982 Douglas (Doug) S. Severson was hired full-time. He had been working part-time at Handyman's for five years while going to school and earning a B.S. degree in finance. In 1983 Doug became a shareholder in the company and was named vice president.

Ground breaking for new addition to Handyman's.

Debra A. Backus joined Handyman's in 1984 and soon became a shareholder and the company's secretary treasurer.

In 1984 the company put additional emphasis on the outside sales of its products. This allowed Handyman's employees to go directly to the customers to better meet their needs. Some of these new customers included schools, factories and healthcare facilities. Also in 1984 an additional salesperson, Marvin Neu, was added to the staff along with a 4,500-square-foot warehouse that allow for additional inventory.

Handyman's had a staff of eight full-time and six part-time employees by 1992 when management realized that in order for continued growth another building expansion was inevitable. By summer 1993, 6,000 square-feet of additional sales area and office space were completed. Handyman's now offered 32 parking spaces to better serve the increased customer traffic. Also in 1993, Doug Severson was named president and Debra Backus became vice president. Stan and Deloris Severson began moving toward a less active role in the company.

The year 2002 brings continued growth at Handyman's with sales figures in the millions plus 10 full-time and 10 part-time staff members. The city of St. Cloud has two hardware stores instead of the nine operating in 1965 when Handyman's first opened its doors. It has many of the same loyal customers it has been serving for upwards of 30 years and currently serves additional customers throughout the state of Minnesota. Its salespeople regularly work with customers within a 70-mile radius of St. Cloud. The tradition of personal customer service continues along with the reputation that "If Handyman's doesn't have it in stock, no one will."

REGENT BROADCASTING

Nestled in the heart of Central Minnesota, the city of St. Cloud was once home to a single radio station. Then in 1950 the FCC granted permission to double this small community's number of radio stations. St. Cloud already had one station and another seemed redundant to the community. In the '50s radio broadcasts differed very little from one station to another. The population expected duplication in the information and entertainment they were already receiving in their homes and cars.

Just over 50 years later that redundant radio station, WJON-AM, has become an anchor in its community and the anchor of Regent Broadcasting in St. Cloud's stable of radio stations. While the original licensee of WJON was a businessman from Duluth, the present owner, Regent Communications continues a strong commitment to serve the citizens of St. Cloud, as did a variety of owners over the last half century.

It was September 8, 1950 when WJON first went on the air, broadcasting from a little concrete building on Lincoln Avenue Southeast, with a small tower adjacent to the building. Broadcasting just across the street from the area's main railroad tracks created an interesting sound problem when the trains went by throughout the day. During live radio shows it was common for listeners to hear the sound of the train rumbling in the background. The trains still rumble by, but due to modern construction and soundproofing, it's not the nuisance it was in the past.

Over the next 20 years WJON changed ownership not once, but twice. An addition was constructed on the building and all of the offices moved into the facility at the Lincoln Avenue site.

In 1970 Andy Hilger, the owner at the time, launched an additional FM station. WWJO-FM, known as "Stereo 98" carried different program-

ming from WJON's news/sports and talk format. Stereo 98 was broadcasting an all-country music format.

The addition of WWJO increased business for the company and with increased business came an augmented need for more employees and space for those employees. In 1979 construction began on a new 12,000-square-foot, state-of-the-art broad-

WJON-AM 1240 received the prestigious Crystal Award for exceptional community service contributions in 1989 and 2002.

Recognized as a state-of-the-art facility, this building continues to house the stations of Regent Broadcasting of St. Cloud.

casting facility. The new building was recognized as one of the finest technical facilities in the nation by national radio and engineering publications. This facility was so state-of-the-art it still serves its purpose today as the location for six stations in the 21st century.

During the 1980s the FCC licensed many new stations across the country, including another half dozen or so in the St. Cloud area. After the period of licensing the FCC then relaxed its ownership rules, allowing one company to own two AM and two FM stations in the same market. This opened the door for KMXK-FM to be purchased. KMXK's format was a form of popular adult music called adult contemporary. It later switched to the oldies music format, playing popular music from the '50s and '60s. Eventually, in the year 2000, the station resurrected one of its former titles as "The Mix" reverted back to a hot adult contemporary radio station.

The 1980s held change for WWJO as well. Now known as "98 Country," WWJO improved its signal with the construction of the highest tower in the area, a 1,000-foot structure located in north central Benton County. This tower boosted 98 Country's 100,000-watt signal over a 17-county area.

In the summer of 1999 WJON, WWJO and KMXK were sold to Regent Communications, a company in the radio broadcasting business based out of Covington, Kentucky. Terry S. Jacobs and William L. Stakelin incorporated Regent in Delaware in November 1996 with the objective of acquiring radio properties that have a history of growing revenues in medium to smaller sized radio markets. Stations under consideration must also have capable operating management and be leaders in their communities or have the prospect of becoming a leader. Regent acquired its first group of stations in June of 1998. Pending the close of all announced transactions, Regent Communications will own and operate 61 stations clustered in 12 markets in California, Illinois, Louisiana, Michigan, Minnesota, New York, Pennsylvania and Texas. This purchase of WJON, WWJO and KMXK allowed for more growth and more possibility for the three-station St. Cloud cluster.

Regent Communications doubled the size of its group of St. Cloud stations the following year. Due to the FCC again broadening ownership rules in 1996, one company was allowed to own seven radio stations in a market of St. Cloud's size. Three additional radio stations were purchased and integrated into the family. KLZZ-FM "The Loon" (a classic rock format), which at one time was known as "The Power Loon" a rock-and-roll station; KKSR-FM "Kiss 96" (a rhythmic-CHR format) which when purchased was known as Star 96 a softer form of adult contemporary radio; and KXSS-AM "Classic Hit Country" which was a nostalgia/big band format. Now Regent was able to serve the entire population of Central Minnesota.

As the number of stations grew, the staff also increased. Initially, WJON had only nine employees. That number later increased to 18 in the year 1975 and to 40 in 1980. Currently, Regent Broadcasting of St. Cloud employs 60 full- and part-time employees for six radio stations.

That single AM radio station that started it all on Southeast Lincoln Avenue is still there, but it is now part of a larger family of radio stations that provide the same service to the St. Cloud community that WJON has been doing since 1950.

The proof is in the recognition. In addition to awards from the *Associated Press*, Minnesota Broadcasters Association and others, WJON-AM has won the prestigious National Association of Broadcasters' Crystal Radio Award for Excellence in Community Service. WJON accepted this award not once but twice, first in 1989 and again in 2002.

The stations of Regent Broadcasting of St. Cloud continue to grow and change, but their mission is one in the same: to inform, entertain and support the communities of Central Minnesota for many years to come.

ST. CLOUD HOSPITAL

It all began in 1857 when four Roman Catholic nuns of a Benedictine order in Pennsylvania and two candidates for the order, traveled to St. Cloud to establish schools in the frontier community. They left St. Paul July 2 on the *North Star;* they were within two miles of their destination the following day when low water brought their steamboat to a halt. On July 4 the six women were ferried ashore and walked to the city.

While much of their activity during the first 30 years was devoted to education, in 1885 the Sisters of the Order of St. Benedict were persuaded to take over the operation of a hospital started by A.C. Lamothe Ramsay, M.D., three years prior.

On February 22, 1886 St. Benedict's Hospital opened on Ninth Avenue North in a three-story home the sisters had purchased for $2,000. A devastating tornado struck the area April 14, 1886 and left 58 people dead and hundreds injured. For two days the Sisters worked around the clock until help arrived from other cities. Their efforts brought grateful recognition

Nursing school graduating classes from 1924–1926 pose in front of St. Raphael's Hospital.

and the hospital was no longer considered a place to go just to die.

Rapidly the number of patients increased, and by 1889 the Sisters had accepted a gift of land southeast of the city for a larger hospital, St. Raphael's. Failure of the city to extend roads and bridges to the area made it virtually inaccessible. The hospital never held more than seven patients at a time. After 10 years a new hospital was constructed adjacent to the original building on Ninth Avenue North and formally dedicated in July 1900.

From 1912 to 1914 more than 1,600 patients were admitted, nearly 1,100 surgeries were performed and 72 babies were born. It became evident by 1926 that a larger facility was needed. At a cost of $2 million, building started on St. Cloud Hospital's current site, 1406 Sixth Avenue North.

With 315 patient rooms and medical specialties ranging from anesthesiology to X-ray, the facility was intended

The community helped evacuate the second St. Raphael's Hospital, which was on Ninth Avenue North, during a fire in 1905.

to be more than adequate for many years to come. But, as in the past, by 1944 the wing previously devoted to housing student nurses was required for patient care and a two-story nurses' home, plus classrooms, was constructed adjacent to the hospital. Eight years later that structure was expanded with the addition of four floors.

In 1962 the sisters gave St. Cloud Hospital to the community by having it separately incorporated. It remains a Catholic hospital whose mission is "to improve the health and quality of life for the people of Central Minnesota in a manner that reflects the healing mission of Jesus and supports the dignity of those providing services and those being served." A board of volunteer directors from the community governs the hospital and has overseen many exciting advances, such as:
• In 1970 Harold Windschitl, M.D., joined the medical staff as the first oncologist in St. Cloud. Five medical oncologists and four radiation oncologists provide cancer services in seven Central Minnesota communities in addition to 1,200 new cancer patients annually at Coborn Cancer Center.
• St. Cloud Hospital dialysis units in

St. Cloud Hospital continues its commitment to quality health care, close to the home that the Sisters of the Order of St. Benedict began 116 years ago.

Alexandria, Brainerd, Little Falls, Monticello, Princeton, St. Cloud and Staples provide more than 32,000 dialysis procedures each year.

• In 1988 the first open-heart surgery was performed at St. Cloud Hospital. Thousands of cardiac procedures have been performed since then. The Heart Center provides outreach to 16 communities. The hospital's Central Minnesota Heart Center has been recognized as one of Solucient's 100 Top Hospitals for Cardiovascular Care in 1999, 2000 and 2001.

• St. Cloud Hospital itself received top-100 hospital status nationwide three times.

• Established in 1996, St. Cloud Hospital/Mayo Family Practice Residency Program is fully accredited by the Accreditation Council for Graduate Medical Education (ACGME). The program's goal is to train residents with the skills needed to work in rural practice.

• The Level II & III Neonatal Intensive Care Unit, which opened in 1988, has 20 beds.

• After experiencing an increase in the demand for complex services close to home, St. Cloud Hospital's Emergency Trauma Center (ETC) expanded. In 1998 the ETC became a verified Level II Trauma Center. The ETC serves more than 40,000 people each year.

In response to the growing needs of the community, CentraCare Health System, an integrated health care delivery system, was formed in 1995. The system was formed via the merger of St. Cloud Hospital and the St. Cloud Clinic of Internal Medicine.

As part of CentraCare Health System, St. Cloud Hospital has become a regional hospital providing service to a 12-county area. The past 20 years have also seen a significant growth in St. Cloud Hospital's medical staff from 130 physicians in 1985 to 330 in 2002. About 135 of those physicians are CentraCare Clinic physicians. Physicians with St. Cloud Hospital medical privileges provide care for residents throughout Central Minnesota in more than 30 communities.

CentraCare Health System is a collaborative group of Central Minnesota health care professionals working together to provide comprehensive, high-quality care, close to home. This group enables St. Cloud Hospital to specialize in services such as orthopedic or neurological medical and surgical care.

Mid-Minnesota Family Practice Center, a St. Cloud Hospital clinic, is dedicated to serving people who have little or no insurance. As part of that effort, volunteers from Mid-Minnesota provide free health screenings as part of Project H.E.A.L. (Health, Education, Access, Link). The volunteers ensure that if further care is needed, hurdles such as transportation are overcome. If patients are uninsured or ineligible for Minnesota health care programs, Mid-Minnesota uses a sliding fee scale.

Project H.E.A.L. partners with area churches, which provide a volunteer base; community service sites, which provide space in the immediate community of the under-served; and government agencies, which provide access to public insurance to bring healthcare screening services and a link to primary care to the uninsured or underinsured people in the St. Cloud area.

St. Raphael's Hospital eventually became a long-term care facility for the Sisters of the Order of St. Benedict.

SENTINEL PRINTING COMPANY

Sentinel Printing Company's legacy is woven from a long and rich history in the St. Cloud and Sauk Rapids, Minnesota, area. It has been almost 150 years since the company opened its doors, and in that time Sentinel has evolved from a small community newspaper to a multi-million dollar printing firm.

Sentinel's origins as a newspaper, *The Frontiersman*, created the foundation for a viable company that would survive the turning of two centuries. George Washington Benedict and Jeremiah Russell established the weekly paper in 1854. Both men served as editors, producing an informative news medium by subscription for 16 years. They sold the paper in 1860 to W.H. and Minnie Wood, who changed the name to *The New Era*. Benedict, a Sauk Rapids pioneer, repurchased the paper in 1868, renaming it *The Sauk Rapids Sentinel.*

In April 1886 a tornado devastated the area and completely demolished the plant. Benedict returned to save the company due to his concern for

Today, jobs are provided electronically on a computer disk or over the internet, which is a far cry from the days of lead type and hand composition.

A corner of the workshop in 1929 where Sentinel published a newspaper. At that time the company and the newspaper went under the name "Sauk Rapids Sentinel."

the employees and the community's need for a viable news source. He strongly believed that they had not received due support through local relief efforts. In 1889 he opened the doors again and got the business back on its feet, offering gainful employment for some of the town's people.

In 1891 Benedict sold the paper to S.A. Clark. Benedict rejoined the paper that same year and continued to serve as editor through many changes in ownership.

The paper merged with *The Free Press* and the *Democrat* in 1903, creating *The Sentinel-Free Press*, and Benedict decided it was time to retire. George Benedict remained active, retaining interest in the paper until his death in February 1910.

That same year *The Free Press* portion of the name was dropped, and the paper became known as the *Sauk Rapids Sentinel* once again.

Eight years later, Ed Vandersluis joined the *Sentinel*, bringing with him many years of publishing and editing experience. He eventu-

ally moved the plant to East St. Cloud and renamed it the *St. Cloud Sentinel*. After more than 28 years with the paper, Vandersluis retired in 1946.

At that time, Richard "Dick" Manthey took the helm of the paper, along with two other partners. In 1948 Manthey became president by buying out the existing partners and introducing three new ones. The rights to publish and print the newspaper were sold to a local man, who published the paper under the name of *The Sauk Rapids Herald*. The company continued with the commercial printing business as the St. Cloud Sentinel Publishing Company.

Manthey served 47 years with the company. He joined the paper after being hired in 1931 as a sports writer and advertising sales person. In the mid-'40s he became a stockholder and in the late-'60s became president. Dick Manthey saw the firm change with the times and grow to meet the needs of his hometown area.

Through the '50s and '60s the partnership arrangement changed many times, but the integrity of the company remained the number one goal.

In 1967 the plant returned to Sauk Rapids as the Sentinel Printing Company, Inc., and local businessman Austin "Doc" Harren joined Dick Manthey at the firm as general manager.

In 1977 Dick Manthey retired, but the firm remained in the family. Dolores, his wife, took his place and in '81 their son Charles, "Chuck," joined the company as an estimator. Dolores served as president for six years before retiring.

Over the past 20 years, many changes in the operational structure occurred. The company was acquired by Gronseth Directory Service Corporation, which had just been purchased by North-West Telecommunications, shortly before Dolores Manthey retired. North-West Telecommunications was then sold to Pacifictel Communications and again to GTE Directories. Through these and other changes, Sentinel survived as a subsidiary of large and diverse businesses.

In November 1991 Chuck Manthey, along with five other employees—Douglas Walter, Norb Fischer, Tom

Forner, Greg Harren and Marv Bauer—bought the company from GTE Directories. Marv Bauer retired in 1998 and Dale Olmscheid and Marcia Goss became partners in the business following Marv's retirement.

Although half of the contracts were absorbed by GTE in the final sale, Chuck and the other owners knew the company could have a future as strong as its past. Sentinel had, after all, proved to be a resilient and viable company.

Since 1991, Sentinel Printing Company has more than tripled in terms of sales revenue, continuing to specialize in printing books, catalogs and telephone directories. It has grown to employ 65 full-time staff members and adds an extra 75 employees for seasonal work.

The staff has remained a valued asset through the years. Sentinel was named one of the Best Workplaces in America in 2001 by the Printing Industry of America. The company was selected for this honor because of the superior environment and business culture it provides for its employees, as well as progressive training, finan-

Sentinel Printing Company's current owners (standing, left to right) Marcia Goss, human resources manager; Dale Olmscheid, plant manager; Doug Walter, vice president/general manager; Norb Fischer, sheet fed press supervisor; and (seated, left to right) Greg Harren, secretary treasurer/St. John's plant manager; Chuck Manthey, president/sales manager; Tom Forner, quality control/safety coordinator.

cial security and additional recognition and rewards.

The company has given back to the community it has called home for so many years. Employees are encouraged to be active in organizations and programs such as United Way at Work, School to Work activities, Chamber sponsored tours to area staff, students, and parents, and involvement in other trade and professional organizations. The company has also established a scholarship fund for graphic arts students at the St. Cloud Technical College.

From a community newspaper to a commercial printer, Sentinel weathered the change because its focus was always to produce a first-rate product. After all, the company name Sentinel does denote assurance, strength, and protection. People like George Benedict, Ed Vandersluis and the Mantheys have cultivated this tradition of excellence since 1854 while building St. Cloud's oldest firm.

A recent view of the perfect binder which collates and binds soft cover books.

A Timeline of St. Cloud's History

1853 John Lyman Wilson purchased the squatter claim of Ole Bergeson for $100. He platted and filed the town site as St. Cloud. This area (between two ravines—Middle Town) became the business center of the new community. Sylvanius B. Lowry, a fur trader at Watab obtained the rights to the land above the Upper Ravine.

1854 George Fuller Brott, "a professional townsite promoter . . . secured the rights to land south" of the Lower Ravine. John W. Tenvoorde came seeking a location for German settlers from Evansville, Indiana. They came the following year and settled in Wilson's Middle Town.

1855 Father Francis X. Pierz, a Catholic missionary to the Ojibwe, conducted the first services in St. Cloud on May 22. He wrote extensively about the beauty and opportunities in St. Cloud and played a significant role in attracting German Catholic settlers to the area; the Baptists organized the first Protestant group in St. Cloud; on August 16 the first post office was opened.

1856 The Church of the Immaculate Conception (German Catholic) was established; April 2, St. Cloud was granted authority by the Minnesota Territorial Legislature to incorporate; August 20, cornerstone laid for St. John's Episcopal Church; June 8, Mrs. Z. H. Morse hosted eight women who agreed to found a Library Association. It would meet every second week with dues of 10 cents per meeting or $2.60 annually.

The Everett School House was built during the winter of 1856–1857 with private donations. One or two private school terms were held before the birth of the public tax education system was established.

1858 September, the first term of the tax supported school opened with 42 students attending—M.P. Noel was the teacher.

1859 Clarke and McClure opened the first bank. It was located above Edelbrock's store.

1862 Fort Holes was erected as a refuge for settlers fearing attack by the Dakota.

1864 St. Cloud Pioneer Fire Company No. 1 was organized with John L. Wilson as foreman.

1865 The Little Giant Engine Company No. 1, the first real company of firefighters, was organized.

1866 The St. Paul and Pacific Railroad reached St. Cloud on the east side of the Mississippi River.

1868 The first Minnesota granite quarry was opened by Breen and Young, on what became part of the St. Cloud Reformatory grounds.

1869 St. Cloud was selected by the state legislature as the site for the

Above: The United States Land Office in St. Cloud, Minnesota, circa 1858. MS6.9/SC3.1/r12, Photo by E.F. Boyd, courtesy, Minnesota Historical Society

Right: St. Cloud hook and ladder truck, 1877. MS6.9/SC8/r5, Photo by Newton J. Trenham, courtesy, Minnesota Historical Society

third Normal School.

1876 Twenty-five women voted in the May election, the first school board election since Minnesota legalized female suffrage in local school elections. The press reported that "They were quite well behaved and created no disturbance."

1880 Forty-four women met at the home of Mrs. Helen Moore to organize the St. Cloud Reading Room Society on February 12.

1886 Mrs. Loren W. Collins and Mrs. T. C. Allen were the first women elected to the St. Cloud school board.

1882 The Granite Cutters form a union.

1883 The St. Cloud Public Library was established by the city council. It accepted a donation of 835 volumes from the Library Association. The city appropriated $500 the following year to support the library; Church of the Holy Guardian Angels was built for English speaking Catholics.

October 10, St. Cloud Electric Light and Power Company turned on 29 electric street lights. Five years later the city ordered 12, 2,000-candle-power lamps to be installed along Main Street. The city agreed to pay $125 annually.

1884 St. Cloud installed a water works station. The major purpose was to provide water from the river "for the extinguishment of fires."

1885 Dr. A. C. Lamonthe Ramsey started a hospital. He asked the Sisters of St. Benedict to take over. It gradually evolved into the St. Cloud Hospital.

1886 Cyclone (tornado) hit the area causing major destruction in St. Cloud and even worse destruction in Sauk Rapids. It helped change local attitudes about a hospital being a place where people went to die. The rise of the St. Cloud business district

replaced Sauk Rapids as the area's major retail center.

1887 Horse-drawn street cars were introduced. Four years later the cars were converted to electrical. Lines of the Granite City Railway Company ran from East St. Cloud to the railroad car shops in Waite Park.

1888–1889 The rapid population growth in the area east of the Mississippi River led to its annexation as the Seventh Ward of the city and school district. The rigorous expansion of the granite industry by the 1880s drew many Swedish granite workers to the area.

While the early settlers located near the Breen-Young quarry, a few families—the Albert Johnsons, the August Williams, and the Lindbergs—made their homes in a hollow between 11th Avenue Southeast and Michigan Avenue. It became known as "Svenska-dalen" or Swede Hollow. The Swedish organized the Calvary Baptist and Salem Lutheran churches.

1889 Lincoln school was built. The Church of the Holy Guardian Angels became the cathedral when Bishop Otto Zardetti arrived and St. Cloud became his residence.

The city's two school districts merge. From 1875 to 1889 the two public schools each had their own building, teachers and board. The Independent school district, sometimes called the German School, reflects the strong influence of culture and language in 19th century Minnesota education. The "German," or Independent School, on the block northwest of St. Germaine and 11th Street North, was renamed Franklin. It was replaced by a new building in 1898, which was razed in the 1950s.

Land donated to the Benedictine sisters in East St. Cloud, became the site of the city's first hospital, St. Raphael. Because it was too far from most inhabitants it was replaced by a new hospital west of the Mississippi River. During the 20th century it was converted to a retirement home. The area developed as a major retirement center with a wide range of housing, and care levels, for seniors by the latter decades of the century.

Matthew Hall Lumber opened at its current expanded location in downtown St. Cloud; October 1, first

The St. Cloud Boys Band in St. Paul for the Kiwanis Convention in 1925. N5.21/r35, courtesy, Minnesota Historical Society

Granite quarry, circa 1890. HD6.2/p21, courtesy, Minnesota Historical Society

delivery of the U.S. mail began in St. Cloud. Letter carriers George A. Dickinson had Lower Town, Michael Miller had Upper Town and J. J. Jackson had the east side of the Mississippi River and the Reformatory as their respective routes.

1890 The Great Northern Railroad built its car shops in Waite Park. It was converted to a commercial district in the last quarter of the 20th century.

1893 Saint Cloud Humane Society was formed "to care for neglected and abused animals, especially horses;" the letter carriers organized a union. Early members included Joe Koshiol, Emil Henneman, M. J. Honer, and H. J. Saunders.

1897–1898 Colonel E. T. (Bill) Davidson built the Davidson Theater, "a well-managed Opera House which brings many of the best theatrical and musical entertainment from the east." It was destroyed by fire in 1912. A new Davidson Theater opened in January, 1914.

1901 There were five automobiles in St. Cloud and two garages: A. A. Eich and Steve Tenvoorde, who had converted his bicycle shop and started selling Saxons, Oldsmobiles, Chalmers and Fords. Very quickly only the Ford dealership remained

and it is still operating a century later.

Polish pioneers settling Third Street and 15th Avenue built their own Polish Catholic church, St. John Cantius.

November 6, 24 members were installed as Local No. 930 of the United Brotherhood of Carpenters and Joiners under the charter issued October 28. Membership fee was one dollar. The minimum wage was 25 cents an hour with a maximum work day of 10 hours—nine hours on Saturday, with 10 hours pay. Overtime was paid at one and a half times and work performed on Sunday was double time. The local celebrated its centennial in 2001.

1903 The International Brotherhood of Teamsters Local No. 586 received their charter; local unions formed the Trades and Labor Council.

1906 The eight-hour work day went into effect for federal workers.

1907 The voting age for women was raised to 24. They were still limited to voting in school and library board elections.

1908 The Good Cheer Branch of the International Sunshine Society formed "to care for neglected and abused humans, especially children."

1910 The Princess, an up-to-date motion picture theater opened at 15 Seventh Avenue South. Admission to the daily seven, eight or nine p.m. showings was five and 10¢.

1912 A second, this time successful, attempt was made to begin telephone service. An earlier 1883 attempt had failed. It grew from one to 13 operators before the end of the year. There were 1,412 customers by the end of the year including 409 farm families.

The city adopted a commission form of government. December 19, "The White Way" was opened with a

---

The Technical High School in St. Cloud, circa 1915. MS6.9/SC5.2/r5, courtesy, Minnesota Historical Society

great celebration. The button was pressed at eight o'clock. St. Germain street was lit by electric lights from Ninth to Fifth Avenues and Fifth South to Second Street South.

1913 Mrs. E. F. Moore was appointed as the "City Pure Food Inspector" in response to the Reading Room Society agitation against the "lack of sanitation where groceries and meats were sold." The Reading Room Society also played a prominent role in the successful agitation "for systematic collection of garbage."

1915 The city purchased the former sawmill site on the east side of the Mississippi. It became Riverside Park. During the 1930s one local Works Progress Administration included a series of tree planting, flower gardens, rock-lined paths, a lily pond and a greenhouse in a section that was renamed Munsinger Gardens.

1918 December 23, St. Cloud's First American Federation of Labor affiliate was chartered.

1921 On Christmas eve the Sherman Theater, which later became the Paramount, held its grand opening with tickets at 50 cents each. It was described as "St. Cloud's Largest and Finest Playhouse." The event featured D. W. Griffith's silent film, *Way Down East*, accompanied by a live orchestra. The theater seated 1,700, had state-of-the-art air conditioning, and a large stage. It was located next to St. Cloud's "finest" hotel, the Breen (the St. Germain), also built in 1921.

1924 Veterans Administration Hospital dedicated.

1928 The present St. Cloud Hospital was built. It has been expanded and remodeled many times. In 1995 it became part of the CentraCare Health System, by 2000 the largest employer in St. Cloud.

1931 Alice Wheelock Whitney traded the Whitney-Cable Airports tract 143 for a larger tract north of St. Cloud. Whitney Memorial Airport opened in June, 1935. A new airport opened in 1969 on 1,400 acres purchased by the city east of town. The old airport has become Whitney Park with an extensive system of ball parks—old airport buildings have been converted to other uses including Whitney Senior Center, opened in 1977.

1936 April 29, the last run of the streetcar from St. Cloud to Waite Park

Bernice Skeate being trained as part of the machine shop defense training program, circa 1940. I.51.10, courtesy, Minnesota Historical Society

Nineteen forty street scene in St. Cloud. MS6.9/SC2/p9, courtesy, Minnesota Historical Society

and back. Buses operated by Raymond Brothers took over.

1946 A main hangar and office for Van's Air Service was built on the land donated to the city by the Whitney family for an airport.

1947 St. Cloud Municipal Band received public funds, uniforms and a full-time director, as well as stipends for band members. It gave regular summer performances at Barden Park. Predecessors included the St. Cloud Union Band, about 1887; the Bicycle Band, about 1900; the Military Band and the Granite City Band during WWI; the Legion Band and the Brewery Band (10 member "Little German Band"), the Elks Band and the Eagles Band after WWI; and the Boys Band organized by G. Oliver Riggs at the invitation of local businessmen in 1923.

1952 The city adopted the mayor-council form of government; presidential candidate Dwight (Ike) Eisenhower made a campaign appearance in St. Cloud.

1956 The local AFL-CIO became the St. Cloud Trades and Labor Assembly.

1968 St. Cloud Human Rights Commission was organized.
1969 A new airport opened east of the city in Sherburne County. The former Whitney Airport was converted to other uses, including a large park and recreational areas.
1972 The Municipal Athletic Complex (MAC) opened on the northwest side of town with one sheet of ice—it was renovated in 1994. A second arena opened in December 1997.
1977 Whitney Senior Center opened in a former airport hanger.
1990 Bill Clemens, the founder of Bankers Systems, and his wife Virginia Rose, donated land for development of a rose garden to the east of Munsinger Gardens. They established an endowment and the park was expanded. It includes six gardens: Virginia Clemens Rose Garden, Rest Area Garden, Formal Gardens, The White Garden, The Perennial Garden and the Treillage Garden along Kilian Boulevard.
1995 St. Cloud Township is merged with the cities of St. Cloud and Waite Park.
1998 Mayor Larry Meyer invites 27

Dwight D. Eisenhower in a parade in St. Cloud on October 4, 1952. J2/1952/p27, photo by Clint Dean Photography, courtesy, Minnesota Historical Society

Swimming pool at an old quarry site, circa 1950. MS6.9/SC4/p1, courtesy, Minnesota Historical Society

community leaders to discuss racial diversity in the community; February 7, Meyer proposes a "Minority Speak Out" forum on racial issues; February 27, Meyer announces he would seek charges against apartment owners who discriminate; August 1, Justice Department official visits St. Cloud to assess racial issues at the request of minority residents.

September, the renovated and refurbished Paramount Theater reopened and became the center of the Paramount Arts District. It includes a 700-seat theater, visual arts studios and classrooms, administrative offices for local arts organizations and supports events presented by groups as the Central Minnesota Children's Theater, County Stearns Theatrical Company and the Troupe Theatre.
2002 January 26 Federated Department Stores, Inc. announced that it planned to sell or close the entire Fingerhut catalog business, including operations that emply 2,670 people in St. Cloud.

St. Cloud State President Roy Saigo and Mayor Ellenbecker joined in addressing issues of diversity and equality.

Sources

Carley, Kenneth. *The Sioux Uprising of 1862.* St. Paul: The Minnesota Historical Society, 1976.

Carter, Jerry L., "Mayor opens diversity talks: Leaders gather, Meyer, asks for help to curtail racism," *St. Cloud Times,* January 29, 1998.

Carter, Jerry L., "Evidence of racism abounds: Emotional speak-out fuels mayor's effort," *St. Cloud Times,* March 5, 1998.

City of St. Cloud documents and resources: Avery, Paula Van, Human Rights Director, City of St. Cloud; "A year of Opportunity—2000–2001 Annual Report of the Human Rights Division City of St. Cloud;" pp 3–19, 14; 2001. Planning Office. "St. Cloud Comprehensive Plan Update: Demographic Survey" 2002; "Comparison of 2001 and 1981 Community Surveys," 2002. Web site: http://ci.stcloud.mn.us//web/mainindex.html provides a link to various city departments and other local government, education, economic, media, arts, etc. sites. This site provided quick access to a wide range of information including city department information and reports such as the Comprehensive Plan. It also provides links to many area government, arts groups, business and economic organizations like the St. Cloud Business Partnership, especially valuable for "Economic Profile: St. Cloud Area Profile 1999–2000: Executive Summary;" and other studies and reports; the areas schools and universities; and such other public agencies as the St. Cloud Metropolitan Transit Commission, "History of the MTC: A Historical Perspective on Transit through the Years," 2002; area media.

Cooper, Myrle, Davis, Michael and Tadema, Tamarat letter, "Letter to Guidance Counselors," *University Chronicle,* March 21, 2002.

Daley, Dave, "COG becomes APO; feud officially ends," *St. Cloud Times,* June 29, 1978 and "New planning panel pact approved," *St. Cloud Times,* May 25, 1978.

Dietz, Charlton. "Henry Behnke: New Ulm's Paul Revere," *Minnesota History* (St. Paul), (Fall 1976), 111–115.

Dominik, John J. "Sam Pandolfo: Minnesota's *Almost* Auto Magnate," *Minnesota History,* (St. Paul), (Winter 1982),138–152.

_____. *Three Towns into One City.* St. Cloud: St. Cloud Area Bicentennial Commission, 1978.

Drazenovich, Dana, "Route change rankle East Side: Shorter parade goes a long way to attract top bands for Wheels, Wings & Water Festival," *St. Cloud Times,* June 23, 1999.

Glasrud, Clarence A. (ed.) *Roy Johnson's Red River Valley.* Moorhead, Minnesota: Red River Valley Historical Society, 1982.

Gove, Gertrude B. *A History of St. Cloud in the Civil War.* St. Cloud: Stearns County Historical Society, 1976.

_____, editor and compiler, *St. Cloud Centennial Souvenir Album 1856–1956,* published by the St. Cloud Centennial Committee, 1957.

_____. *St. Cloud Centennial Souvenir Album.* St. Cloud: St. Cloud Centennial Committee, 1956.

Halena, Sue, "Rapid growth gives Central Minnesota [a] new look, young face." *St. Cloud Times,* May 23, 2001.

Henig, Gerald T. "A Neglected Cause of the Sioux Uprising," *Minnesota History,* (St. Paul), (Fall 1976), 107–110.

Henry, Edward L. (ed.) *Micropolis in Transition.* Collegeville, Minnesota: Center for the Study of Local Government, 1971.

Hiertmaier, Christine, "Learning, fun cross paths at powwow: Local American Indian center joins festival to cultivate understanding," *St. Cloud Times,* July 10, 1997.

Johnson, Ann Marie, "St. Cloud's Munsinger and Clemens Gardens: a Public Legacy'" Master of Arts thesis, St. Cloud State University, August, 1998.

Keillor, Garrison, *In Search of Lake Wobegon,* Viking Studio (2001), pp 12, 16.

Local Union #930 Centennial Anniversary, Rengel Printing, St. Cloud, 2001.

Lundgren, Renee, Great River Interfaith Partnership grant application quoted from an email, April 15, 2002.

Mattern, Patty and Inglebrett, Julie, "Gangs bang on St. Cloud's door," *Times,* December 31, 1992.

Meyer, Larry Papers, "Into the Third Millennium: An analysis of issues facing the City of St. Cloud and some practical responses to take us into the year 2000 and beyond," October, 1993, pp 9–11 (Stearns County Heritage Center Archives).

"Minnesota counties by per-capita personal income," Minneapolis *Star Tribune,* March 11, 2002.

Minnesota State Demographic Center, Minnesota State Planning Office, publications: "2000 Profiles of General Demographic Characteristics: St. Cloud city, Minnesota;" "Census, 2000: Households;" "Census 2000: Minnesota Age Profile;" Carlson Gail, "Asians in Minnesota, 2000," March, 2002; Hibbs, James, "Strong population growth continues in Minnesota," February, 2000 and "Unprecedented Population Growth Revealed by Census," December, 2001; "Minnesota Household Profile of General Demographic Characteristics from Census 2000;" McMurry, Martha, "2000 Census Shows a More Racially and Ethnically Diverse Minnesota," May, 2001; "Race Population by County, Census 2000." Web site: http://www.mnplan.state.mn.us/demography/census 2000.html.

Mitchell, William Bell. *History of Stearns County.* 2 vols. Chicago: H. C. Cooper, Jr., & Co., 1915.

Molene, John, "Churches' inaction bother residents: Second meeting setting to continue race discussions," *St. Cloud Times,* March 26, 1998.

Molene, John, "Family structure is changing in Central Minnesota," *St. Cloud Times,* May 25, 2001.

Moses, George. *Minnesota in Focus.* Minneapolis: University of Minnesota Press, 1974.

Nelson, Eric, *History of the St. Cloud Public Library or How a Great Book on the Frontier Grew Into the Great River Regional Library,* n.p., 1976.

Newcombe, Barbara T. "'A Portion of the American People': The Sioux

Sign a Treaty in Washington in 1858," *Minnesota History,* (St. Paul), (Fall 1976), 82–96.

Nistler, Mike. *Outlook,* Winter, 2002, outlook@stcloudstate.edu, March 27, 2002.

"Overall Housing Study for the St. Cloud Metro Area" prepared by Admark Resources for Central Minnesota Task Force on Affordable Housing, Minnesota Housing Partnership, St. Cloud Area Economic Development Partnership, City of St. Cloud, City of St. Joseph, City of Sartell, City of Sauk Rapids, City of Waite Park, Benton County, Sherburne County and Stearns County, February, 2001.

Russo, Priscilla Ann. "The Time to Speak is Over: The Onset of the Sioux Uprising," *Minnesota History,* (St. Paul), (Fall 1976), 97–106.

Sáez, David, "Church group goal: Uproot oppression (Congregations, agencies launch GRIP to deal with local issues)," *St. Cloud Times,* May 18, 1998.

Sáez, David, "Fathering . . . from a distance," *Times,* June 21, 1998.

Schumacher, Lawrence, "New 6th District surges into Minnesota spotlight," *St. Cloud Times,* April 29, 2002.

Sherwood, Charles, "The St. Cloud Municipal Band," summer, 1985 typescript courtesy of the St. Cloud Park and Recreation Department.

Smith, G. Hubert. "A Frontier Fort in Peacetime," *Minnesota History,* (St. Paul), (Fall 1976), 116–128.

Times, January 1, 1980–April 20, 2002. Web site: http://www.sctimes.com.

Unze, David, "Area's Asian population expands," *St. Cloud Times,* May 27, 2001.

____ "Hispanic boom reshapes Stearns," *St. CloutTimes,* March 29, 2001.

Utley, Robert M. and Washburn, Wilcomb E. *The American Heritage History of the Indian Wars.* New York: American Heritage Publishing Co., Inc. Bonanza Books, 1977.

Voigt, Robert J. *Holy Angels in St. Cloud.* St. Cloud: Sentinel Printing Co., Inc., 1983.

Winchell, N. H.; Neill, Edward D.; Willimas, J. Fletcher; Bryant, Charles S. *History of the Upper Mississippi Valley.* Minneapolis: Minnesota Historical Company, 1881.

Wocken, Chuck, director, Stearns County Parks Department, parkinfo@co. stearns.mn.us.

Zisla, Jake, "Report: SCSU lacks credibility," *University Chronicle,* February 14, 2002.

Acknowledgments

I am grateful for the chance to thank publicly a number of people whose gracious help has made this a pleasant assignment: to Ed Stockinger, whose deft handling of the manuscript for the bicentennial history of St. Cloud, *Three Towns into One City*, resulted in its being an infinitely more interesting book than it would otherwise have been and whose untimely death ended a long period of unselfish service to St. Cloud and, incidentally, deprived this manuscript of his wit, wisdom, and wealth of words; to the entire staff of the Stearns County Historical Society for allowing me unfettered access to their abundant files and material and for suggesting avenues of research I would not have had the sense to explore unbidden; to Mary Cannon, editor of *Minnesota History*, not only for her kind words and gentle advice but for her encouragement in a matter and manner I will always remember and cherish; to a number of people, especially Ed Lauermann, Alcuin Ringsmuth, and Dick Statz, who made extra efforts to obtain information or supply rare pictures; to Patricia Morreim, who generously consented to read the manuscript for historical accuracy; and finally to my wife Shirley and my children who tolerated my long absences—or my long silences when present—for the many months of research and writing. They helped when they were asked and didn't when they weren't.

John J. Dominik

The difficult task of organizing and selecting among the many events which seem so crucial to the discussion of the Cental Minnesota Region during the closing decades of the 20th, and the opening years of the 21st centuries was made easier through the assistance of many individuals both in answering questions and providing access to sources. Former St. Cloud Mayor Larry Meyer and current Mayor John Ellenbecker added valuable perspectives of public officials directly involved as council members and mayors in shaping the city's history. City staff including: Paula Van Avery, Human Rights Director; Prentiss Foster, assistant director of the Park Department; and David Broxmeyer, St. Cloud Planning Office kindly cooperated. These, and other public employees, helped in many ways by providing access, and often copies of, public documents and photographs and in giving valuable suggestions to other sources of information.

Dan Finn, chair of the multi-city task force on affordable housing assisted in providing copies of relevant studies. Renee Lundgren, executive director of the Great River Interfaith Partnership was a valuable resource for reviewing the development of interfaith cooperation. Dan Green, faculty member, the College of Education at St. Cloud State University and advisor to recent city administrations and businesses on human rights issues, provided valuable insights into understanding the dynamics of the changing racial and ethnic issues. The archive staff of the Stearns County History Museum were also most cooperative and helpful. The St. Cloud Area Economic Development Partnership's studies cover a wide range of relevant economic and social analysis. The St. Cloud Convention and Visitors Bureau has also been very helpful in providing photographic records of the area at the turn of the new century.

John C. Massmann

Index

CHRONICLES OF LEADERSHIP INDEX

Antioch Company, The/Creative
    Memories, 146-147
Bankers Systems, Inc., 148-149
Bauerly Bros, Inc., 150-151
Capital Granite & Marble, Inc., 176-177
Catholic Charities, 178-179
CentraCare Health System, 180-181
Coborn's, Inc., 182-183
Continental Press, 152-153
Gold'n Plump Poultry, 154-155
Great Steps Orthotic & Prosthetic Solutions,
    156-157
Handyman's Hardware Inc., 184-185
Liberty Savings Bank, fsb
    Liberty Loan and Thrift Corporation,
    158-159
Lumber One, Avon Inc.
    and Lumber One, Cold Spring Inc.,
    160-161
Nahan Printing, Inc., 172-174
Regent Broadcasting, 186-187
Resource Training & Solutions, 162-163
St. Cloud Hospital, 188-189
St. Cloud Regional Airport, 164-165
St. Cloud Surgical Center, The, 166-167
Sentinel Printing Company, 190-191
Sisters of the Order of Saint Benedict
    St. Benedict's Monastery, 168-169
Tenvoorde Ford, 170-171

GENERAL INDEX

Italicized numbers indicate illustrations.

A

Abolition, 87, 88, 89
Abbott Northwestern Hospital, 141
Acadia, 13
Acton, 36, 37
Adams Cigar Factory, Julius, *44, 57*
AFL-CIO, 197
Albany, 129
Allen, Mrs. T.C., 193
All America City, 110, 112
American Federation of Labor, 196
American Legion, 77
Andrews, Christopher C., 15, 19, 30, 32, 90
Angus Acres, 104
Antietam, 35
Antioch Company, The/Creative
    Memories, 146-147
Appomattox, 43
Associated Press, 90
Atkinson, Rodney, 129

B

Ballantine, Dennis, 137
Bankers Systems, Inc.,141, 142, 148-149, 197
Barden Park, 196
Barr Canning, 77
Barritt, John, 61, 66
Bauerly Bros, Inc., 150-151
Beaver, 20

Beaver Islands, 86, *94*
Beer and Breweries, 12, 33, 34, 47, 71
Benton County, 130, 131, 133, 141
Bergeson, Ole, 10
Bicycle Band, 196
Big Eagle, *37*
Big Squeak, 21, *21*
Big Woods, 142
Boerger, William, *91*
Boys Band, 196
Breckenridge, John, 32
Breen, 192
Breen-Young quarry, 193
Brewery Band, 196
Brick, Leo, 92
Brick, Peter, 91
Briggs, Joshua, 16
Briggs, Mrs. Joshua, 16
Brokaw, N.H., 59
Broker's Block, 40, *40*
Brott, George Fuller, 13, *13*, 15, 17, 18, 45,
    86, 112, 192
Brower, Ripley B., 66
Brown, Leroy, *67*
Buchanan, James, 15
Bull Run, Battle of, 35
Bunnell, Charles, 61
Burbank, Henry Clay, 23, *24*, 25, 47, 112
Burbank, James Crawford, 22, *24, 25*, 47, 112
Bureau of Census, 104. *See also* Census
Byers, George, 104, 105

C

C.F.&W. Powell's Hardware, *2*
Calhoun, Thomas, 30
California, 134, 135
Campbell, Elgy Van Voorhis, 81
Calvery Baptist Church, 193
Capital Granite & Marble, Inc., 176-177
Carter Building, 77
Cass, Lewis, 10, *11*
Catholic Charities, 178-179
Census: 1990, 130; 2000, 133; 2001, 133
CentraCare Health System, 141, 180-181, 196
Central House, *26*
Central Minnesota Children's Theater,
    142, 197
Central Minnesota Group Health, 141
Central Minnesota Heart and Emergency
    Trauma Centers, 141
Central Minnesota Heart Center, 141
Central Minnesota Youth Soccer
    Association, *133*
Central Park, *120*
Chamber of Commerce, 61, 69, 105
Chicago, 142
Churches, 81, *82*, 99, 121, 195. *See also*
    individual churches
Church of the Holy Gaurdian Angels,
    193, 194
City government, 95, 99, 100, 101, 102, 103
City Hall, *44*

Civilian Conservation Corps, *77*
Civil War, 13, 29, 31, 32, 33, *33*, 34, 35, 36,
    43, 81
Clark, Nehemiah P., 58, 61
Clarke, 192
Clemens, Bill, 142, 197
Clemens, Virginia Rose, *128*, 142, 197
Clemens Gardens, *127*
Coates, John, *90*
Coborn Cancer Center, 141
Coborn's, Inc., 141, 182-183
Cold Spings, 135
Collignon, Phil, 109
Collins, Mrs. Loren W., 192
Columbian Book Store, *97*
Commercial Club of St. Cloud, 61, 69
Community Conversations meeting, 138
Continental Press, 152-153
County Stearns Theatrical Company and
    the Troupe Theater, 142, 197
Crime-Free Multi Housing Program, 138
Crossroads Shopping Center, 107, *107*, 111
Cultural diversity, 136, 137, 138, 139

D

Dakota, 192; War, 35
Dave Torrey Arena, 142
Davidson, E.T., 194
Davidson Theater, 194
Davis, Christopher Donte, 137
Davis, Josephine, 139
DePalma, Ralph, 68
Department of Commerce, 104
Depression, 72, 75, 76, 77, 78
DeSoto Bridge, 25
DeVlieg, Ray, *67*
Dickenson, George H.,194
Dobyns, Fletcher, 71, 72
Dole, William P., 38
Douglas, Stephen, 32
Duluth, 53

E

Eagles Band, 196
Eastman, Alvah, 90
East Plains Trail, 20
Edelbrock, Joseph, 30; his store, *31*, 192
Eich, A.A., 194
Eisenhower, Dwight D., 196, *197*
Elks Band, 196
Ellenbecker, John D., 129, 137, 140
Emergency Relief Administration, 78
Engdahl, Paula, *134*, 136
Ernest, Christopher, 136
Ervin, Hal C., 61
Evans, Hugh, 61
Everett, Edward, 15
Everett School House, 192

F

Fair-housing, 138
Farmers Loan and Investment Company, 61

Farmers State Bank, 61, 62
Fandel, 141
Fargo, 134
Federal agents, *70, 74, 75*
Federal Communications Commission, 93
Fernwood, 104
Fire Department, 30, *96*
1st Minnesota Volunteers, 35
First National Bank, 62
First Presbyterian Church, *139*
Fitness, Ray J., *67*
Forest City, 41
Formal Garden, 197
Forrest, Vincent, 106
Forsyth, Ben, 68
Fort Abercrombie, 42
Fort Garry, 20
Fort Holes, 40, 192
Fort Ripley, 18
Fort Snelling, 10, 18, 20, 21
4th Minnesota Regiment, 33
Franklin Manufacturing, *62*, 69
Franklin School, 194
Freeman, Ambrose, 38, 41
Freeman, Dan, *90*
Fremont, John C., 32
Freeport, 129

G
Gales & Strohel, *46-47*
Gang violence, 142
Garlington, Lawrence, 35
Gaurreau, Victor, 66, *67*
German School, 194
Gettysburg, 35
Gilman, Charles A., *90*; his house, *100*
Golden Corridor, 140
Gold'n Plump Poultry, 154-155
Gordon, Hanford Lennox, *90*
Gorman, Willis A., 13
Grand Central Hotel, *26*
Grange, 27
Granite City Band, 196
Granite City Railway Company, 193
Granite Cutters Union, 193
Granite industry, 48, 49, *49*, 51, 52, 53, 75, 78, 193; quarry, *194, 197*
Grant, Devon, *133*
Great Northern Railroad, 194
Great River Interfaith Partnership (GRIP), 129, *131*, 138; task force, 138
Great Steps Orthotic & Prosthetic Solutions, 156-157
Greeley, Horace, 89
Green, Les, *134, 139*
Griffith, D.W., 196; *Way Down East*, 196

H
Halena, Sue, 131
Handyman's Hardware Inc., 184-185
Hanscom, George, 61
Has-a-War-Club, *37*

Haven Township, 131
HealthPartners, 141
Health services, 141
Heidman, George, 61
Henneman, Emil, 194
Henry, Edward L.,104, 105, 106, 107, 108, 109
Herberger, Conrad, 23
Herbergers, 141
Hester Park, *100*, 106
Hill, James Jerome, 54, 55, 58
Historic Places, 142
Holdingford, 129
Hole-in-the-Day, 38, 39
Holes, Samuel, 23, 40
Holy Angels Procathedral, 117
Home Depot, 141
Home Guards, 42
Honer, M.J., 194
Housing Descrimination, 138
Human Rights Division, 137, 138
Human Rights Office, 137, 138
Human Rights Ordinance, 137
Humphrey, Hubert H., 106

I
Immaculate Conception Church, *117, 192*
Independent Schoool, 194
Indians, 9, 10, 24, 35, 36, 37, *37*, 38, *39*, 41, 42, 43, 192
International Brotherhood of Teamsters Local No. 586, 195
International Sunshine Society, 195; Good Cheer Branch, 195
Ireland, John, 52

J
Jackson, J.J., 194
Janey Crane Foundation, *128*
Johnson, Albert, 193
Jones, Thomas, 17
Justice Department, 197

K
Kaiser, Peter, 91, 92
Keillor, Garrison, 120, 129
Kelley, Oliver Hudson, 27, *27*
Killian's Landing, 19
Klu Klux Klan, 139
Knoblach, Jim, *131*
Koshiol, Joe, 194

L
Ladner, Charles F., 61, 68
Lake George, 12, *113, 124*
Lake Itasca, 10
Lake Wobegon, 129, 131, 142; Regional Trail, *120*
Lam, Owen Long, 133, *134*
Lam, Vy, 133
Landis, Kenesaw Mountain, 67, 68
Laraway, George W., 58
Lee, Robert E., 43

Legion Band, 197
Leighton, Al, 93
Letter Carriers: union organized, 194
Le Sauk Township, 131
Liberty Savings Bank, fsb
    Liberty Loan and Thrift Corporation, 158-159
Library Association, 192
Lincoln, Abraham, 29, 31, 32, 34, 35
Lincoln, Mary Todd, 35
Lindberg, 193
Little Crow, 36, 37, 38, *39*, 42, 43
Little Giant Engine Company No. 1, 192
Loehr, Alcuin G., 104, 109
Loop, *107, 110-111*, 111
Lower Town, 12, 13, 15, 17, 18, 19, *34-35*, 45, 56, 81, 85, 86
Lowry, Sylvanus B., 13, 19, 23, 29, 30, *31*, 87, 90, 112, 192
Lumber One, Avon Inc.
    and Lumber One, Cold Spring Inc., 160-161
Lundgren, Renee, 129

M
Macdonald, Colin F., 90, *90*, 91
Mahowald, Betsy, 136
Mathew Hall Lumber, 194
McClure, 192
McIntee, Art, *76*
McKelvy, James M., 17, 32, 35
Mall Germain, 108, 109, *109*, 111
Manassas, Battle of, 35
Mankato, *37*
Marlatt, Silas,17
May, Gerhard, 92
Medicine Light, 37
Melrose School District, 135
Menards, 141
Merchants National Bank, 61
Merrill Corporation, 141
Mesabi, 66
Metcalf, Lee, 106
Métis, 23
Metropolitan Planning Commission, 112
Metro Transit Commission, 112
Metzroth, 141
Meyer, Joseph, 92
Meyer, Larry, *131, 134*, 136, 137, 138, 142, 197
Mezroth Clothing Bazaar, J.W., 2
Middle Town, 12, 13, 18, 81, 192
Military Band, 196
Miller, Michael, 194
Miller, Stephen, 17, *28*, 32
Mills Farm Fleet, 141
Minden Township, 131
Miner Theater Company, 61
Minneapolis, 9, 51, 53, 129, 130, 140, 141, 142
Minneapolis, 18
Minnesota 13, 72, 129, 130, 131, 132, 133, 135, 140, 142
Minnesota, University of, 72, 135

Minnesota Correctional Facility, 48
Minnesota Department of Economic Security Research and Statistics Office, 141
Minnesota Department of Trade and Economic Development, 141
Minnesota House, 27
Minnesota River Valley, 37
Minnesota State Reformatory for Men, 52-53, 53
Minnesota Territorial Legislature, 192
Minnesota Territory, 10
Missionary Ridge, Battle of, 33
Mississippi & Rum River Boom Co., 48, 49
Mississippi River, 9, 18, 20, 47, 48, 48, 49, 53, 57, 59, 64, 78, 89, 105, 116, 123, 124, 128, 130, 131, 141, 193, 194
Mitchell, Elizabeth, 15, 15
Mitchell, Henry Z., 15, 15, 16, 17, 25, 42, 89
Mitchell, Mary C., 25
Mitchell, William Bell, 17, 25, 35, 58, 89, 90, 90
Mockenhaupt, August, 12
Molene, John, 133
Molitors Trout Heaven Park, 125
Montana gold rush, 24
Moore, Helen, 193, 195
Moore, R. Chaning, 90
Morse, Mrs. Z. H., 192
Motor Hotel, 64
Municipal Arena, 111, 112
Municipal Athletic Complex (MAC), 142, 197
Municipal Commission, 108
Munsinger Gardens, 126, 142, 143, 195, 197; Lily Pond, 143. See also individual Gardens
Munsinger Park, 78, 79, 126
Murphy, James, 76

N
Napoleon, 10, 12
Nahan Printing, Inc., 141, 172-174
National Association for the Advancement of Black People (NAACP), 139
National Municipal League, 110, 111, 112
Newspapers, 17, 18, 31, 33, 35, 41, 61, 76, 86, 87, 88, 89, 89, 90, 91, 92. See also individual newspapers
Nichols, Edward, 137
Nicolay, John G., 38
9th Minnesota Regiment, 42
Noel, M.P., 192
Normal School, 193
Northern Rangers, 41
Northern States Power, 106, 107
North Side Park, 64-65
Northwest Daily Press Association, 90
Northwestern Bell, 106
Northwestern Express Company, 23
Northwestern Fur Company, 17
Norway Lake, 38

O
Office of Cultural Education, 136
O'Keefe, Dennis, 139
Ole Bergeson, 192
Ojibew, 192
Opatz, Joe, 131

P
Palmer, Benjamin R., 16
Pandolfo, Samuel Conner, 59, 60, 61, 61, 62, 63, 63, 64, 66, 67, 68, 69, 71, 112
Pandolfo Manufacturing Company, 68
Pan Motor Company, 59, 60, 61, 62, 62, 64, 66; Model A of, 67, 68, 69
Pan Sewer Trust, 69
Pan Town, 64, 69
Paramount Arts District, 197
Paramount Theater, 142, 197
Paynesville, 38, 40
Pembina, 21, 24, 25
Perennial Garden, The, 197
Phoenix Iron Works, 56, 57, 59
Pierz, Francis X., 12, 18, 192
Pike, Zebulon Montgomery, 10, 86
Pius IX, 71
Pleasant Lake, 131
Pope, John, 21, 22
Population: Asian, 133, 134, 135, 136, 135, 137; family household, 129, 130, 131, 133, 134, 136; growth chart, 132; minority, 135, 136, 138; hispanic 133, 134, 135, 136; national median ages, 132, 133; non-Hispanic, 135, 136; rate of growth, 131, 140; Vietnamese, 133, 134, 138
Potter, David, 139
Powell, Charles F., 17
Powell, William, 17
Princess, The, 195
Prohibition, 71, 72, 74, 75

Q
Quarry Park & Nature Preserve, 121
Querales, Ramon, 135

R
Radio and Television, 90, 92, 93, 106
Railroads, 18, 25, 53, 54, 55, 56, 75
Ramsey, Alexander, 29, 30, 30, 38
Ramsey, C. Lamonthe, 193
Rao, Nishta, 135
Raymond & Dunnewold, 46-47
Raymond Brothers, 196
Reasbeck, George, 106
Red Legs, 37
Red Owl, 37
Red River Trail, 20; carts, 21, 22, 23
Red River Valley, 24
Regent Broadcasting, 186-187
Reinhard, Bernard, 90
Reiter, David, 139
Religious denominations, 129, 138, 192, 193, 195. See also individual churches

Resource Training & Solutions, 162-163
Rest Area Garden, 197
Richmond, 41, 42
Riggs, G. Oliver, 196
Ritsche Arena, 142
Riverside Park, 104, 195
Rockville, 131; Township's, 131
Rocori Area Schools, 135; English as a Second Language (ESL), 135
Roosevelt, Franklin D., 77
Rox Ball Park, 111, 112

S
Sago, Roy, 139
St. Anthony, 19
St. Augusta, 131; Township, 131
St. Benedict's College, 133
St. Boniface Catholic Church, 135
St. Cloud Annihilators, 34
St. Cloud Area Planning Organization, 112, 131
St. Cloud Area School District 742, 135
St. Cloud Boys Band, 194
St. Cloud Brass Band, 34
St. Cloud City, 13
St. Cloud Electric Light and Power Company, 193
St. Cloud Environmentally Sensitive Areas Ordinance, 142
St. Cloud Fibre Ware Company, 56, 57, 58, 59
St. Cloud Grocery Company, 61
St. Cloud Guards, 32, 33
St. Cloud Hospital, 188-189, 141, 196
St. Cloud Human Rights Commission, 137, 197
St. Cloud Humane Society, 194
St. Cloud Iron Works, 61
St. Cloud Medical Group, 141
St. Cloud Municipal Band, 196
St. Cloud Opportunities, Inc., 105
St. Cloud Paper Mill Company, 58, 59
St. Cloud Pioneer Fire Company No. 1, 192
St. Cloud Public Library, 102, 103, 118, 193
St. Cloud Public Schools, 136; District Number 742's, 135; English as a Second Language (ESL), 135
St. Cloud Reading Room Society, 193
St. Cloud Reformatory, 48, 192, 194
St. Cloud Regional Airport, 164-165
St. Cloud Surgical Center, The, 166-167
St. Cloud State University, 122, 123, 133, 134, 135, 136, 137, 138, 139, 139, 140, 142; Chronicle, 139; Cultural Center, 139; Huskies, 140; international studies program, 135, 136; racism and anti-Semitism on campus, 140; student population, 134, 136; Survey: crime in the community, 142; overall quality of life, 142
St. Cloud Technical College, 133, 136
St. Cloud Times, 129, 131, 133, 135, 139

St. Cloud Township, 197
St. Cloud Trades and Labor Assembly, 197
St. Cloud Union Band, *6, 196*
St. Cloud Volunteer Company, 32
St. Cloud Water Pollution Control
    System, 112
St. Cloud Water Treatment Plant, *105*
St. John Canitus, 195
St. John's Episcopal Church, 192
St. John's University, 133
St. Joseph, 131, 132, 133; Township, 131
St. Mary's Cathedral, *131*, 138
St. Mary's School, *117*
St. Paul, 9, 15, 20, 51, 52, 89, 93, 194
St. Raphael, 194
St. Rosa, 129
Salem Evangelical Lutheran Church, *139*, 193
Sartell, 131, 132, 133, 141
Sauk Rapids, 131, 132, 141, 193
Sauk Rapids Bridge, 12
Sauk River, 20, 55, 64, 141, 142
Sauk Valley, 18, 47
Schaefer, Peter, *97*
Schaefer, Robert, *97*
Schaefer's Book Store, *97*
Schilplin, Fred, 61, 66, 90, 92, 93
Schilplin, Frederick C., 90
Schoolcraft, Henry R., 10, *11*
Schools and Universities, 14, 15, 19, 78, 79,
    80, 81, 82, *82*, 83, 83, 84, *84*, 85, *85*, 86,
    87, 106, *118, 121, 122. See also* individual
    schools and universities
Schumacher, Lawrence, 129
Searle, F.E., 58
2nd Minnesota Regiment, 32, *33*
Security State Bank, 61
Selke Field, 78
Sentinel Printing Company, 190-191
7th Minnesota Volunteers, 35
Seventh Congressional District, 129
Seward, William H., 31
Shepley, James, 87, 88, 89
Shepley, Mrs. James, 89
Sherburne County, 130, 131, 133, 141, 197
Sherman Theater, 142, 196
Sibley, Henry J., 42, *42*
Sisters of Saint Benedict, 193, 194
Sisters of the Order of Saint Benedict
    St. Benedict's Monastery, 168-169
Sixth Congressional District, 129
Skeate, Bernice, 196
Special Life Saving Award, 137
Smith, E.C., 17
Spofford & Simonton, 90
State Supreme Court, 85
Statz, Dick, 106
Stearns, Charles T., 13, 14
Stearns County, *121*, 129, 130, 131, 133,
    135, 141
Stearns County Courthouse, *98, 99, 118*
Stearns House, 14, *14*, 15, *84*, 85
Stills, *70*, 71, *73*, 74, 75

Street, Norman, 61
Swede Hollow, 193
Swisshelm, Henry, 16, 17, 112
Swisshelm, Jane Grey, 14, 17, 22, 29, 30, 31,
    32, 35, 45, 87, 88, *88*, 89, 90, 112

T
Taconlipeiyo, *37*
Talcott, Amelia, 15
Talcott, Francis, 18
Taoyatedutah, 36, 37, 38, *39*, 42, 43
Taylor, John, 15, 17
Technical High School, *195*
10th Street Bridge, 10, *123*
Tenvoorde, John W., 12
Tenvoorde, Steve, 194
Tenvoorde Ford, 141, 170-171
Texas, 133, 134, 135
Thief, The, *37*
Thielman, Peter B., 61
3rd Minnesota Regiment, 32, *36*
Thompson, Clark W., 38
Tileston, George, 56
Tileston Flour Mill, *58-59*
Tornado of 1886, 48, *193*, 193
Trades and Labor Council, 195
Traveling Hail, *37*
Treillage Garden, 197
Twin Cities, 129, 137

U
United Brotherhood of Carpenters and
    Joiners, 195; Local No. 930, 195
U.S. Mail: delivery begins, 194
United States Land Office, *192*
Unze, David, 133, 134, 135
Upper Town, 8, 9, 12, 13, 16, 18, 19

V
Van Avery, Paula, 137
Van's Air Service, 196
Veteran's Administration, 105
Veteran's Administration Hospital, 196
Veteran's Administration Medical
    Center, 141
Viet-Tien Market, 133, 134
Virginia Clemens Rose Garden, *128, 197*
Volstead, Andrew, 71
Voting age, 194
Volz & Wever, 25

W
Wabasha, *37*
Waite, Henry Chester, 90
Waite Park, 55, 108, *121*, 130, 131, 132, 133,
    141, 194, 196, 197
Waite's Crossing Bridge, 20
Walker, Mari, 135
Watab, 192
West, Caleb, 87
West, Josiah Elam, 17; Water & Power
    Company of, 56, 58, 90

Westerhaus, Tom, 135
White, Clarence, *131*
White Cloud, 137
White Garden, 197
"White Way, The," 195
Whitney, Alice Wheelock, 196
Whitney, Wheelock, 77
Whitney Memorial Airport, 196, 197
Whitney Memorial Park, *125*, 196
Whitney Recreation Center, *125*, 142
Whitney Senior Center, *125*, 142, 196, 197
Wilkinson, Morton Z., 38, *38*
Williams, August, 193
Williams Gardens, 77
Wilson, Harriet Corbett, *11*
Wilson, John Lyman, *8*, 10, 12, 13, 19, *192*;
    and home, *19*, 33
Wilson, Joseph, 13, 112
Wimer, Boniface, 71
Winkleman, Charles, 137
Witschen, Robert, 92, 93
Women's rights, 87, 88, 193
Woodland Hills, 104
Wooley, Martin, 13, 18
Works Progress Administration, 77, 78, 195
World War I, 92, 196
World War II, 56, 69, 78, 86, 104
Wounded Knee, 42

Y
Yokota, Kiyoko, 135
Young, 192

Z
Zardetti, Otto, 193

2